Palgrave's Critical Policing Studies

Series Editors
Elizabeth Aston, School of Applied Sciences, Edinburgh Napier
University, Edinburgh, UK
Michael Rowe, Department of Social Sciences Newcastle City Campus,
Northumbria University, Newcastle upon Tyne, UK

In a period where police and academics benefit from coproduction in research and education, the need for a critical perspective on key challenges is pressing. Palgrave's Critical Policing Studies is a series of high quality, research-based books which examine a range of cutting-edge challenges and developments to policing and their social and political contexts. They seek to provide evidence-based case studies and high quality research, combined with critique and theory, to address fundamental challenging questions about future directions in policing.

Through a range of formats including monographs, edited collections and short form Pivots, this series provides research at a variety of lengths to suit both academics and practitioners. The series brings together new topics at the forefront of policing scholarship but is also organised around who the contemporary police are, what they do, how they go about it, and the ever-changing external environments which bear upon their work.

The series will cover topics such as: the purpose of policing and public expectations, public health approaches to policing, policing of cyber-crime, environmental policing, digital policing, social media, Artificial Intelligence and big data, accountability of complex networks of actors involved in policing, austerity, public scrutiny, technological and social changes, over-policing and marginalised groups, under-policing and corporate crime, institutional abuses, policing of climate change, ethics, workforce, education, evidence-based policing, and the pluralisation of policing.

Danielle Watson · Loene Howes ·
Sinclair Dinnen · Melissa Bull · Sara N. Amin

Policing in the Pacific Islands

Danielle Watson
School of Justice
Queensland University of Technology
Brisbane, QLD, Australia

Loene Howes
School of Social Sciences
University of Tasmania
Hobart, TAS, Australia

Sinclair Dinnen
Department of Pacific Affairs
Australian National University
Canberra, ACT, Australia

Melissa Bull
School of Justice
Queensland University of Technology
Brisbane, QLD, Australia

Sara N. Amin
School of Law and Social Sciences
The University of the South Pacific
Suva, Fiji

ISSN 2730-535X   ISSN 2730-5368 (electronic)
Palgrave's Critical Policing Studies
ISBN 978-3-031-10634-7   ISBN 978-3-031-10635-4 (eBook)
https://doi.org/10.1007/978-3-031-10635-4

© The Editor(s) (if applicable) and The Author(s) 2023. This book is an open access publication.
Open Access This book is licensed under the terms of the Creative Commons Attribution 4.0 International License (http://creativecommons.org/licenses/by/4.0/), which permits use, sharing, adaptation, distribution and reproduction in any medium or format, as long as you give appropriate credit to the original author(s) and the source, provide a link to the Creative Commons license and indicate if changes were made.
The images or other third party material in this book are included in the book's Creative Commons license, unless indicated otherwise in a credit line to the material. If material is not included in the book's Creative Commons license and your intended use is not permitted by statutory regulation or exceeds the permitted use, you will need to obtain permission directly from the copyright holder.
The use of general descriptive names, registered names, trademarks, service marks, etc. in this publication does not imply, even in the absence of a specific statement, that such names are exempt from the relevant protective laws and regulations and therefore free for general use.
The publisher, the authors, and the editors are safe to assume that the advice and information in this book are believed to be true and accurate at the date of publication. Neither the publisher nor the authors or the editors give a warranty, expressed or implied, with respect to the material contained herein or for any errors or omissions that may have been made. The publisher remains neutral with regard to jurisdictional claims in published maps and institutional affiliations.

Cover credit: © Melisa Hasan

This Palgrave Macmillan imprint is published by the registered company Springer Nature Switzerland AG
The registered company address is: Gewerbestrasse 11, 6330 Cham, Switzerland

Acknowledgements

This book, *Policing in the Pacific Islands*, is the product of a collaboration among the five co-authors, which spanned more than two years. The content of the book has developed and evolved over the course of the collaboration into the finished product that we share with our readers.

We would like to acknowledge the police organisations, civil society organisations, and regional bodies of the Pacific Island countries and territories that have shared their data and experiences that have allowed us to write this book.

We thank our respective universities and the schools and departments within them for supporting our efforts to publish this book, including making it available as an open access publication. Specifically, we thank the School of Justice, Queensland University of Technology; School of Social Sciences, University of Tasmania; Department of Pacific Affairs, Australian National University; and School of Law and Social Sciences, University of the South Pacific.

Finally, we thank the reviewers of this book for their helpful feedback, Natasha Broadstock for her assistance with editing our manuscript, and the team at Palgrave Macmillan, for their guidance and support with this exciting project.

Contents

1	Introduction to Policing in the Pacific	1
2	Context-Specific Issues and Challenges of Policing in the Pacific	9
3	Trends in and Social Dynamics of Crime in the Pacific	37
4	Plural Policing in the Pacific	83
5	The International Policing Agenda in the Pacific	111
6	Women and the Institution of Policing in the Pacific	151
7	Conclusion	187
Index		193

About the Authors

Danielle Watson is a Senior Lecturer and Research Training Coordinator in the School of Justice, Queensland University of Technology. Her research focuses on security, policing, police–community relations, policing culturally and linguistically diverse communities, and plural regulatory systems in the Caribbean and the Pacific. She conducts research on (in)security in Pacific Island countries, capacity building for security service providers, and recruitment and training, as well as many other areas specific to improving security in developing country contexts.

Loene Howes is a Senior Lecturer in Criminology in the School of Social Sciences and a Senior Researcher in the Tasmanian Institute of Law Enforcement Studies (TILES) at the University of Tasmania. Her research aims to foster increased effectiveness of communication in the criminal justice system in ways that enhance access to justice. It explores topics such as the relational dynamics of police investigative interviews, interprofessional communication about forensic science evidence, and policing partnerships in Pacific contexts.

Sinclair Dinnen is a Senior Fellow in the Department of Pacific Affairs at the Australian National University. He previously lectured in law at the University of Papua New Guinea (PNG) and was Head of Crime Studies at PNG's National Research Institute. His Ph.D. investigated urban crime, resource conflict, and election-related violence in PNG. He has conducted extensive research in the Melanesian Pacific and published widely on legal pluralism, crime and policing, security and development, conflict and peacebuilding, and hybrid social and political orders.

Melissa Bull is an Interdisciplinary Scholar and the Director of Queensland University of Technology Centre for Justice. She has expertise in the fields of sentencing and punishment, drug and alcohol policy and regulation, policing diversity, and policing in differently organised states. She has conducted research focused on the principles of punishment, sentencing and serious drug supply offences, sentencing and disability, criminal justice diversionary programs targeting drug- and alcohol-related offending, international drug regulation, and policing in diverse communities including the policing of gender violence in the global South.

Sara N. Amin is a Senior Lecturer and the Discipline Coordinator of Sociology at the University of the South Pacific. Her research and teaching interests centre on the intersections of power, identity, and resistance, with a special focus on dynamics related to the politics of violence, gender, religion, and migration in South Asia and Pacific Island countries. Her research has been funded by various organisations including the British Academy, the Australian Research Council, Canadian Social Science and Humanities Research Council, the Fulbright Foundation, and the Ford Foundation.

Acronyms

3P	Partnership for Pacific Policing
AAP	Australian Assisting Police
AFP	Australian Federal Police
AIPM	Australasian Institute of Police Management
ANU	Australian National University
APEC	Asia-Pacific Economic Cooperation
APG	Asia/Pacific Group on Money Laundering
AusAID	Australian Aid
CEDAW	Convention on the Elimination of All forms of Discrimination Against Women
COVID-19	Coronavirus Disease of 2019
DAC	Development Assistance Committee
DFAT	Department of Foreign Affairs and Trade
DHS	Demographic and Health Surveys
DPKO	Department of Peacekeeping Operations
DSM	Deep Sea (or seabed) Mining
ECP	Enhanced Cooperation Program
FIUs	Financial intelligence units
FRANZ	France, Australia, and New Zealand
FSM	Federated States of Micronesia
HRW	Human Rights Watch
ICTs	Information and Communication Technologies
ILGA World	International Lesbian, Gay, Bisexual, Trans and Intersex Association
IPV	Intimate Partner Violence

LGBTQA+	Lesbian, Gay, Bisexual, Transgender, Queer/Questioning, Asexual, and Others
MDGs	Millennium Development Goals
MFAT	Ministry of Foreign Affairs and Trade
MICS	Multiple Indicator Cluster Surveys
MTRT	Mid-Term Review Team
NGOs	Non-Governmental Organisations
NZAID	New Zealand Aid
OCO	Oceania Customs Organisation
PICs	Pacific Island countries
PICP	Pacific Islands Chiefs of Police
PICP WAN	Pacific Islands Chiefs of Police Women's Advisory Network
PICTs	Pacific Island countries and territories
PIDC	Pacific Immigrant Development Community
PILON	Pacific Islands Law Officers Network
PNG	Papua New Guinea
PPDP-R	Pacific Police Development Program—Regional
PPDVP	Pacific Prevention of Domestic Violence Programme
PPF	Participating Police Force
PTCCC	Pacific Transnational Crime Coordination Centre
PTCN	Pacific Transnational Crime Network
RAMSI	Regional Assistance Mission to Solomon Islands
RNZ	Radio New Zealand
RPNGC	Royal Papua New Guinea Constabulary
RSIP	Royal Solomon Islands Police
RSIPF	Royal Solomon Islands Police Force
SDGs	Sustainable Development Goals
SIA	Security Industries Authority
SIDS	Small Island Developing States
SPC	Secretariat of the Pacific Community
TCUs	Transnational Crime Units
TPDP	Tonga Police Development Programme
TSOC	Transnational Serious and Organised Crime Pacific Taskforce
UN	United Nations
UNDP	United Nations Development Programme
UNFPA	United Nations Population Fund
UNICEF	United Nations Children's Fund
UN-INSTRAW	UN International Research and Training Institute for the Advancement of Women
UNODC	United Nations Office on Drugs and Crime
UNSCR	United Nations Security Council Resolution
US	United States
USSR	Union of Soviet Socialist Republics/Soviet Union
VAW	Violence Against Women
WAN	Women's Advisory Network
WHO	World Health Organization

LIST OF FIGURES

Fig. 2.1 The Pacific Islands (*Source* CartoGIS College of Asia and the Pacific, Australian National University) 13

Fig. 3.1 Total police-recorded criminal offences in 2013/2014 vs. 2018/2019 (*Sources* Fiji: Fiji Bureau of Statistics, 2013; Fiji Police Force [personal communication, 2019]; Solomon Islands: Royal Solomon Islands Police Force, 2014, 2018; Vanuatu: Nichols et al., 2019; Samoa: Samoa Bureau of Statistics, 2013; R. Boodoosingh [personal communication, 2021]; Tonga: Tonga Police, 2014, 2019; Tuvalu: Tuvalu Police Service [personal communications, 2013, 2019]; Guam: Guam Police Department, 2015, 2020; Kiribati: Kiribati Police Service [personal communication, 2020]) 45

Fig. 3.2 Crime rates in PICTs per 500 habitants in 2013/2014 vs. 2018/2019 (*Sources* Fiji: Fiji Bureau of Statistics, 2013; Fiji Police Force [personal communication, 2019]; Solomon Islands: Royal Solomon Islands Police Force, 2014, 2018; Vanuatu: Nichols et al., 2019; Samoa: Samoa Bureau of Statistics, 2013; R. Boodoosingh [personal communication, 2021]; Tonga: Tonga Police, 2014, 2019; Guam: Guam Police Department, 2015, 2020; Kiribati: Kiribati Police Service [personal communication, 2020]) 46

Fig. 3.3 Property crimes and crimes against the person as a proportion of total crimes in 2013/2014 vs. 2018/2019 (*Sources* Fiji: Fiji Bureau of Statistics, 2013; Fiji Police Force [personal communication, 2019]; Solomon Islands: Royal Solomon Islands Police Force, 2014, 2018; Vanuatu: Nichols et al., 2019; Samoa: Samoa Bureau of Statistics, 2013; R. Boodoosingh [personal communication, 2021]; Tonga: Tonga Police, 2014, 2019; Guam: Guam Police Department, 2015, 2020; Kiribati: Kiribati Police Service [personal communication, 2020]) 47

Fig. 3.4 Homicide rates in 1990 vs. 2017 in Oceania (*Source* Global Burden of Disease Collaborative Network, 2018; Institute for Health Metrics and Evaluation, 2018; Roser & Ritchie, 2013. *Note* Homicide rates are measured as the number of deaths from homicide per 100,000 individuals) 53

Fig. 3.5 Estimated percentage of children (1–14 years) experiencing violent discipline (psychological and physical) at home (*Source* Suthanthiraraj, 2019) 56

Fig. 3.6 Proportion of ever-partnered women disclosing experience of IPV (physical and/or sexual) (*Source* See Table 3.1) 57

Fig. 3.7 Comparison of lifetime experience of women and girls since age 15 of physical and sexual violence by intimate partner vs. non-partner (*Source* See Table 3.1) 58

Fig. 4.1 Growth of licensed security companies, PNG (*Source* Adapted from Isari [2019], p. 4) 100

List of Tables

Table 3.1	Years, survey methodologies, and age groups of IPV data in Figs. 3.6 and 3.7	57
Table 3.2	Criminalisation of homosexuality in PICTs	60
Table 5.1	Broad categories and roles of international policing	119
Table 5.2	Examples of discrete police capacity development initiatives	133
Table 5.3	Pacific partnerships for addressing transnational crime	138

CHAPTER 1

Introduction to Policing in the Pacific

Abstract Research on policing in the Pacific Islands draws from multiple disciplines, reflecting the multifaceted nature of policing in local contexts that neither fit a Western model of statehood nor adopt an analytic position from the global North. This chapter sets the scene for a focused, contextualised and interdisciplinary discussion of policing in Pacific Islands countries and territories. It recognises the need to analyse policing both within the broader context of the global dynamics of policing, crime and (in)security, and within the specific, complex, and diverse countries and territories of the region. The chapter outlines the structure of the book and provides an overview of the chapters that follow.

Keywords Pacific policing · Policing landscape · Policing themes

Background

Police, as the most visible arm of government and the primary interface between a state and its population, signify and implement a state's right to engage in actions intended to ensure legislated acceptable behaviours from its populace (Dunham & Alpert, 2010; Pollock, 1998). The power and authority assigned to state police place police and acts of (and associated with) policing at the forefront of criminological and other popular discourses. Contemporary policing scholarship has shifted away from a basic focus on police use of authority, power, persuasion, and force to broader multidisciplinary and prismatic understandings of policing as complex (Hughes et al., 2013; Prenzler & Sarre, 2002), evolving (Kelling & Wycoff, 2001), non-singular (Dinnen & Braithwaite, 2009; Greener, 2009; Jones & Lister, 2015; Jones & Newburn, 2006; Loader, 2000), and impacted by contextual variables (Dempsey & Forst, 2015; Newburn, 2012; Watson, 2018; Watson & Kerrigan, 2018). While these topics continue to be explored extensively by policing scholars in developed countries with a history of dominance in knowledge production, the growing body of literature on policing in developing countries, particularly Pacific Islands countries and territories (PICTs), is not as extensive.

Pacific scholars have typically taken an indirect or parallelistic approach to policing that shifts the primary focus away from criminological positioning to an adapted hybridised disciplinary mix more suited to the multifaceted nature of policing in contexts that do not fit neatly into Western models of state(hood). This, in part, serves as an acknowledgement of police as an imported security mechanism that evolves to suit the context. Research from different interdisciplinary camps, specifically anthropology, gender, cultural, and environmental studies—which also account for the majority of sources with a specific focus on policing in the Pacific—draw attention to the myriad of societal manifestations of dysfunctions and threats to security across the Pacific region. These dysfunctions and threats are primarily in relation to marginalised groups, climate, natural resources, and cultural capital. Interdisciplinary scholarship also highlights the inadequacy of responses and the need to expand the scope of discussions aimed at generating actionable solutions. The secondary positioning of policing by scholars in these fields means that scholarly literature is dispersed among multiple de-linked sources with no particular focus on presenting a holistic view of policing in PICTs. This, on the one hand, may be interpreted as a signal to researchers of a need to cover more criminological ground; while, on the other, it might highlight the need for greater collaborative efforts. *Policing in the Pacific Islands* is a combination of both interpretations.

Policing in the Pacific Islands examines a large body of secondary data from multiple sources to draw attention to the multifaceted nature of policing in contemporary Pacific Island societies. We explore selected themes relevant to an understanding of the complex roles of policing, both specifically as critical to governance and service delivery, and more generally in terms of broader issues and future directions in Pacific policing. The political and legal relationship between policing organisations and other government departments, police relationships with women, youth and vulnerable groups, responses to crime and criminality, and the increasing requirement for human resource deployment in a limited or resource-constrained environment are discussed. We provide a contextualised account of policing and how it is practised in small island developing states across the Pacific region, and elaborate on emerging global issues within policing discourses such as terrorism, and transnational and cross-border crimes, and how these issues can affect regional security and governance.

Beyond the focus on policing, we aim to unpack the sometimes singular and historic representations of the Pacific region, which can lead to flawed assumptions about regional uniformity and overshadow the realities of the complexity and diversity of the region. We do this not to deny the existence of similarities across the region, nor to undermine the value of regional discussions and presentations, but to caution against assumptions about the creation of an all-inclusive narrative with applicability for all PICTs. Attention is drawn to the region's rich and varied colonial past (and present), existing complexities between nationalism and dependence, and reliance on external entities and cooperation. Pacific policing is explored as the maintenance of law and order within a specific geographic remit, with local, regional, and international stakeholders that can have competing or conflicting geopolitical agendas. We also highlight the multifaceted nature of policing beyond well-known enforcement roles, as well as the place of different types of regulatory authorities and actors in the Pacific, which are informed by not only law, but also community norms—often referred to as *kastom*—associated with local forms of customary or traditional authority, religion, and Indigenous arbitration practices.

Chapter Organisation

While we acknowledge the multifaceted nature of policing and the wide range of themes covered in policing scholarship, we do not claim to cover all policing-related topics or realities specific to all PICTs. Instead, we discuss five priority themes to provide scholars and practitioners with an overview of the complex issues that are at the forefront of local, regional, and international Pacific security discourses. These themes are security challenges, the changing crime landscape, multiple security actors, the internationalisation of responses to crime and criminality, and women in security. These themes are discussed in five chapters as follows.

Chapter 2 discusses context-specific issues and challenges faced by police officers in PICTs. It draws on examples from Melanesia, Micronesia, and Polynesia to show that police officers in the Pacific are faced with conventional policing challenges as well as 'unconventional' issues specific to island territories with strained resources, strong cultures and traditions, reliance on external support, unconventionally policed spaces, and large and often fragmented jurisdictions. It also examines formal and informal policing roles underscored by tradition, culture, and religion, and shows that policing in the Pacific is as much about improvisation as it is about discretion and professional practice. In addition, this chapter highlights the need for literature based on research evidence that is historically, contextually, and socially specific, if solutions are to be derived to address local and regional policing challenges.

Critical to an understanding of policing in any context are insights into the crime prevention and response mandate. Chapter 3 explores the changing face of crime, disorder, and law enforcement in PICTs. Police organisations across the globe have undergone significant changes in an attempt to respond to the new and emerging threats with which they are faced. This is also true for the Pacific region as climate change induced population displacements, expanded food insecurity, rapid urbanisation, and new technologies are changing crime, disorder, and policing practices. We describe changes in the types of crimes police officers are required to respond to and discuss how these 'new' crimes prompt specific types of organisational shifts. We also elaborate on internal adjustments, as well as international partnerships forged as a response to the changing face of crime and disorder.

Chapter 4 provides an overview of the plural dimensions of policing provision in the Pacific. This includes the role of diverse policing actors operating at different scales—local, regional, international, and transnational—as constituent parts of broader security assemblages. As well as the familiar form of public police organisations, these actors include informal policing arrangements drawing on local *kastom* and faith-based authority, as well as the expanding domains of transnational and private policing in recent years. The chapter also discusses how growing recognition of pluralisation by scholars has encouraged a more expansive conceptualisation of policing as a network of power and regulation involving multiple actors and a variety of institutional forms, thereby moving beyond a conventional focus on the police as a discrete organisation. In doing so, the chapter examines how the notion of plural policing unsettles longstanding assumptions about the primacy of states in security governance.

Chapter 5 examines the complex endeavour of international policing. In the Pacific, where countries are typically categorised as developing nations, and some additionally as fragile or conflict-affected states, capacity development has long been a focus of international policing. Additionally, since the beginning of the twenty-first century (and particularly since 11 September 2001), security threats such as terrorism and transnational crime have become increasingly prominent. Resolving such complex internal and external security threats is beyond the capacity of a single jurisdiction; partnerships are crucial, but they are shaped by various social and political forces. This chapter examines the forms of international cooperation that shape and contribute to policing organisations in the Pacific. It provides specific examples of policing partnerships in the Pacific region, discusses the fragility and variances that underpin them, and highlights strengths identified in research and practice on which to build.

Chapter 6 examines women and the institution of policing in the Pacific. Gender equality has been a primary focal area for international, regional, and local organisations working in the Pacific, largely because of high numbers of documented cases of gender inequality and the prevalence of crimes against women. The gender agenda has resulted in significant attention being drawn to police organisations as the most visible arm of governance and because of their role in responding to violence against women and girls. One proposed solution to advancing the gender agenda has been to increase the number of female police officers. Achieving this goal has been hampered by many challenges: professional, institutional, and social. Here, we explore the place of women in highly gendered policing organisations and provide a general overview of the multiple roles they negotiate as women in policing in the Pacific Islands.

We conclude with a summary of key issues presented throughout the book and a discussion about the ways forward for policing in the Pacific Islands. We consider what the preceding chapters together tell us about policing in the Pacific and how these arguments are situated within (or come into conflict with) broader discourses and theories about contemporary policing practice. We also propose an agenda for future directions for dialogue, research, and scholarship on policing in the Pacific Islands.

REFERENCES

Dempsey, J. S., & Forst, L. S. (2015). *An introduction to policing*. Cengage Learning.

Dinnen, S., & Braithwaite, J. (2009). Reinventing policing through the prism of the colonial kiap. *Policing & Society, 19*(2), 161–173.

Dunham, R. G., & Alpert, G. P. (2010). The foundation of the police role in society. In Dunham, R. G., Alpert, G. P., & McLean, K. D. (Eds). *Critical issues in policing, contemporary readings*. Waveland Press.

Greener, B. K. (2009). *The new international policing*. Palgrave Macmillan.

Hughes, B., Hunt, C. T., & Curth-Bibb, J. (2013). *Forging new conventional wisdom beyond international policing: Learning from complex political realities*. Martinus Nijhoff Publishers.

Jones, P. D., & Lister, D. H. (2015). Antarctic near-surface air temperatures compared with ERA-Interim values since 1979. *International Journal of Climatology, 35*(7), 1354–1366.

Jones, T., & Newburn, T. (Eds.). (2006). *Plural policing: A comparative perspective*. Psychology Press.

Kelling, G. L., & Wycoff, M. A. (2001). *The evolving strategy of policing: Case studies of strategic change*. National Institute of Justice.

Loader, I. (2000). Plural policing and democratic governance. *Social & Legal Studies, 9*(3), 323–345.

Newburn, T. (Ed.). (2012). *Handbook of policing*. Routledge.

Pollock, J. M. (1998). *Ethics in crime and justice: Dilemmas and decisions*. West/Wadsworth.

Prenzler, T., & Sarre, R. (2002). The policing complex. In A. Graycar & P. Grabosky (Eds.), *The Cambridge handbook of Australian criminology* (pp. 52–72). Cambridge University Press.

Watson, D. (2018). *Police and the policed: Language and power relations on the margins of the global south*. Springer.

Watson, D., & Kerrigan, D. (2018). Crime, criminality, and north-to-south criminological complexities: Theoretical implications for policing 'hotspot' communities in 'underdeveloped' countries. In K. Carrington, R. Hogg, J. Scott, & M. Sozzo (Eds.), *The Palgrave handbook of criminology and the global south* (pp. 611–632). Palgrave Macmillan.

Open Access This chapter is licensed under the terms of the Creative Commons Attribution 4.0 International License (http://creativecommons.org/licenses/by/4.0/), which permits use, sharing, adaptation, distribution and reproduction in any medium or format, as long as you give appropriate credit to the original author(s) and the source, provide a link to the Creative Commons license and indicate if changes were made.

The images or other third party material in this chapter are included in the chapter's Creative Commons license, unless indicated otherwise in a credit line to the material. If material is not included in the chapter's Creative Commons license and your intended use is not permitted by statutory regulation or exceeds the permitted use, you will need to obtain permission directly from the copyright holder.

CHAPTER 2

Context-Specific Issues and Challenges of Policing in the Pacific

Abstract Issues and challenges are not uncommon to policing organisations across the globe. For those in Pacific Islands countries and territories (PICTs), common issues such as functioning in a limited or resource-constrained environment and adapting to continuously increasing stakeholder demands are further compounded by geographic context. The region presents unique policing spaces, which means that policing challenges characterised as normal or conventional must be dealt with alongside unconventional policing issues specific to PICTs with varied governance arrangements, strained resources, diverse cultures and traditions, reliance on external support, spaces that are policed by alternative means, and large and often fragmented jurisdictions. This chapter provides an overview of the challenges faced by police organisations in PICTs and shows that policing in these contexts is as much about improvisation as it is about discretion and professional practice. It establishes a context for later discussions about crime in PICTs; formal and informal policing roles across the region underscored by geography, tradition, culture, and religion; international policing agendas; and contemporary shifts in arguments about women in policing.

Keywords Policing challenges and complexities · Organisational capacity · Colonial policing · Policing jurisdictions · Donor funding

Introduction

Policing in Pacific Island countries and territories (PICTs) is situated in a context that melds traditional practices with Western models of law-and-order maintenance. The region's rich history of governance along traditional and cultural lines means that systems of upholding law and order preceded states and state policing models, which were later introduced through colonialism, contact or the adoption of Western constabulary replicas of governance (Jolly, 2016; Putt et al., 2018; Sai, 2007). Prior to the introduction of colonial models, the maintenance of order primarily involved a range of approaches to social conflict management led by non-state authorities (families and communities) headed by male elders, chiefs, or individual 'big-men'.[1] Order maintenance included, but was not limited to, physical action (e.g., warfare and revenge attacks), the sanction of sorcery, the involvement of local leaders (usually representative of extended families within the community), and payments of compensation (Goddard, 2010, pp. 6–9 as cited in Allen et al., 2013; MacDonald, 2001; Pratt & Melei, 2018; Uakeia, 2016). The roles of these individuals took on more of a restorative character rather than one of power, and there was a primary focus on collective dispute resolution in contexts where the priority was peace at the community level (Chambers & Chambers, 2001, p. 63 as cited in Pratt & Melei, 2018). In PICTs where the arrival of religious missionaries preceded that of colonial authorities, the idea of centralised councils was promoted and council positions were often filled by traditional leaders who retained influence in their communities (MacDonald, 2001). The integration of customary approaches with Christian beliefs and Western-style legal adversarialism meant that a hybrid model of justice and governance was in place when colonial authorities later arrived (MacDonald, 2001; Pratt & Melei, 2018). In many colonies (in the Pacific and elsewhere) legal dualism prevailed, where there were in effect two very different systems that applied to Europeans and 'natives', respectively. It is important to note that while formally separate (legal) systems existed in many countries and territories, considerable interaction occurred between them in practice. Justice and policing under colonialism were very different to the modern justice and policing systems in independent PICTs.

---

[1] 'Big-men' are commonly associated with Melanesian societies and distinguished from chiefly Polynesian societies.

Contemporary police organisations across the region primarily reflect Western institutional legacies associated with the establishment of states and the sanctioning of the police as the most visible instrument of government authority (Watson & Dinnen, 2020). The constabulary model was the standard initial policing import across the British colonies (Bell, 2013; Dinnen, 2008; Emsley, 2014). Specifically, the Royal Irish Constabulary was paramilitary in form and perceived by colonial administrators as most appropriate for large and sparsely populated places (Emsley, 2014). It was also seen as appropriate for policing (and suppressing) Indigenous populations (primarily in Melanesian countries, such as PNG, where it was largely about extending government influence and implementing 'native administration') (Bell, 2013; Dinnen, 2008). The primary focus of these 'State Military Forces' (Emsley, 2014) was the protection of the power of the colonial state through internal security and public order maintenance (Bell, 2013). Initially, colonisation undermined local systems and leadership by removing the autonomy and authority of existing leaders and enforcing punishment (Allen et al., 2013). Often, those appointed by colonial authorities, as was the case in Solomon Islands, were not recognised by locals, and those whom the locals wanted to be appointed did not meet requirements set by colonial authorities (Allen et al., 2013). In Solomon Islands, as was the case in other PICTs, local councils were formed to manage customary matters and were managed by British-appointed individuals (Allen et al., 2013). In many PICTs, imported systems eroded traditional hierarchies, then reincorporated them (Allen et al., 2013). Some powers were lost, some were gained, and the Indigenous people, in many instances, adapted to enforce colonial laws (Emsley, 2014).

While the uniqueness and diversity of the Pacific region makes it problematic to articulate an all-encompassing policing narrative about the former or current state of policing, generalisations can be made about the issues and challenges specific to PICTs with strained resources, diverse cultures and traditions, reliance on external support, unconventionally policed spaces, and large and often fragmented jurisdictions. This chapter presents an overview of these challenges and further elaborates on how they impact on policing in specific PICT contexts. It builds on dialogue about the resilience of PICTs, and draws on examples from Melanesia, Micronesia, and Polynesia to show that in addition to the common issues and challenges faced by police organisations, the Pacific landscape presents context-specific realities to be navigated and negotiated by police organisations. This chapter establishes the context for much of what is discussed in the ensuing chapters. It moves from a provision of historical insights into policing in PICTs to a brief discussion of organisational shifts impacting on policing across the region. Issues and challenges related to jurisdiction, funding, and organisational capacity are also explored before an overview of these issues and challenges is presented.

Pacific Policing Historical Insights

The Pacific Islands region is often viewed as comprising three broad cultural and geographic sub-regions—Melanesia, Micronesia, and Polynesia. Scattered across an enormous expanse of ocean, each country has its own distinct history and socio-political characteristics, making it difficult to generalise across the region as a whole. Differences exist in terms of political status and population size, as well as in key social and economic indicators. Most Pacific Island countries are microstates with small populations dispersed across numerous low-lying islands. Approximately 90% of the region's population of around 11 million people live in the independent Melanesian states of Papua New Guinea (PNG), Fiji, and Solomon Islands (United Nations Population Fund [UNFPA], 2014, p. 5). Approximately 9 million of these live in PNG alone, which dominates the region in terms of land mass and population size (Department of Foreign Affairs and Trade [DFAT], 2021) (Fig. 2.1).

Variations in population sizes are reflected in those of Pacific police organisations, which range from fewer than 20 officers in tiny Niue to around 7000 in PNG (Putt et al., 2018). Other differences include levels of crime and insecurity in different countries, as well as in policing traditions derived from the histories of police development in each country, including legacies from colonial pasts and the continuing influence of external powers providing policing assistance in the post-colonial present.

Colonial Policing

Prior to colonisation and contact with the West, traditional policing mechanisms upheld order and security in PICTs (Boodoosingh & Schoeffel, 2018; Jolly, 2016; Putt et al., 2018; Sai, 2007). Differentiations between precolonial policing and broader justice mechanisms are not readily available in Pacific policing literature. However, scholarly

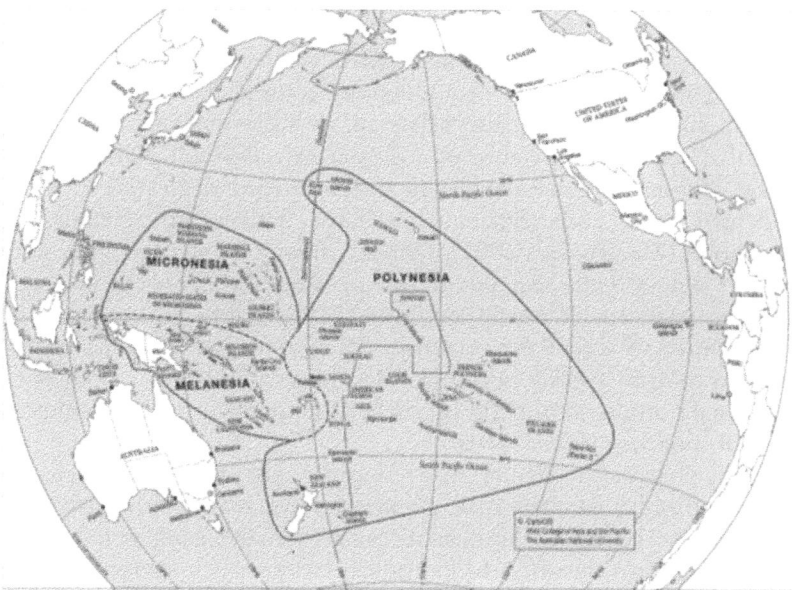

Fig. 2.1 The Pacific Islands (*Source* CartoGIS College of Asia and the Pacific, Australian National University)

accounts allow us to make informed interpretations about the mechanisms that preceded what is now known as policing across the region. Precolonial or traditional policing mechanisms largely consisted of peacemaking between tribes or families, which was usually brokered by elders or community/tribal/clan leaders (Jolly, 2016). Such undertakings included the resolving of disputes between individuals (MacDonald, 2001). Variances in these policing mechanisms can be seen in examples drawn from Melanesia, Micronesia, and Polynesia.

In the Melanesian islands that became Solomon Islands, there were a range of social and regulatory systems, which involved leadership roles being occupied by hereditary chiefs or individual big-men, or a combination of both (Putt et al., 2018). Similarly, in PNG, headmen, big-men, or chiefs provided clan leadership and guidance, with nuances of titles and terms differing across regions (Sai, 2007). Fiji also had a hierarchical society with hereditary tribal chiefs who maintained order using customary law based on traditional social order (Jowitt, 2009).

In the Micronesian country of Kiribati, communities were governed by an *Unimwane* or group of male elders who represented a family or clan, and by the *maneaba* or community council (MacDonald, 2001; Uakeia, 2016). *Maneaba* also refers to a village meeting house, and the social and political centre of a district (MacDonald, 2001; Uakeia, 2016). *Maneaba* was associated with several *kainga*, which were the basic residential units—each containing extended families and a number of households (MacDonald, 2001). Disputes among *kainga* members were handled out of *maneaba*, but if two or more *kainga* were involved, *maneaba* involvement usually occurred (MacDonald, 2001). If participants refused to accept the consensus decision reached (Uakeia, 2016), recourse to arms usually occurred (MacDonald, 2001). In addition to maintaining order, *maneaba* disseminated and implemented government (council) policies (Uakeia, 2016).

In the Polynesian country that was to become Tuvalu, maintenance of law and order involved male community elders (*taumatua/te sina o fenua/matai*) acting as representatives of extended families to resolve disputes and provide advice to individuals charged with leadership roles. These leadership roles included the council of chiefs (*kau aliki* or *kaiga aliki*) and reigning chiefs[2] (*ulu aliki*) who represented a number of extended families in a district and had the authority to make final decisions (Pratt & Melei, 2018).

Similar systems existed across the Pacific with a common purpose of maintaining order at the family, village, community, district, or island level; resolving disputes; determining appropriate reprisal or compensation; and ensuring the maintenance of societies (Goddard, 2010, pp. 6–9 as cited in Allen et al., 2013; Pratt & Melei, 2018; Uakeia, 2016).

Colonisation and Policing

The colonial history of the Pacific region documents various interfaces with Christianity before the presence of colonial authorities. Examples of this were evidenced in Kiribati and Tuvalu (MacDonald, 2001; Pratt & Melei, 2018). As was the case in other countries, Christian missionaries encouraged the formation of centralised councils to oversee the maintenance of law and order. A merger between traditional and

---

[2] The reigning chief for each island served on the council of chiefs.

foreign practices of order maintenance occurred in places such as Kiribati and Tuvalu, as council positions were often filled by traditional leaders who, therefore retained influence in their communities in new ways (MacDonald, 2001). MacDonald (2001) states that Kiribati was less welcoming of imported structures and values, and did so only as a means of controlling or mitigating colonial influence. The integration of customary approaches with Christian beliefs fostered a hybrid model of justice and governance prior to the arrival of British authorities in the late 1890s, which is discussed further in Chapter 4 (MacDonald, 2001; Pratt & Melei, 2018).

Missionary influence and Christianisation also impacted Solomon Islands. However, the missionaries had less significant influence in shaping law and order in some parts of Solomon Islands compared with their role in the early colonisation of Tuvalu and Kiribati. Early missionary efforts in Solomon Islands were mainly coastal and more widespread efforts did not commence until the introduction of the British Protectorate in 1893 (Hilliard, 1974). Colonial leaders viewed the disparate centralised council systems in Solomon Islands as lacking order and saw a society in need of other governance methods (Putt et al., 2018). In 1970, there were about 50 local courts in Solomon Islands and their main role was to resolve land matters according to customary law and to address minor criminal issues (Cox et al., 2012). The courts operated according to colonial authority guidelines (Nanau, 2017). Local councils were scrapped in 1998 (Allen et al., 2013) and local courts dwindled, with active numbers limited to around five by 2008 (Cox et al., 2012). In Tuvalu, in 1997, local councils on eight islands obtained power over their own administrative affairs (Fraenkel & Corbett, 2016). These councils are mainly dominated by (male) elders and chiefs, sometimes with influence from church leaders; however, there are indications that roles for women on island councils are increasing (Fraenkel & Corbett, 2016).

Colonial administrators recruited Indigenous people as policemen to serve as intermediaries between colonisers and Indigenous people (Allen et al., 2013; Putt et al., 2018; Sai, 2007). Countries such as Fiji and Solomon Islands had small armed constabularies, with European officers and 'native' police (Putt et al., 2018). The legitimacy of headmen appointed by the colonisers was often challenged because of non-adherence to Indigenous hierarchies of authority, and those nominated by locals for appointment were often deemed unworthy by the colonisers (Allen et al., 2013). Local councils managed by British-appointed headmen were formed to manage customary matters (Allen et al., 2013). In many instances, colonial systems were perceived to erode the traditional hierarchies, before reincorporating them (Allen et al., 2013) and empowering Indigenous people to enforce colonial laws (Emsley, 2014). Different forms of resistance to colonial rule resulted in an acknowledgement of the need to reorient or train local leaders within established jurisdictions to provide a middle ground for law-and-order maintenance discussions, decisions, and actions, and to validate colonial structures involving local elders, chiefs, and councils (Allen et al., 2013).

Pluralised regulatory arrangements often cause challenges for police and local leaders. Chiefs of police across the region have in the past commented on officers being confused about governance and formal processes among local leaders (Boswell, 2010). Efforts to decentralise and work with local systems while still working with colonial models of governance usually translated to police officers being unclear on formal processes (Boswell, 2010). In some parts of the Pacific, there was (and continues to be) a lack of understanding among local leaders about how to work with formal systems, despite efforts by governments to educate, and police are placed in the awkward position of navigating interactions (Boswell, 2010). Challenges usually presented where traditional leaders acted both formally and informally. As expressed by Farran, discussing Vanuatu, the blurred lines between customary practices and codified law refer to whether 'traditional leaders involved in rule making, law enforcement, and dispute resolution are acting in a public capacity as agents of the state' (2006, p. 102). If they were not acting as state agents, they could not be held legally responsible for decisions that violated the constitution (Farran, 2006), complicating legal culpability.

From Independence to Modern-Day Policing

Despite independence, British colonial systems continued to shape policing in many PICTs (Bull et al., 2019). Fiji, Kiribati, Solomon Islands, and Tuvalu (and arguably other PICTs) all feature some hybrid of customary and colonial (or non-state and state) policing systems, with various levels of international policing present (Watson, 2020). Non-state authorities (i.e., family, church, and community) continue to play a significant role in addressing most conflict and security matters in PICTs. The geographical spread of populations in PICTs means that state policing does not reach all areas, and minor disputes and daily security needs continue to be managed locally by councils in most rural and some urban spaces, without the engagement of central authorities (Allen et al., 2013; Putt et al., 2018). Central policing authorities across the region continue to improve their legitimacy and distance themselves from negative images. For example, in Kiribati, the Commissioner of Police changed the name from the Kiribati Police Force to the Kiribati Police and Prison Services, respectively, to reflect a shift towards community collaboration in crime prevention and solving (Carswell & Loughlin, 2016).

Despite continued attempts at rebranding and strategising to disassociate from a longstanding colonial, paramilitaristic image, police organisations—primarily in Melanesia (but also in other parts of the Pacific)—continue to be viewed by international bodies, non-governmental organisations, and scholars as state apparatus of suppression and control of those deemed less powerful or those adhering to practices or behaviours that contradict the ideologies of state power brokers or rule of law. In Melanesian countries such as Fiji, Solomon Islands, and Vanuatu, strong remnants of the constabulary model remain in the police forces. Reference to human rights protections and civil liberties is absent from police Acts of Parliament, which instead focus on the role of police in law-and-order maintenance (Prasad, 2006). Other problematic aspects of colonial (state) policing include the absence or weakness of external civilian governing bodies and external methods of accountability (Prasad, 2006). For example, the Fiji Police Force is not subject to external oversight (Amnesty International, 2016), whereas in Samoa the Ombudsman's office is responsible for investigating complaints against the police (Ombudsman Samoa, 2020).

In much of Micronesia and Polynesia, state policing organisations have undergone multiple adaptations to foster more community-oriented approaches to policing. Initiatives include inviting and incorporating feedback from community stakeholders to inform organisational change, adapting foreign policies to suit local communities, and organisational restructuring to align with international best practices. Examples can be seen in Tuvalu, Guam, Fiji, Solomon Islands, Vanuatu, and more generally in the greater Pacific region. In 2013 and 2017, the Tuvalu Police Service requested country-wide research to elicit feedback from community stakeholders about their views on the state of policing in Tuvalu and ways to improve service delivery (Watson, 2018). A similar initiative was undertaken in Guam in 2018 (Watson et al., 2019). In 2013 and 2017, respectively, the Fiji Police Force and the Guam Police Department introduced the Duavata Community Policing Concept and the Mandaña Community-Oriented Policing Strategy (Fiji Police Force, 2013; Watson et al., 2019). Both reflect adapted versions of international community policing models to suit local policing contexts, and both are premised on established partnerships with local communities. Solomon Islands' adaptation of New Zealand's Crime Prevention Policy and No-Drop Policy are other examples of borrowing policing strategies and adapting and implementing them with consideration of local alignment. International shifts have resulted in the police organisations of PICTs reviewing gender policies and practices (Carswell & Loughlin, 2016; Goldsmith & Dinnen, 2007), revising or revisiting information-sharing arrangements and agreements (Putt et al., 2018), and increasing the emphasis on fostering community partnerships and empowering local stakeholders (Goldsmith & Dinnen, 2007; Turnbull, 2011). Against a backdrop of longstanding issues and challenges impacting policing operations, there continues to be a general consensus among PICTs' police leaders about the need for the advancement of policing practices within their respective jurisdictions.

Key Challenges for Policing in the Pacific

Challenges for policing roles across the Pacific region are underscored by geography, tradition, culture, and religion; international policing agendas; and contemporary shifts surrounding arguments about women in policing.

Organisational Shifts

The organisational mandates for policing organisations in some PICTs differ in important ways from those of policing organisations in the global North, from which Pacific policing organisations borrow operational frameworks, policies, and practices. Police organisations comprise one of multiple arms of national security service providers. As is the case with many metropolitan police organisations, they work alongside other stakeholders, including but not limited to immigration, national coast guard, and customs. The arrangements that exist in PICTs vary. Some PICTs maintain strong remnants of the colonial policing models as reflected in the police forces of Fiji and PNG, while others—such as Tuvalu Police Service (Government of Tuvalu, 2016; Pratt & Melei, 2018) and the Federated States of Micronesia Police—have been expanded to take on greater security service provision roles within their jurisdiction, such as border security and maritime offences. At the same time, others have shifted to adapt more service-oriented models, as reflected in the police services of Kiribati and Samoa (see e.g., Carswell & Loughlin, 2016; Samoa Police Service, 2021). Like policing organisations across the globe, those in PICTs are required to adapt in response to global shifts, international conventions, legislative advancements, crime evolution, and ever-increasing stakeholder demands.

Policing Large and Fragmented Jurisdictions

As a region with small populations inhabiting numerous islands and atolls dispersed across approximately 15% of the globe (World Bank, n.d.) policing organisations in PICTs face multiple challenges associated with large and often fragmented jurisdictions (Newton, 1998). For many police organisations across the region, the policing of large expanses of surrounding waters is one of many responsibilities, which include but are not limited to support for other arms of security, disaster response, and responding to public calls for service. Reference to the situation in Tuvalu provides contextual insights into one example.

Tuvalu has a population of approximately 11,000. The population is spread across nine islands and atolls, and over 26 square kilometres of land, dispersed over the 1.3 million square kilometres of the central Pacific Ocean (DFAT, 2020b; Fraenkel & Corbett, 2016). Tuvalu has a 900,000-square-kilometre exclusive economic zone (Fraenkel & Corbett, 2016). With a total of 101 sworn officers, the Tuvalu Police Service has responsibility for all calls for services within its jurisdiction on land and sea, as well as responsibility for managing disaster responses. Until Australia gifted a patrol boat to the Tuvalu Police Service in 2019, the organisation had just one boat for patrol purposes, responding to maritime calls for services, inter-island supply and communication, disaster support, and all other required policing purposes (DFAT, 2019). More than 80% of police personnel are based on the main island of Funafuti, where the capital is situated. The remainder is posted on seven of the outlying islands, and the remaining island has no police presence. Police posts on five of the outlying islands are staffed by one sworn officer who is supported by one unsworn community police member (Watson, 2018; Watson et al., 2021). There are also strong police–community relations for the maintenance of law and order, with communities having primary responsibility for dispute resolution and state police being involved as deemed necessary or appropriate at the community level. Further information on parallel policing arrangements in other PICTs is provided in Chapter 4. The realities for policing of PICTs with multi-island or otherwise geographically fragmented jurisdictions are very similar. For example, Solomon Islands, which is significantly larger in scale and population size than many other PICTs, has a land area of 28,400 square kilometres consisting of a double chain of six large islands and hundreds of smaller ones, forming nine main island groups (DFAT, 2020a; Putt et al., 2018). Similarly, Kiribati has a population of approximately 117,606 across 33 islands (Uakeia, 2016; World Bank, 2020). The policing challenges across their respective jurisdictions are numerous.

The constraints of resources available to policing organisations—including the limited range, upkeep, and usage of available technological resources—often translate to the allocation of the majority of resources to the most densely populated areas or immediate organisational priorities (Watson, 2020). Some organisations face challenges such as inadequate budgets to fund essential operations (Watson, 2020)—a challenge that can be further compounded by poor resource management (Stretem Rod blong Jastis mo Sefti, 2016). Such resource prioritisation results in a lack of immediate access to local police in many outlying islands and villages across the region (Boswell, 2010).

Policing arrangements across fragmented jurisdictions differ throughout the region. In some contexts, police posts on outlying islands or in remote regions exist with minimal staffing and minimal operational capacity (Allen et al., 2013; Evans et al., 2011; Putt et al., 2018). In PNG, communities based in rural and remote mountain areas, as is the case in most parts of Melanesia, have little or no police contact (Peake & Dinnen, 2014). While officers in such postings usually have full police powers, they are often supported by—or seen by residents as secondary to—non-state policing arrangements that exist at the community level (Bull et al., 2019; Farran, 2006; Lievore & Fairbarn-Dunlop, 2007; Pratt & Melei, 2018). There are also instances where no police posts are present on sparsely populated outlying islands or isolated regions (Boswell, 2010; Evans et al., 2011; Peake & Dinnen, 2014). Notwithstanding differences in consequences based on place, population size, and historical conflicts, such examples can be found across all of Melanesia, Micronesia, and Polynesia. Many countries in the Pacific include outlying islands and villages with small populations and no police posts (Boswell, 2010). In some of these contexts, partnerships exist between the police and communities to maintain law and order, whereas in others, extended family units determine accepted standards for behaviours and self-regulatory practices (Bull et al., 2021; Evans et al., 2011; Howes et al., 2021; Pratt & Melei, 2018). While these arrangements vary from one context to another, they generally involve community leaders or elders presiding over disputes, grievances, or perceived breaches of upheld laws and referring matters to formal policing authorities as they deem necessary (Pratt & Melei, 2018; Putt et al., 2018).

A limited police presence or the lack of a police presence in outlying islands and regions introduces issues of police legitimacy. The presence and functionality of alternative (largely customary) forms of law-and-order maintenance render the police (usually regarded as an external authority) a role as a state-centric entity that is unfamiliar and its members as unwarranted strangers (Bull et al., 2019; Peake & Dinnen, 2014). Several other factors also influence the effect of imported justice systems. These include regulatory pluralism, which formally and legally recognises customary laws and/or structures (Boodoosingh & Schoeffel, 2018; Fraenkel & Corbett, 2016; Siikala, 2014); informal norms around customary practices and other social and community norms (Lievore & Fairbarn-Dunlop, 2007; Pratt & Melei, 2018). All of these are bolstered by strong ties to culture and local identity (Putt et al., 2018). While policing hierarchy and state justice models remain largely Westernised, the complexities of law-and-order maintenance in many PICT contexts challenge the authority of the colonial systems (Bull et al., 2019).

The inability of the countries' legal systems to handle the types or magnitude of crimes taking place within them is further compounded by limitations in the resources needed to facilitate the policing of large geographic expanses (Boswell, 2010; DFAT, 2017a; Newton, 1998; Watson et al., 2021). For example, DFAT states that Fiji's 'geographic spread is a challenge, with some difficulty in providing advanced police capabilities to remote islands' (2017a, p. 27). Similarly, Connery and Claxton stated (with reference to 2014 figures): 'The [Royal Papua New Guinea Police Force] numbers around 6000 sworn and unsworn members, plus reserves and auxiliaries. This makes it a very small force when the size of PNG's population [9 million] and the complexity of the nation's geography are considered' (2014, p. 8). Patrolling within marine borders presents a significant challenge for police across the region. Increases in criminal activities in the surrounding waters of many PICTs highlight the vulnerabilities of the region by opportunistic criminal elements who attempt to capitalise on the challenges police face in detecting, monitoring, investigating, and responding to illegal activities (McNulty, 2013; United Nations Office on Drugs and Crime [UNODC], 2016). Criminal activity, and the transportation of contraband items and unauthorised fishing catches over long distances with little detection from law enforcement, are enabled by the transnational mobility of fishing boats (McNulty, 2013). In 2012, a yacht that had been tracked from South America became stranded in Tongan waters. A dead man was found on-board and 200 kilograms of cocaine were found in the hull (McNulty, 2013).

Despite regional attempts to address some of these challenges, collaboration is often overshadowed by varying national interests (Rosser, 2016; Schweble, 2009–2010), non-complementary national legislature, differing priorities of collaborators (Anderson, 2010; Boswell, 2010), and capacity mismatches or shortcomings of some partners (Boswell, 2010; Carswell & Loughlin, 2016; McLeod & Herrington, 2016). Partnerships can be seen as self-serving. For example, Australian interests in Pacific policing may be undergirded by concerns about broader Pacific security due to the close association with Australia's own national security (Rosser, 2016; Schweble, 2009–2010). Concerns around business agendas also emerge—with labour contracts given to those from donor countries, rather than to local workers as an opportunity for strengthening the local economy (Anderson, 2010). In interviews with Pacific Island chiefs of police, some participants identified political tensions between the Australian Federal Police (AFP) and New Zealand Police in terms of who was in charge in Pacific policing programs (Boswell, 2010). Similarly, police officers who had received training as part of the Pacific Prevention of Domestic Violence Programme (PPDVP) noted a lack of coordination between the AFP and New Zealand Police, and that duplication needs to be avoided (Carswell & Loughlin, 2016). Participants in police leadership training also noted challenges in applying new skills when there are constant struggles to meet basic policing resource needs (McLeod & Herrington, 2016)—an experience also found in general skills training, such as training around forensic techniques that did not consider the facilities or financial resources available (Boswell, 2010).

For PICTs with uninhabited islands, concerns exist that these islands may be used for illegal activities. Strained resources and resource allocation to other operational priorities account for the low or non-prioritisation of patrols of uninhabited areas. These factors, which are elaborated upon in Chapter 5, partly account for the Pacific being deemed a financially viable transshipment point or corridor for organised and transnational crime (Watson et al., 2021). Authorities in Fiji, Solomon Islands and Vanuatu have reported on challenges in responding to illicit drug and other unauthorised activities on outlying islands and unpatrolled waters in their respective jurisdictions (Australian Fisheries Management Authority, 2019; McDonald & Torrens, 2020). The natural growth of criminalised flora (Bourke & Allen, 2009; Devaney et al., 2006; Halvaksz & Lipset, 2006) also presents a challenge for authorities that are charged with responsibilities for harvesting and destroying feral cannabis. The challenges with large jurisdictions go well beyond those discussed in this chapter, as individual PICTs also face context-specific challenges such as lack of substance-testing facilities, dated (or non-availability of) resources, corruption, and others not elaborated upon here. Some of the common challenges related to funding and organisational capacity are discussed below.

Foreign-Funded Local Police

The Pacific is often described as one of the world's most aid-reliant regions, with many countries being categorised by the Development Assistance Committee (DAC) as eligible for Official Development Assistance (Dornan & Pryke, 2017). Three PICTs have been identified on the list of least developed countries in the world (Tuvalu, Solomon Islands and Kiribati), three as lower middle-income countries and territories (Tokelau, PNG and Vanuatu) and seven as middle-income countries and territories (Fiji, the Republic of the Marshall Islands, Nauru, Niue, Palau, Tonga, and Wallis and Futuna Islands) (Organisation for Economic Co-operation and Development, 2020). The list of developed countries and economies identified in the United Nations' *World Economic Situation and Prospects* (2020) does not include any PICTs. Many of these developing countries rely on external international sources for foreign aid and development assistance to fund police organisations operational budgets, resources and training. The Australian Government committed

$79 million over four years (July 2017 to June 2021) to the Solomon Islands Police Development Program and continues to fund the Royal Solomon Islands Police Force's (RSIPF) operational budget (through assistance provided to the law and justice sector (DFAT, 2017b).

In many (or arguably all) instances, the provision of external support is conditional upon various factors, which include but are not limited to alignment with donor-country priorities, policy revision or implementation guided by international standards, adaptation of external reporting frameworks, and use of donor-country specialists. This conditionality has implications for the operation of the respective Pacific police organisations. In keeping with internationally established standards for the provision of international assistance to less developed countries, aid agendas largely prioritise development assistance and promote self-sufficiency and improved conditions for at-risk groups. Regional assistance to Pacific policing organisations from Australia and New Zealand is primarily channelled through established organisations such as the Pacific Islands Forum Secretariat the Pacific Islands Chiefs of Police Secretariat (PICP), the Secretariat of the Pacific Community and the Pacific Islands Law Officers' Network. Within many of these bodies, there are sub-groups with a specialised focus on specific areas. For example, the PICP has a subgroup devoted specifically to capacity building and the provision of training for police officers from PICTs referred to as the Pacific Police Training Advisory Group. In addition to existing regional support channels, arrangements exist between smaller groups of PICs and donor organisations. For example, the Pacific Police Development Program— Regional (PPDP-R) is an Australian Government initiative whereby the AFP provides in-country development support to police organisations in Kiribati, Niue, Tuvalu, the Republic of the Marshall Islands, Palau, Cook Islands and the Federated States of Micronesia (AFP, 2016). This is further discussed in Chapter 5. Further fly-in, fly-out assistance is provided as required, to meet the specific needs of these seven PICTs (AFP, 2016). The AFP also assists police organisations in smaller countries such as Tuvalu to develop training plans to strengthen police service provision (Government of Tuvalu, 2016).

Other well-known arrangements exist across the region. For example, Fiji signed a memorandum of understanding on police cooperation with China's Ministry of Public Security (Hill, 2018). Practical support from China has been in the form of vehicles, communication equipment, anti-riot equipment and drones (Hill, 2018). Training support has occurred in the form of specialist senior officers working with Fiji police for a period (Lacanivalu, 2017) and officers travelling to China for specialist training (Kumar, 2018). The Fijian Police Commissioner noted that China was one of the force's biggest donors (Lacanivalu, 2017). In addition to providing support to Fiji, China has provided policing support to Samoa, Cook Islands, Vanuatu and PNG in the form of equipment, vehicles and infrastructure (Hill, 2018). Led by the New Zealand Police, the Partnership for Pacific Policing is a four-year program for capacity development. It involves seven PICTs (Cook Islands, Kiribati, Niue, Tokelau, Tuvalu, Samoa and Vanuatu), and was established to provide support for police around technical policing skills, management and leadership (New Zealand Police, 2020). Several PICTs were also members of the now complete PPDVP led by the New Zealand Police. This provided mentoring and support from both the New Zealand Police and AFP (Carswell & Loughlin, 2016). Several PICTs were provided with domestic violence coordinators as part of this program (Ronald, 2014).

The commonality among providers of aid to police organisations is an expressed desire to contribute to regional development and democratic policing through the provision of a wide range of support to enhance the rule of law, access to justice, and improved national and regional security. Despite the existence of the Paris Declaration on Aid Effectiveness, which highlights the need for mutual agreement and commitments among donors and recipients, differing perspectives or a mismatch between donor and recipient priorities is not uncommon. Challenges can be identified across studies of donor invention in policing in the Pacific. Areas prioritised for funding by donors, though valid from donor perspectives, do not always present as the main priorities for aid recipients. As mentioned earlier, a notable study on the perceived impacts of this issue, which involved interviews with 14 representatives from the PICP, documented a number of challenges with aid from Australia and New Zealand to Pacific policing organisations (Boswell, 2010). Similar sentiments were expressed by other scholars in their discussions of themes related to a lack of donor flexibility to local needs and contexts, limited consideration of political context and climate, and limited autonomy and control for local recipients (Cox et al., 2012).

The long-term benefits of policy development funding in contexts where human resources are strained are likely to be overshadowed by the burden of an increased workload. Aid recipients have, in the past, raised concerns about the challenges of accountability and monitoring in regard to aid from Australia and New Zealand, which can place an added strain on limited human resources (Boswell, 2010). A contrast is provided in the aid provided by China and Taiwan, which was able to be accessed with relative ease and under relatively flexible conditions (Boswell, 2010). In countries such as Solomon Islands, a challenge exists in working within uncertain economic and fiscal environments. This issue is compounded by complex externally managed and operated procurement and accountability systems that impact the police organisation's operational capacity. Recipients of donor aid have also been described as hesitant to criticise donors due to political sensitivities (Boswell, 2010), which limits the opportunity for informative feedback. In addition, power in relation to donor aid is believed to give donor countries the ability to force decisions that benefit themselves (Boswell, 2010).

Donor conditions may not reflect contextual sensitivity and honest dialogue about issues; they may be viewed as detrimental to aid agreements. Furthermore, broader arguments have been raised about a regional approach to external policing inventions. These arguments include the risks of a standardised approach to interventions (Manuel et al., 2013) that may not encourage technical thinking and may lack the necessary engagement to address strategic, political and cultural concerns (Manuel et al., 2013). This position on foreign aid and external policing interventions was common across studies where interviewees also raised the issue of a lack of understanding of local cultures and the country's needs (Boswell, 2010; Cox et al., 2012; McLeod & Herrington, 2016). The relevance of metropolitan policing to PICTs is also a specific issue (Boswell, 2010; Watson & Dinnen, 2020), which raises further concerns about the value of punitive or retaliatory approaches that are based on international occurrences not necessarily impacting the places where they are being introduced (Anderson, 2010; Dinnen & Watson, 2021; Watson & Dinnen, 2020). Examples can be seen across the region, with policy development aid to match those that exist in donor countries, such as New Zealand's discontinued domestic violence 'no drop' policy being implemented in countries without the capacity to provide victim support. Productive partnerships and a strong understanding of local cultures, though crucial, continue to be underemphasised (Anderson, 2010; Boswell, 2010).

Capacity Growth and Development
As is the case globally, police organisations in PICTs face capacity growth and development challenges. With relatively small organisations, the limited number of officers available to meet operational challenges has implications for capacity growth and development. Estimates of police human resource capacity in the Pacific Island Forum states list organisations with numbers ranging from around 20 sworn officers for a population of approximately 1642–4700 officers for a population of 9 million (Putt et al., 2018). As discussed in Chapter 5, the challenges faced by police are acknowledged by local as well as international stakeholders—as evidenced in continued partnership and support arrangements, collaborative initiatives, and regional and national joint ventures (Boswell, 2010; McLeod & Herrington, 2016). In the Southwest Pacific, the primary support for police organisations comes from Australia and New Zealand, with countries in Asia, Europe and the United States of America typically providing smaller-scale and one-off interventions. PICTs located further north receive greater support and aid from the United States.

The AFP provides capacity growth and development to police organisations in PICTs through various means. Other initiatives include training provided through the Australian Institute of Police Management (AIPM), Pacific Faculty of Policing, which includes in-country training, and professional development training for executives and for women in policing (AIPM, 2020).

These partnerships can have unintended negative impacts on policing in PICTs. Although some international policing providers (including the AFP) have gained valuable insight from previous endeavours and have tried to revise and adapt their capacity growth and development activities accordingly, issues with human resource management, ineffective performance management and lack of transparency have been known to impact negatively on such initiatives (DFAT, 2017b; Prasad, 2006). Those selected by their respective organisations for training are not always best suited to ensure knowledge transference or capacity development (Anderson, 2010; DFAT, 2017b). Training, whether conducted locally or abroad, also has direct impacts on available human resources. The timely replacement of skilled and seconded officers, especially individuals with specialist administrative and technical roles, presents major operational challenges. Despite considerable attempts to upskill personnel within organisations, the limited numbers of skilled personnel available within the organisations make it difficult to ensure appropriate levels of transfer. Capacity shortfalls also affect ongoing implementation, monitoring, enforcement, and review of initiatives to ensure that ideas, policies, and procedures become embedded as necessary (DFAT, 2017b).

Retention of skilled personnel is an ongoing challenge for police organisations in PICTs. While maintaining the required human resource capacity is an issue faced by police organisations across the globe, in PICTs this issue is further exacerbated by decreased prioritisation of resources for police organisations in many countries and territories (as climate change, natural disaster support, health care, and education take precedence), increasing demands for better-qualified officers, a mismatch between the supply of—and demand for—female officers, generally high non-completion rates of recruit training programs (Mou, 2015), low incentives relative to job requirements and undoubtedly a plethora of further issues (Wilson et al., 2010).

The best intentions do not always reflect cognisance of context. In smaller countries with no training facilities, there is reliance on other countries to train police officers (using training models likely developed for and suited to the provider country's context). The extent to which measures are in place to adapt training received to suit local contexts is unknown. The imposition of foreign ideologies with little relevance to local contexts can undermine good intentions and have far-reaching negative implications. For example, the implementation of a gender-balancing 50/50 recruitment strategy by the RSIPF in Solomon Islands (see Chapter 6) to align with international gender equality agendas demonstrates ambitions ahead of in-country advances in gender relations and conditions for women (RSIPF, 2019). A follow-up report indicated higher rates of training non-completion for female recruits, who identified domestic challenges as the primary reason for this. There are also concerns about delays in moving from aid-dependency to sustainability (Manuel et al., 2013), and fears about developing an aid-dependent culture (Anderson, 2010). Often, services related to capacity development are contracted by the aid donor, which sees about 70% of donor aid return to the country of origin (Boswell, 2010). Funds from donors are also sometimes managed independently of the police organisations, which presents challenges for the intended recipients of the funds. The Solomon Islands Police Development Program report (DFAT, 2017b) identified the use of externally managed corporate services for budgeting and human resource management as a challenge to the emergence of strong policing capabilities.

Conclusion

As is the reality for policing organisations in other parts of the world, policing in PICTs is not without issues and challenges. Drawing on examples from across the Pacific, this chapter has highlighted the primary challenges faced by policing organisations, and elaborated on how these challenges impact on the manner in which policing is actioned and the character it takes on in varied contexts. Arguments have been presented to show that the issues and challenges faced by policing organisations are contextually embedded and are as much a part of the local landscape as other issues specific to governance—or, more specifically, law-and-order maintenance. Despite continued attempts by many police organisations in PICTs to improve service provision and engagement with communities, addressing issues of strained resources, limited access to justice and police legitimacy remains a work in progress. Communities identify heavily with customary justice mechanisms and with their own geographical and language grouping, and this complicates the role of central government and police (Putt et al., 2018). For example, in Solomon Islands, '[l]ocal identities and allegiances remain strong, while national institutions are relatively weak, as compounded by a small population dispersed across a fragmented archipelago' (Putt et al., 2018, p. 17). Similarly, Dinnen and colleagues (2006) suggest that traditional mechanisms in Solomon Islands have been drawn upon and adapted in response to the weaknesses of the state becoming apparent. Minor conflicts and everyday security remain local and informally managed in communities, with little resort to police agencies (Lievore & Fairbairn-Dunlop, 2007; Pratt & Melei, 2018; Putt et al., 2018). Social behaviour continues to be viewed as the informal jurisdiction of the village, and local leadership has a strong influence on norms (Meibusch, 2019). The social authority of customary justice systems ensures community participation and agreement on outcomes (Harper, 2011). The legitimacy of these systems in PICTs impacts police legitimacy.

While the historical, traditional, social, political, and economic distinctiveness of PICTs make it impractical to generalise, assume similarities, or transfer inferences, there exist commonalities across PICTs with regard to a number of challenges faced by police organisations. The specific character of the challenges, however, varies based on context and country-specific operational agendas. It is therefore important to acknowledge that the challenges discussed in this chapter, except in instances where specific examples are provided, may not apply to all PICTs or may not adequately represent the magnitude of the issues. Further challenges, which are not outlined or elaborated upon here, are likely to exist. Additional sources should therefore be consulted for country-specific information as necessary.

REFERENCES

Allen, M., Dinnen, S., Evans, D., & Monson, R. (2013, August). *Justice delivered locally: Systems, challenges, and innovations in Solomon Islands*. Justice for the Poor research report. World Bank. https://openknowledge.worldbank.org/handle/10986/16678

Amnesty International. (2016). *Beating justice: How Fiji's security forces get away with torture*. Amnesty International Ltd.

Anderson, T. (2010). *The limits of RAMSI*. AID/WATCH.

Australian Federal Police (AFP). (2016). A helping hand: The Pacific Police Development Program-Regional is a perfect case of 'for the Pacific, by the Pacific' cooperation. *AFP Platypus Magazine*, pp. 6–10.

Australian Fisheries Management Authority. (2019). Commonwealth Southern Bluefin Fishery—Application 2019. https://www.awe.gov.au/environment/marine/fisheries/commonwealth/southern-bluefin/application-2019

Australian Institute of Police Management (AIPM). (2020). *Pacific chiefs join the AFP and AIPM to officially launch the Pacific Faculty of Policing*. https://www.aipm.gov.au/pacific-faculty-policing-opening

Bell, E. (2013). Normalising the exceptional: British colonial policing cultures come home. *Mémoire(s), Identité(s), Marginalité(s) dans le Monde Occidental Contemporain. Cahiers du MIMMOC, 10*.

Boodoosingh, R., & Schoeffel, P. (2018). *Community law-making and the codification of customary laws—Social and gender issues in Samoa*. National University of Samoa.

Boswell, B. M. (2010). *The evolution of international policing in the Pacific: A critical analysis* [Master's thesis]. School of History, Philosophy, Political Science and International Relations, Victoria University of Wellington. https://researcharchive.vuw.ac.nz/handle/10063/1520

Bourke, M. R., & Allen, B. (2009). Stimulants. In M. R. Bourke & T. Harwood (Eds.), *Food and agriculture in Papua New Guinea* (pp. 223–230). ANU Press.

Bull, M., George, N., & Curth-Bibb, J. (2019). The virtues of strangers? Policing gender violence in Pacific Island countries. *Policing and Society, 29*, 155–170.

Bull, M., Watson, D., Amin, S. N., & Carrington, K. (2021). Women and policing in the South Pacific: A pathway towards gender-inclusive organizational reform. *Police Practice and Research, 22*(1), 389–408.

Carswell, S., & Loughlin, S. (2016). *Evaluation of capacity development for police on child protection in Fiji, Kiribati and Vanuatu*. Carswell Consultancy for UNICEF Pacific.

Connery, D., & Claxton, K. (2014, October). Shared interests, enduring cooperation: The future of Australia—PNG police engagement. *Strategic Policing and Law Enforcement Program: Special Report*. Australian Strategic Policy Institute.

Cox, M., Duituturaga, E., & Scheye, E. (2012). *Solomon Island case study: Evaluation of Australian law and justice assistance*. Australian Agency for International Development.

Department of Foreign Affairs and Trade (DFAT). (2017a). *DFAT country information report Fiji*. Australian Government.

Department of Foreign Affairs and Trade (DFAT). (2017b). *Solomon Islands Police Development Program 2017b–2021 design document*. Australian Government. https://www.dfat.gov.au/sites/default/files/sipdp-design.pdf

Department of Foreign Affairs and Trade (DFAT). (2019). *Tuvalu country brief*. Australian Government. https://www.dfat.gov.au/geo/tuvalu/tuvalu-country-brief

Department of Foreign Affairs and Trade (DFAT). (2020a). *Solomon Islands country brief*. Australian Government. https://www.dfat.gov.au/geo/solomon-islands/solomon-islands-country-brief

Department of Foreign Affairs and Trade (DFAT). (2020b). *Tuvalu*. Australian Government. https://www.dfat.gov.au/geo/tuvalu

Department of Foreign Affairs and Trade (DFAT). (2021). *Papua New Guinea country brief*. Australian Government. https://www.dfat.gov.au/geo/papua-new-guinea/papua-new-guinea-country-brief

Devaney, M., Reid, G., & Baldwin, S. (2006). *Situational analysis of illicit drug issues and responses in the Asia–Pacific region*. Australian National Council of Drugs.

Dinnen, S. (2008). The Solomon Islands intervention and the instabilities of the post-colonial state. *Global Change, Peace & Security, 20*(3), 339–355.

Dinnen, S., McLeod, A., & Peake, G. (2006). Police-building in weak states: Australian approaches in Papua New Guinea and Solomon Islands. *Civil Wars, 8*(2), 87–108.

Dinnen, S., & Watson, D. (2021). Police reform in a post-conflict context: The case of Solomon Islands. *Policing: A Journal of Policy and Practice, 15*(1), 387–398.

Dornan, M., & Pryke, J. (2017). Foreign aid to the Pacific: Trends and developments in the twenty-first century. *Asia & the Pacific Policy Studies, 4*(3), 386–404.

Emsley, C. (2014). *The English police: A political and social history.* Routledge.

Evans, D., Goddard, M., & Paterson, D. (2011). *The hybrid courts of Melanesia: A comparative analysis of village courts of Papua New Guinea, island of Vanuatu and local courts of Solomon Islands* (Justice and Development Working Paper Series 3). World Bank. https://openknowledge.worldbank.org/handle/10986/18107

Farran, S. (2006). Is legal pluralism an obstacle to human rights? Considerations from the South Pacific. *The Journal of Legal Pluralism and Unofficial Law, 38*(52), 77–105.

Fiji Police Force. (2013). *Fiji Police Duavata community policing model.* Police Annual Report.

Fraenkel, J., & Corbett, J. (2016). Tuvalu. In S. Levine (Ed.), *Pacific ways: Government and politics in the Pacific Islands* (2nd ed.). Victoria University Press.

Goldsmith, A., & Dinnen, S. (2007). Transnational police building: Critical lessons from Timor-Leste and Solomon Islands. *Third World Quarterly, 28*(6), 1091–1109.

Government of Tuvalu. (2016). *National strategy for sustainable development 2016 to 2020.* Government of Tuvalu.

Halvaksz, J., & Lipset, D. (2006). Another kind of gold: An introduction to marijuana in Papua New Guinea. *Oceania, 76*, 209–219.

Harper, E. (2011). *Customary justice: From program design to impact evaluation.* International Development Law Organization.

Hill, C. (2018, April 6). China's policing assistance in the Pacific: A new era? *Flagpost.* Parliamentary Library, Australian Parliament House. https://www.aph.gov.au/About_Parliament/Parliamentary_Departments/Parliamentary_Library/FlagPost/2018/April/china-pacific-police

Hilliard, D. (1974). Colonialism and Christianity: The Melanesian mission in the Solomon Islands. *The Journal of Pacific History, 9*(1), 93–116.

Howes, L. M., Watson, D., & Newett, L. (2021). Police as knowledge brokers and keepers of the peace: Perceptions of community policing in Tuvalu. *Police Practice and Research, 22*(1), 745–762.

Jolly, M. (2016). Men of war, men of peace: Changing masculinities in Vanuatu. *The Asia Pacific Journal of Anthropology, 17*(3–4), 305–323.

Jowitt, A. (2009). Fiji. In S. Katz (Ed.), *The Oxford International encyclopedia of legal history.* Oxford University Press.

Kumar, A. (2018, August 18). Our cops to train in China regarding meth, synthetic drugs. *Fiji Sun.* http://fijisun.com.fj/2018/04/29/our-cops-to-train-in-china-regarding-meth-synthetic-drugs/

Lacanivalu, L. (2017, July 27). Chinese attaches boost police work. *Fiji Sun.* http://fijisun.com.fj/2017/07/27/chinese-attaches-boost-police-work/
Lievore, D., & Fairbairn-Dunlop, P. (2007). *Pacific prevention of domestic violence programme: Tonga report.* Victoria University of Wellington.
MacDonald, B. (2001). *Cinderellas of the empire: Towards a history of Kiribati and Tuvalu.* The University of the South Pacific.
Manuel, C., Biddle, K., Shields, D., van der Heyden, J., & Hooper, R. (2013). *Strategic evaluation of police work funded under the New Zealand aid programme 2005–2011.* Ministry of Foreign Affairs and Trade.
McDonald, J., & Torrens, S. M. (2020). Governing Pacific fisheries under climate change. In J. McDonald, J. S. McGee, & R. Barnes (Eds.), *Research handbook on climate change, oceans and coasts.* Edward Elgar Publishing.
McLeod, A., & Herrington, V. (2016). Fostering police leadership capacity in Solomon Islands: Understanding the challenges to organizational reform. *Policing: A Journal of Policy and Practice, 10*(1), 44–54.
McNulty, J. (2013). Western and Central Pacific Ocean fisheries and the opportunities for transnational organised crime: Monitoring, control and surveillance (MCS) Operation Kurukuru. *Australian Journal of Maritime and Ocean Affairs, 5*(4), 145–152.
Meibusch, C. (2019). *South Pacific domestic violence legislation: What changes could encourage victims to report domestic violence? The case for reform Samoa, Kiribati and Solomon Islands* [Master's thesis]. School of Law Faculty of Arts, Law and Education, The University of the South Pacific.
Mou, F. (2015, July 27). Samoa Police to gain new recruits but remain short-handed. *Loop.* https://www.loopsamoa.com/content/samoa-police-gain-new-recruits-remain-short-handed
Nanau, G. L. (2017). Solomon Islands. *The Contemporary Pacific, 29*(2), 354–361.
New Zealand Police. (2020). *ISG introduction.* https://www.police.govt.nz/about-us/programmes-initiatives/isg/introduction
Newton, T. (1998). Policing in the South Pacific Islands. *Police Journal, 71*(4), 349–352.
Ombudsman Samoa. (2020). *About our work.* https://ombudsman.gov.ws/about-us/
Organisation for Economic Co-operation and Development (OECD). (2020). *DAC list of ODA recipients.* http://www.oecd.org/dac/financing-sustainable-development/development-finance-standards/DAC-List-ODA-Recipients-for-reporting-2021-flows.pdf
Peake, G., & Dinnen, S. (2014). Police development in Papua New Guinea: The need for innovation. *Security Challenges, 10*(2), 33–52.
Prasad, D. (2006). Strengthening democratic policing and accountability in the Commonwealth Pacific. *Sur. Revista Internacional De Direitos Humanos, 3*(5), 110–135.

Pratt, J., & Melei, T. (2018). One of the smallest prison populations in the world under threat: The case of Tuvalu. In K. Carrington, R. Hogg, J. Scott, & M. Sozzo (Eds.), *The Palgrave handbook of criminology and the global south* (pp. 729–750). Palgrave Macmillan.

Putt, J., Dinnen, S., Keen, M., & Bately, J. (2018). *The RAMSI legacy for policing in the Pacific region: Research report*. Australian National University.

Ronald, C. (2014). *Pacific prevention of domestic violence programme (PPDVP)* [Conference presentation]. 40th Pacific Islands Chiefs of Police Conference.

Rosser, A. (2016). Asia's rise and the politics of Australian aid policy. *The Pacific Review, 29*(1), 115–136.

Royal Solomon Islands Police Force (RSIPF). (2019). *RSIPF gender strategy 2019–2021*. Royal Solomon Islands Police Force.

Sai, A. (2007). *Tamot: Masculinities in transition in Papua New Guinea* [PhD thesis]. Faculty of Arts, Education and Human Development, Victoria University of Wellington.

Samoa Police Service. (2021). *About*. https://www.samoapolice.ws/about/

Schwebel, A. (2009–2010). The influence of national interest in aid policy making: A South Pacific illustration. *Melbourne Journal of Politics, 34*, 106–131.

Siikala, J. (2014). Hierarchy and power in the Pacific. *Anthropological Theory, 14*(2), 215–230.

Stretem Rod blong Jastis mo Sefti (SRBJS). (2016). *Vanuatu-Australia Policing and Justice Program 2017–2020, program design document*. https://www.dfat.gov.au/sites/default/files/vanuatu-australia-policing-and-justice-program-design-document.pdf

Turnbull, B. (2011). *Pacific Prevention of Domestic Violence Programme: Independent evaluation report*. Ministry of Foreign Affairs and Trade.

Uakeia, T. (2016). Kiribati. In F. Barrowman (Ed.), *Pacific ways: Government and politics in the Pacific Islands*. Victoria University Press.

United Nations. (2020). *World economic situation and prospects*. https://www.un.org/development/desa/dpad/wp-content/uploads/sites/45/WESP2020_Annex.pdf

United Nations Office on Drugs and Crime (UNODC). (2016). *Transnational organized crime in the Pacific: A threat assessment*. Pacific Islands Forum Secretariat.

United Nations Population Fund (UNFPA). (2014). *Population and development profiles: Pacific Island countries*. United Nations Population Fund Pacific Sub-Regional Office. https://pacific.unfpa.org/sites/default/files/pub-pdf/web__140414_UNFPAPopulationandDevelopmentProfiles-PacificSub-RegionExtendedv1LRv2_0.pdf

Watson, D. (2018). *Tuvalu Police stakeholder perceptions study 2017*. The University of the South Pacific.

Watson, D. (2020, September). *Pacific policing in the COVID-19 era: Overworked and under-supplied.* Policy Forum: Asia and the Pacific Policy Society (APPS). https://www.policyforum.net/pacific-policing-in-the-covid-19-era/

Watson, D., Boateng, B., & Miles-Johnson, T. (2021). Legitimizing policing practices: A study of stakeholder perceptions of police trustworthiness, effectiveness and relationship with the community. *Police Practice and Research, 22*(1), 623–639.

Watson, D., & Dinnen, S. (2020). History, adaptation and adoption problematised. In Amin, S., Watson, D., & Girard, C. (Eds). *Mapping security in the Pacific: A focus on context, gender and organisational culture.* Routledge.

Watson, D., Rivera, J., & McNinch, R. (2019). *Stakeholder perceptions about Guam Police Department service provision: Community perceptions survey.* The University of the South Pacific.

Watson, D., Sousa-Santos, J. L., & Howes, L. M. (2021). Transnational and organized crime in Pacific Island countries and territories: Police capacity to respond to the emerging security threat. *Development Bulletin, 82,* 151–155.

Wilson, J. M., Dalton, E., Scheer, C., & Grammich, C. A. (2010). *Police recruitment and retention for the new millennium.* RAND Corporation.

World Bank. (n.d.). *The World Bank in Pacific Islands.* https://www.worldbank.org/en/country/pacificislands

World Bank. (2020). *Climate change knowledge portal for development practitioners and policy makers: Kiribati.* https://climateknowledgeportal.worldbank.org/country/kiribati

Open Access This chapter is licensed under the terms of the Creative Commons Attribution 4.0 International License (http://creativecommons.org/licenses/by/4.0/), which permits use, sharing, adaptation, distribution and reproduction in any medium or format, as long as you give appropriate credit to the original author(s) and the source, provide a link to the Creative Commons license and indicate if changes were made.

The images or other third party material in this chapter are included in the chapter's Creative Commons license, unless indicated otherwise in a credit line to the material. If material is not included in the chapter's Creative Commons license and your intended use is not permitted by statutory regulation or exceeds the permitted use, you will need to obtain permission directly from the copyright holder.

CHAPTER 3

Trends in and Social Dynamics of Crime in the Pacific

Abstract An understanding of policing dynamics requires an examination of not only the landscape of criminal activities that police encounter and work in, but also the socio-political processes that produce crime in a given community and context. This chapter provides an overview of crime trends in Pacific Islands countries and territories (PICTs) in the twenty-first century and discusses some key social dynamics producing various crimes. It pays special attention to crimes and violence experienced by young people and women, as well as how neoliberal globalisation has produced new vulnerabilities in PICTs, including expanding organised and transnational crime, such as drug trafficking and cybercrime. The chapter includes suggestions for where there are research and data gaps, and how future research and policy should aim to close these gaps to further inform crime-related policies.

Keywords Crime in the pacific · Youth and crime · Gender-based violence · Trafficking · Environmental crime · Corruption · Violence

© The Author(s) 2023
D. Watson et al., *Policing in the Pacific Islands*,
Palgrave's Critical Policing Studies,
https://doi.org/10.1007/978-3-031-10635-4_3

Introduction

The study of crime remains a contested field, constituted by theoretical, empirical, and policy debates around trends in, causes of, and responses to crime (Carrabine, 2017). Policymakers, police, and the public engage in these debates through implicit and explicit assumptions about the 'nature' of crime and criminality in their own contexts. A common narrative among police, criminal justice actors, and the public regarding crime in Pacific Islands countries and territories (PICTs) is both that crime rates are increasing and the nature of crimes is changing due to rapid social change, related to urbanisation, marketisation, and a weakening of communal and Indigenous means of regulating rule-breaking and criminal behaviours. This discourse fits with theorisation of crime in the context of 'modernisation', a weakening of family- and community-based relations and the erosion of moral solidarity through the stresses of modern economic life produces anomie; that is, a lack—or loss of regulation—of human desires, human behaviour, and sense of collective belonging (DiCristina, 2016).

However, crime is also a political construct, reflective of the efforts of political elites to reinforce their privilege and interests, as well as expressions of various social and political contradictions or conflicts in a given society (Blaustein et al., 2018). Moreover, in PICTs, as noted in Chapter 2, criminal law was inherited from colonial rule that often worked in the interests of colonial powers, rather than local communities and, as such, further reinforces class-based inequalities and oppression (Forsyth, 2009; Sumner, 1982). In PICTs, there are also tensions related to how enforcement of customary forms of justice can become criminal or criminalised, especially in situations where specific customary forms of punishment may violate human or individual rights embodied in legal frameworks (see e.g., Amin, Trussler, et al., 2022). Key in critical perspectives on crimes is that activities of poor and marginalised groups tend to be both more criminalised and punished, while crimes and harms committed by economic and political elites tend to be ignored, and may not even be defined as crime (Wacquant, 2009). Therefore, there is often both more focus and data on violent crimes, property crimes, theft and crimes against state authority, while corruption, state-based crimes, and corporate crimes are less documented.

A critical perspective centres on ongoing global politics and inequalities between nations in understanding crime dynamics. Post-colonial societies, such as PICTs, continue to be impacted by colonial histories and legacies in the structure of legislation, criminal justice systems, and policing (Cunneen, 2011). Thus, unlike in the global North, countries in the global South, including PICTs, often face foreign pressures regarding reform of and/or prioritisation in their criminal law and justice systems that also distort alignment with local interests, priorities, values, and understandings of crime. These pressures come from different sources, including international conventions to which countries are party, aid dynamics, and the continued exploitation of resources in PICTs by Northern powers (Watson et al., 2021). We see these dynamics especially in relation to crimes related to gender-based violence, child abuse, and the environment (Carrington et al., 2018).

Legacies of colonialism for crime and violence also include the racialised and ethnicity-based divisions and inequalities produced under colonial rule and reproduced in post-colonial societies (Carrington et al., 2018). In addition, the use of post-colonial societies as playgrounds for super-power geo-politics has impacted on political stability and political violence dynamics. As such, police in PICTs are located in a context that includes violence against ethnic and political minorities and their property. The threat of group violence in the form of inter-tribal/ethnic, racialised, and/or political violence continues to be an issue in some PICTs. While this is beyond the scope of the chapter, some important implications for policing are discussed in Chapters 4, 5, and 6.

This chapter discusses some of the data trends and social dynamics of crime in the context of PICTs. It first examines the challenges of analysing crime data in the region and the subsequent difficulty for police and policymakers to produce data-driven policing action. This is followed by a discussion of trends and dynamics related to non-violent and violent crimes in the region, with a special focus on crime-related issues faced by youth, women, and marginalised communities. This section points to the challenging and complex environment PICT police services face, as well as indicating how other societal actors may be relevant and needed. The next section examines dynamics related to organised and transnational crime, looking at how these have become amplified through processes of neoliberal globalisation, and emphasising the need for regional, transnational, and multi-sectoral collaboration for policing. The final section of this chapter looks at state crimes, with a special focus on the use of excessive force by police and how evolving legislation, practices, and norms require greater attention in this regard for police reform, and also larger reforms in governance.

Data on Crime in the Pacific

In PICTs, as in all contexts, there are at least three key sources of crime data—country-level police data, national-level victimisation or stakeholder perception surveys, and judicial records of criminal cases. Discussions of crime data from these sources should always come with important caveats, including the fact that crimes of the state, corruption, and crimes committed by the police in their work tend to be documented (when actually reported) in processes outside of public access, through internal mechanisms. Reports produced by human rights watchdogs, media outlets, and other civil society organisations become important sources regarding many of these latter types of crimes. Criminal codes and classifications also differ across the region and, as such, comparisons of data between national jurisdictions should be interpreted with caution.

Crime volume and rates based on police-based data provide only a partial picture of the actual or population-based true crime rate since police records only reflect law-breaking acts that are reported to the police or caught by police authorities and actually documented by the police. Moreover, the analysis of trends in police-based crime data can be difficult given changes in legislation and record-keeping practices within countries, as well as differential definitions between countries. Significantly in Pacific Island societies, when looking at crime data, it is important to note that the authority and legitimacy of the police have been shifting, especially under urbanising processes and state-building efforts. This has contributed to a general trend of increased reporting to the police of law-breaking behaviour that would not previously have been reported (Cain, 2001; Pratt & Melei, 2018; Putt & Dinnen, 2020). Nevertheless, in both urban and rural or outer islands of PICTs, police continue to be dependent on traditional authorities (such as chiefs and elders) to deal with certain types of law-breaking behaviours (see e.g., Forsyth, 2009; Watson & Dinnen, 2020). Therefore, record-keeping practices in rural and outer islands can vary quite significantly from urban centres and main/larger islands in a given country or territory (Cain, 2001). There can also be delays in communication to metropole headquarters from more remote centres. Therefore, police-based crime data in PICTs for any given year will tend to be more biased towards urban centres and main islands. In many PICTs, record-keeping practices of the police forces have become more regular and professionalised; police-based 'annual trends of crime' reports have become more easily accessible to the public; and, especially since the early 2010s, such reports are also archived online on government websites, as well as on the social media pages of the police departments themselves. However, there are still substantive variations in the regularity and quality of police-based data keeping across the region. Further adding to the problem of incomplete, irregular, and partial crime data at the police level is the fact that police-based crime data is also impacted by the dynamics of policing priorities, which are influenced by funding sources and how budgets are determined (see Chapter 2).

In addition to police-based crime data, reflecting a push towards data and community-driven policymaking there have been several community perception surveys of safety and policing commissioned by the police themselves, other arms of governments or through the Pacific Police Development Programs funded by the Australian Government. Community perception surveys have been undertaken in Solomon Islands (see e.g., the annual 2009–2013 People's Survey by ANU Enterprise/ANU Edge [at ramsi.org], as well as the Royal Solomon Islands Police Force Annual Reports, 2013–2018), Tonga (Koloto & Fowles, 2012), Samoa (Samoa Bureau of Statistics, 2013), Cook Islands (McMurray, 2014), Tuvalu (Watson, 2017), and Guam (Watson et al., 2019). Although these types of surveys do not help measure crime rates, they remain important by providing insights into public perceptions of safety and crime, as well as indicating to what extent trends from police-based data of crime may align with trends from actual crime rates (Hipp, 2013; Maguire & McVie, 2017).

Victimisation surveys are often considered to provide a more reliable and stable picture of the actual crime rate. While various United Nations surveys, Demographic Health Surveys, and World Bank surveys point to victimisation rates in relation to theft, property crimes, and violence against the person, crime victimisation surveys have not been undertaken in a systematic and longitudinal way in any PICTs. Integrating criminal victimisation items into regular national surveys would provide an important mechanism for monitoring crime rates, as well as potentially evaluating policies regarding the policing of crime. This is particularly true because of both the constraints faced by police in data keeping and the fact that, despite changing trends, many crimes continue to go unreported to state institutions, especially outside of urban centres.

It is important to note that, despite the lack of national-level crime victimisation surveys, due to women's movements across the region, donor-driven pressure on policies regarding violence against women

(VAW), and monitoring and evaluation obligations created through international conventions (e.g., the *Convention on the Elimination of All Forms of Discrimination Against Women*) and global development goals (the United Nations Millennium Development Goals and Sustainable Development Goals) there is an emergent body of crime victimisation data on domestic, intimate partner, sexual, and family violence in the region. Regarding VAW, and especially domestic violence and intimate partner violence (IPV), between 2003 and 2013—through funding from different agencies, such as AusAID, the United Nations Population Fund (UNFPA), the Secretariat of the Pacific Community (SPC), and the World Health Organization (WHO), and the work of women's organisations locally—there are country-specific surveys that have produced data, including for Samoa (UNFPA, 2006), Vanuatu (Vanuatu Women's Centre, 2011), Kiribati (SPC, 2009a), Solomon Islands (SPC, 2009b), Tonga (Ma'a Fafine mo e Famili, 2012), Fiji (Fiji Women's Crisis Centre, 2013), Papua New Guinea (PNG) (WHO, 2013), and Tuvalu (SPC, 2009c). There has also been additional, more recent documentation of the prevalence and incidence of family violence in PICTs. For example, in 2017, in Samoa, the Office of the Ombudsman conducted a national public inquiry into family violence (Samoa Office of the Ombudsman and National Human Rights Institution, 2018). Putt and Dinnen (2020) provide a report on family and sexual violence in PNG, which was funded by the Australian Government through the Justice Services and Stability for Development Program. Similarly, due to advocacy by civil society organisations, violence against children has been documented via the 14 country situation analyses commissioned by the United Nations Children's Fund (UNICEF) Pacific, which provides some indication of the level of violence experienced by children in Cook Islands, the Federated States of Micronesia (FSM), Fiji, Kiribati, the Republic of the Marshall Islands, Nauru, Niue, Palau, Samoa, Solomon Islands, Tokelau, Tonga, Tuvalu, and Vanuatu (UNICEF, 2017).

A review of the available data on crime indicates that there are important gaps that need to be addressed. These include developing systematic and regular national victimisation surveys, documenting reports of criminal behaviour to customary authorities, and better integrating police and corrections data that would allow for analyses of recidivism. Additionally, there is a need for research and analyses of crime in corrections systems and crime from the perspectives of perpetrators.

Keeping in mind the above discussion, in this chapter we draw on data from police reports, and available victimisation and stakeholder perception surveys, as well as—when relevant—reports from different civil society organisations and media outlets. Specifically, we have used police-based reports of crime data from Fiji, Tonga, Samoa, Solomon Islands, Vanuatu, Kiribati, and Guam. While Tuvalu Police Service data was made available, there were discrepancies in the data that could not be verified and therefore we have relied mainly on the Tuvalu Stakeholders Perceptions Study (Watson, 2017). For PNG, reports and analyses based on police data and previous victimisation surveys have been used. In discussions of domestic violence and violence against women and children, we have used both police-based data and reports available from victimisation and prevalence surveys in Samoa, Tonga, Tuvalu, Kiribati, Fiji, PNG, Solomon Islands, and Vanuatu. For transnational crime, organised crime, corruption and state crimes, existing studies and reports by human rights watchdogs, civil society actors, and media outlets have been utilised. We have not looked at judicial records of criminal cases since the chapter is focused on discussing trends in criminal behaviour rather than trends in judicial processes, outcomes, or decisions.[1] Data from prisons would also have been useful; however, access to corrections data is constrained across PICTs and gaining access was not possible.

Given the data used in this chapter, crime dynamics are not represented in many parts of Micronesia, including the Republic of the Marshall Islands, Tokelau, Nauru, Palau, and the FSM; nor in some parts of Polynesia, such as the French territories.

Overview of Trends in and Social Dynamics of Crime in the Pacific

Prevalence of crime, especially violent crime, in PICTs is relatively low, with Melanesian countries having higher rates of crime compared to Polynesian and Micronesian countries. Overall, the number of criminal

---

[1] See, for example, the reports on the United Nations Development Programme Access to Justice projects in Fiji and Solomon Islands at https://www.pacific.undp.org/content/pacific/en/home/projects/Fij_A2J.html and https://www.pacific.undp.org/content/pacific/en/home/projects/solomonislands-accesstojustice.html/. Additional reports include the Access to Justice Study commissioned by Sustineo in the Solomon Islands: https://sustineo.com.au/projects/solomon-islands-access-to-justice-study/.

offences and the crime rate,[2] based on police records, have declined since the early 2010s in Fiji, Vanuatu, Kiribati, Tuvalu, and Samoa, but increased in Solomon Islands, Tonga, and Guam (see Figs. 3.1 and 3.2).[3] This is generally true of both property crimes and crimes against the person (see Fig. 3.3), although since 2013 crimes against the person have increased in Samoa and crimes against property have increased in Guam.

While police often find themselves dealing with traffic violations, property crimes, alcohol-related interpersonal violence, and disturbances of the peace, police in PICTs must also respond to context-specific and emerging situations. Thus across PICTs, despite overall low crime rates, crimes related to domestic, intimate partner, and family violence are persistently among the highest in the world, with the prevalence of IPV being 51% in Melanesia, 41% in Micronesia, and 39% in Polynesia (WHO, 2021). Police are increasingly being called to respond to domestic, intimate partner, and family violence. Especially in the Melanesian countries, police have had to also deal with inter-ethnic violence, political violence, and violence between private security providers, as well as violence in sorcery accusations. Across PICTs, cybercrimes are growing, with even governments being victims (Watson, 2021a, 2021b). Some PICTs have also become points of transit for organised and transnational crime related to the smuggling of drugs, wildlife, small arms, and migrants, as well as drug trafficking. Both the location of PICTs as a route from Asia and Latin America towards markets in New Zealand and Australia and the difficulty of policing the vast expanses of ocean that characterise

---

[2] Throughout the chapter, whenever possible, we report counts first, and then rates. This is because crime is a rare event in PICTs and, as such, rates are strongly impacted by population size, which leaves rates of places with small populations extremely volatile. This is true throughout PICTs with population sizes substantively less than 100,000 people. Also, although crime rates in cross-national comparisons are usually reported as per 100,000 habitants, given the small populations of many PICTs we report rates here as per 500 habitants.

[3] In Figs. 3.1 and 3.2, numbers are included for countries for which we were able to access data. Also note that, reflecting some of the challenges of crime data discussed above, based on police records the crime rate for Tuvalu would appear to be 200/500 habitants in 2013 and 198/500 habitants in 2018, which would mean that Tuvalu has the highest crime rate in the PICTs. This seems unlikely. However, despite repeated follow-ups, no clarification was provided by the Tuvalu Police Service or the Tuvalu Ministry of Justice regarding these numbers. It is possible that traffic violations were counted in the crime data even though the data labelling in the reports does not indicate this and suggests otherwise. This is why Tuvalu is not included in Figs. 3.2 or 3.3.

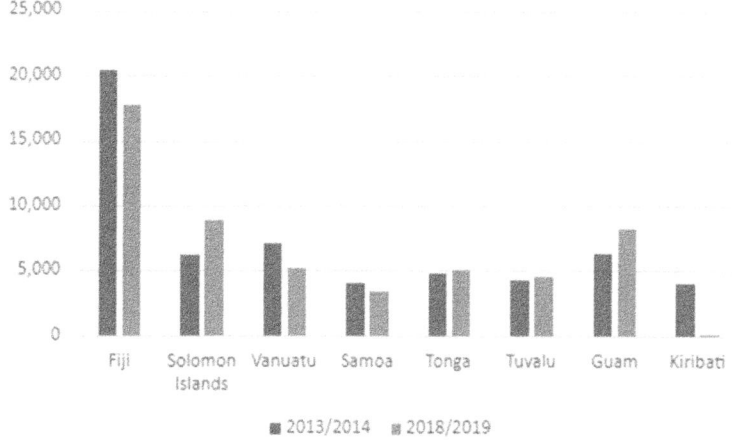

Fig. 3.1 Total police-recorded criminal offences in 2013/2014 vs. 2018/2019 (*Sources* Fiji: Fiji Bureau of Statistics, 2013; Fiji Police Force [personal communication, 2019]; Solomon Islands: Royal Solomon Islands Police Force, 2014, 2018; Vanuatu: Nichols et al., 2019; Samoa: Samoa Bureau of Statistics, 2013; R. Boodoosingh [personal communication, 2021]; Tonga: Tonga Police, 2014, 2019; Tuvalu: Tuvalu Police Service [personal communications, 2013, 2019]; Guam: Guam Police Department, 2015, 2020; Kiribati: Kiribati Police Service [personal communication, 2020])

PICTs have made them attractive for organised crime routes (Watson et al., 2021). Furthermore, in addition to environmental crimes that involve illegal fishing, logging, and trade of wildlife, PICTs continue to witness environmental crimes involving illegal disposal of waste, illegal development of land, and other activities directly harming the environment—often by foreign corporations (with problematic links to local political elites), but by local businesses and actors as well. Publics across PICTs also continue to worry about a range of state crimes, including corruption, police brutality, and other forms of human rights violations by their governments.

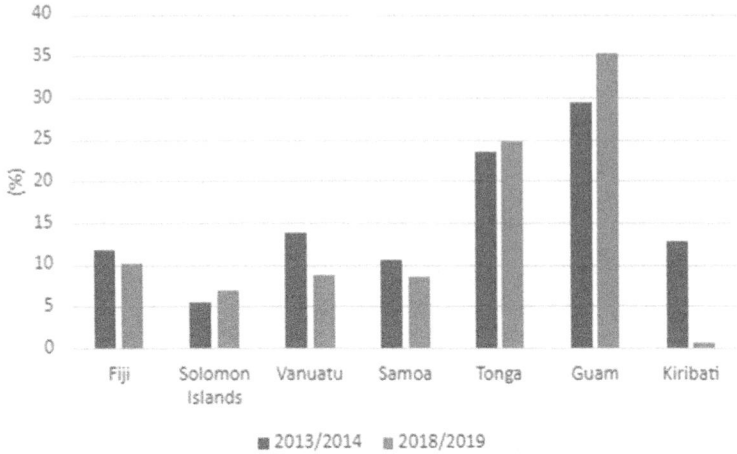

Fig. 3.2 Crime rates in PICTs per 500 habitants in 2013/2014 vs. 2018/2019 (*Sources* Fiji: Fiji Bureau of Statistics, 2013; Fiji Police Force [personal communication, 2019]; Solomon Islands: Royal Solomon Islands Police Force, 2014, 2018; Vanuatu: Nichols et al., 2019; Samoa: Samoa Bureau of Statistics, 2013; R. Boodoosingh [personal communication, 2021]; Tonga: Tonga Police, 2014, 2019; Guam: Guam Police Department, 2015, 2020; Kiribati: Kiribati Police Service [personal communication, 2020])

Non-Violent Crime

Non-violent crime refers to a crime that does not involve the use of force or cause injury to persons. While this type of crime includes a range of offence categories, in this section, we focus on trends in property crime and substance-abuse-related crime, as well as key factors driving these trends, and implications for policing.

Property Crime

Reflecting a global trend (Heiskanen, 2010), there has been a decline in property crime as a proportion of total crimes across the Pacific since the 1990s (Cain, 2001) and in the period 2013–2018 (except in Guam) (see Fig. 3.3). Nevertheless, motor vehicle theft, burglary, and housebreaking continue to be salient issues for the public. For example, the 2013 community perception study in Samoa indicated that crimes of theft and break-ins were considered to be in the top five most worrying crimes

Fig. 3.3 Property crimes and crimes against the person as a proportion of total crimes in 2013/2014 vs. 2018/2019 (*Sources* Fiji: Fiji Bureau of Statistics, 2013; Fiji Police Force [personal communication, 2019]; Solomon Islands: Royal Solomon Islands Police Force, 2014, 2018; Vanuatu: Nichols et al., 2019; Samoa: Samoa Bureau of Statistics, 2013; R. Boodoosingh [personal communication, 2021]; Tonga: Tonga Police, 2014, 2019; Guam: Guam Police Department, 2015, 2020; Kiribati: Kiribati Police Service [personal communication, 2020])

for the population (Samoa Bureau of Statistics, 2013). In Guam, the community identified theft as the most common concern, followed closely by concerns about home invasions, burglaries, and trespassing (Watson et al., 2019). In contrast, however, the 2017 community perception study in Tuvalu (Watson, 2017) indicates that crimes of theft, stealing property, and damage to property remain low on the list of what both police and the public are concerned about.

Most of these crimes are understood to be opportunistic and a product of the high rates of youth unemployment across PICTs, increasing inequality and rapid urbanisation in the region (Adinkrah, 1995; Plange, 2000). However, despite the understanding that they are often opportunistic, it is important to note that the degree of organisation in these types of crime varies across the region—thus while the *raskols* (a generic term for criminals or a group of criminals in PNG) of Port Moresby (PNG) are involved in organised criminal (including violent) activity

(Goddard, 2005), *squads* (gangs) of young men (and sometimes women) in Port Vila (Vanuatu) hang out together and may sometimes engage individually in thefts (Kraemer, 2013). As such, in their work on Port Vila, Stern (2017) and Kraemer (2013) refer to the marginalisation and stigmatisation of especially young men from urban informal settlements in media and a public discourse on their criminality that does not align with the reality on the ground, where many groups of unemployed young men do important unpaid work for community.

Even though domestic vs. commercial property crimes indicate different aspects of (in)security, police-based records of property crimes are not disaggregated by domestic vs. commercial property crimes. Some studies have noted that commercial property crimes have reversed trends since early 2000 in Fiji (Duncan & Sharma, 2005) and since 2010 in PNG (Lakhani & Willman, 2014), with domestic break-ins becoming more common than commercial property crimes. This may be a result of increased investment in private security measures by commercial property owners. Dinnen (2020) notes that in PNG, the increased use of private security may make marginalised groups more likely to experience property crimes compared to privileged elites and corporate actors. This dynamic, which we also see globally, is likely true in the other PICTs. Duncan and Sharma (2005) argue that recorded property crimes (both domestic and commercial) in Fiji may be decreasing because of increased private expenditure by higher-income households and businesses on crime prevention, including security guard firms, and security doors, grilles, wiring, and alarm systems. Like Dinnen (2020), Duncan and Sharma (2005) argue further that the privatisation of self-protection means that lower-income households are more likely to become victims of property crimes and that these crimes are also less likely to be recorded and reflected in police data. Government investment in both more 'boots on the ground' and infrastructure—such as lighting and surveillance cameras—are also referred to when explaining the decrease in property crimes (see e.g., Neimila, 2019). However, these claims need to be examined more systematically and, at the moment, data to do this kind of analysis is missing. Moreover, analysis is also required regarding which neighbourhoods and communities benefit from these public investments and which are excluded. Specifically, crime victimisation surveys with representative samples that allow for neighbourhood-based and socio-economic analysis would be helpful in providing a more accurate and nuanced picture.

Substance-Abuse-Related Crime
Police data indicates that offences related to drunkenness, drug use, and consequent disturbance of the peace have increased across the region. This is supported by community perceptions. For example, in Tuvalu, the police and community identified alcohol-related crimes as the greatest concern (Watson, 2017, 2021). In Guam, 75.1% of the community listed substance abuse and 63.7% placed underage drinking as priorities (Watson et al., 2019). Men and youth are more likely to engage in problematic drug and alcohol use and to commit drug- and alcohol-related crimes; while women and girls involved in illicit drug use or experiencing drug addiction may engage in transactional sex and opportunistic crimes, and be at greater risk of experiencing sexual and physical violence. Accidents and deaths linked to driving motor vehicles under the influence are also a problem in the region.

There is a particular concern about substance abuse by youth and related juvenile delinquency that has been increasing since the beginning of the twenty-first century (Devaney et al., 2006; Noble et al., 2011; Plange, 2000). In the Republic of the Marshall Islands, the top three offences recorded were disturbing the peace, drunk and disorderly conduct, and different types of assault, usually recorded as being under the influence of alcohol (Noble et al., 2011). In Solomon Islands, alcohol-related crimes such as production and sale of *kwasa* (home brew) and drunk and disorderly conduct, as well as theft/property damage motivated by or conducted under the influence of alcohol, were identified as leading offences, especially among young men (Noble et al., 2011). In the FSM, thefts, especially by young people, have been linked to obtaining cash to buy alcohol and drugs (or electronics), and arrests usually note that young offenders are under the influence of alcohol (Noble et al., 2011). Lack of enforcement of regulations limiting access to underage alcohol consumption and single-session binge drinking is considered problematic practices in many parts of PICTs and are linked to disorderly conduct, disturbance of the peace, and sometimes assault. In Samoa, possession of illicit drugs continues to be among the most common crimes, especially among young male offenders. While alcohol and marijuana were the main concerns previously (Devaney et al., 2006), increased availability of methamphetamine (ice) and, to some degree, cocaine/heroin (see 'Organised and Transnational Crime', below) have become a concern and are linked to increased violence in distribution processes, as well as in disorderly or violent conduct under the influence (Lyons, 2019a, 2019b).

Violence in the family, socio-economic inequalities and lack of employment opportunities, and political systems that marginalise large chunks of the population (the poor, cultural/ethnic minorities) continue to have an impact on patterns of substance abuse and related crimes. Persistent underinvestment in addressing substance abuse, at both proximate and holistic levels, is also a problem. Unlike in the North Pacific, where treatment programs specifically for substance addiction are available, treatment programs related to addiction are limited in the South Pacific countries and territories—being provided only in PNG, Fiji and Solomon Islands, and only through psychiatric hospitals (Devaney et al., 2006)—and stigma surrounding addiction continues to make drug users vulnerable to violence and additional criminal activity and violence (Al Jazeera, 2019). While police responses, especially with young people (and particularly young women), have often been to allow elders to mediate the situation, over time increasing concerns (often with links to violent crimes) have led to arrests and sentencing. It is important to note that when non-state interventions are used, they can involve physical forms of discipline, which can contribute to continued substance abuse (Noble et al., 2011). Corrections systems in PICTs do not often address addiction and therefore there is an increased risk of the persistence of addiction and 'falling into' criminal behaviour.

Violent Crime/Crimes Against the Person

Violent crime includes murder, serious sexual offences, grievous bodily harm, armed robbery, and car-jacking. Based on national police data, there is a five-year trend of decline in crimes against the person as a proportion of total crimes across the region, except in Samoa (see Fig. 3.3, under 'Overview of Trends in and Social Dynamics of Crime in the Pacific'). At the same time, it is important to recognise that this trend does not capture the persistently high rates of different kinds of violence that women, men, and young people face across the region, especially within the family (Asian Development Bank, 2016; Eves, 2006; UNFPA, 2019).

Community and stakeholder perception surveys place the use and abuse of alcohol (and other drugs) as key factors in contributing to violent crime. However, research suggests that while alcohol may be used specifically to 'gain courage', to work as a trigger in opportunistic crimes, to enable violence, or to excuse violence, other social factors are considered much more important in understanding the dynamics of violent crime (Carrabine, 2017; Eves, 2006). Recorded homicides and violent crimes usually note the use of weapons, including axes, bush/cane knives, *filipins* (slingshots with metal darts), and firearms. With the exception of PNG (as noted further below, under 'Firearms Trafficking'), the availability and use of small firearms are not considered to be major issues in most of the region; however, in some PICTs small firearms are more commonly used in violent crime than figures would suggest, and their presence may be increasing through transnational crime networks (United Nation Office on Drugs and Crime (UNODC), 2016), which are examined later in the chapter (see 'Organised and Transnational Crime', below). Discussions of violence in PICTs also lead often to questions of violent Pacific cultures/masculinities. However, as Biersack notes, there is a contemporary political economy in the production of violent masculinities:

> Whatever the link between violence and masculinity in the past, contemporary masculinity and its association with violence must be understood, at least to a degree, with respect to contemporary economic realities ... Throughout Pacific Island history, men have competed for prestige. Yet many men today lack a reliable income stream, an education and literacy and/or an ability to speak colonial languages and pidgins; as a result, they find themselves at the bottom of a socio-economic ladder that has no precolonial precedent. As a new underclass, they are ill equipped to operate in the new arenas of male competition and, thus, to perform masculinity, which was and still is crucial to their social standing. (2016, p. 206)

Police in PICTs must also respond to the use of customary practices of dealing with rule breaking, which can include violent forms of discipline. These practices then come into conflict with human rights frameworks that are embedded in the legal structure of many of the PICTs. Violence against children and the rights of the children (as noted further below: see 'Youth Violence and Violence Against Children') is one such area that police are having to negotiate, and another relates to the pluralistic systems of authority/justice that exist in PICTs. For example, in Tuvalu, police had to stop elders on one outer island from administering a physically violent punishment against a pastor who had broken the community's by-laws (Amin, Watson, et al., forthcoming). In these situations, traditional or customary forms of authorities must be sanctioned by the police, but the police may often lack the resources and capacity to do so.

Homicide

Across Oceania, homicide rates on average have gone down since 1990 across all age groups, except in Fiji and Guam where homicide rates have increased since 1990. Figure 3.4 shows homicide rates in 1990 and 2017 in Oceania. Note that while homicide rates are mainly low in PICTs, the small populations of some of the countries mean that isolated incidents will inflate the rate. There is also internal variation in homicide rates. For example, in PNG, while the provinces of Gulf and Milne Bay have low rates compared to the national rate of 10.97 per 100,000 population, the city of Lae in Morobe province has rates of 60 per 100,000 population. Further, the UNODC (2019) *Global Study on Homicide* noted that records of causes of death, including homicide, are poorly recorded across the region and that homicide rates may be higher than measured. This is in part linked to the remoteness of many islands (most PICTs) and interiors (e.g., PNG and parts of Fiji) that lead to underreporting of all types of crimes, including homicide.

The UNODC (2019) study suggests that homicide in PICTs falls into three categories: inter-tribal/ethnic conflict, violent crime (including organised crime, hate crime, and brawls) and domestic violence. The politicisation of ethnicity and subsequent violence produce violent deaths in PNG, Fiji, Solomon Islands, and Tonga. Women account for between 10 and 44% of victims of violent deaths in Melanesia (UNODC, 2019).

Other than homicide, violence against the person occurs in multiple forms and overlaps with other forms of crimes. Unorganised interpersonal violence—such as fights in bars, between neighbours, or after drinking sessions—are usually between men and occur throughout PICTs. Police and publics blame alcohol, especially 'home brew' (Kessaram et al., 2016), and some rural communities in remote islands have banned alcohol during certain hours, days, or events (e.g., in Tuvalu and Kiribati). Other research indicates that while alcohol may be a proximate/immediate factor, rivalries, property contestations, or 'saving face' may also be at play (see e.g., Eves, 2006).

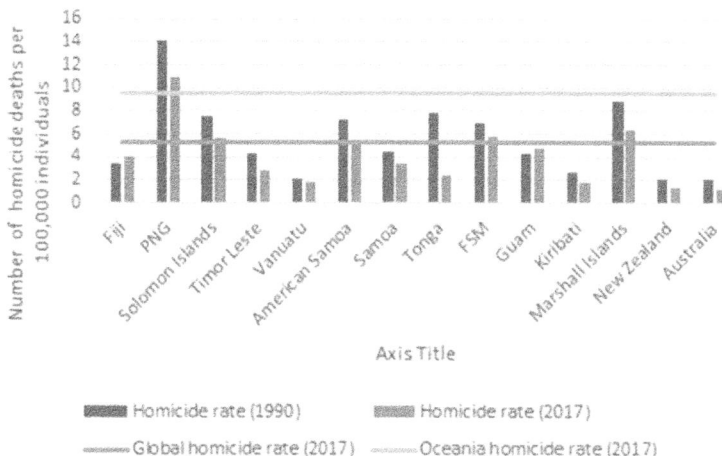

Fig. 3.4 Homicide rates in 1990 vs. 2017 in Oceania (*Source* Global Burden of Disease Collaborative Network, 2018; Institute for Health Metrics and Evaluation, 2018; Roser & Ritchie, 2013. *Note* Homicide rates are measured as the number of deaths from homicide per 100,000 individuals)

Youth Violence and Violence Against Children

One form of violent crime that has become a concern relates to youth[4] rivalries that break out into sporadic occurrences of violence between different secondary schools or gang-like groups (e.g., in Tonga, Samoa, FSM) or between neighbourhoods (e.g., in Fiji, the Republic of the Marshall Islands, PNG). Lee describes these kinds of violent acts in Tonga as:

> intense inter-school rivalries that frequently erupt into violence including large-scale brawls in the streets … [A boy] described being trapped on a bus with boys from a rival school who hit him repeatedly with a piece of

---

[4] Definitions of youth in PICTs vary and tend to include a wider age range than the global definition of 15–24 years. In PICTs, the term 'youth' often includes young adults and is related to whether one is married and has children rather than just a specific age or employment experience and, as such, 15–35 years often captures the cultural meaning of youth better (Lee & Craney, 2019; Plange, 2000).

> wood ... [to the point of requiring] plastic surgery to repair his face ... Some Tongans regard such experiences of violence as an inevitable part of adjusting to Tongan life. (2017, p. 85)

Some of these dynamics also overlap with drug distribution networks (as discussed under 'Organised and Transnational Crime', below). Others, as noted above, are linked to irregular or opportunistic thefts and property damage. Socio-economic inequalities, a discourse of certain groups of youth (e.g., deportees, diasporic youth 'sent back', unemployed youth) as 'troublemakers', and marginalisation of youth continue to be important drivers of these dynamics. For example, in the case of violence in Tongan secondary schools, a significant component relates to the enforcement of social hierarchies based on social status, class, gender, and 'outsider/foreign' (vs. 'local/native') in Tonga (Fa'avae et al., 2017; Lee, 2017). In the case of Fiji, these types of youth gang violence occur most often in social housing communities and informal settlements. Noble and colleagues (2011) confirm that young people were the main participants (though not the leaders) in riots and other forms of public violence/unrest in Tonga in 2006, in the 'Tensions' in Solomon Islands from 1998 to 2003.

Social media has also created a relatively new medium for producing violence (including physical harm or suicide) and harm through cyber-bullying across PICTs (Fa'avae et al., 2017). While the knee-jerk reaction to the more dramatic forms of these incidences is to put more police on the ground or to increase surveillance and (physical) discipline of youth, a much more holistic approach is needed to address these dynamics, including creating more socio-economic opportunities for young people and making more space for youth voice and participation in decision-making forums (Fa'avae et al., 2017; Lee & Craney, 2019; Noble et al., 2011). How rule-breaking behaviour by young people is treated has become an important point of debate and discussion, with civil society organisations and some faith-based organisations advocating for steering away from punitive and exclusionary measures that further alienate and marginalise youth and increase the risk of continued delinquent and criminal behaviour (Heard, 2018; Noble et al., 2011).

Criminological and policy discussions of youth violence and delinquency need to consider how high rates of violence against children by family members and teachers in PICTs produce youth violence (Noble et al., 2011). A 2019 study conducted by Save the Children, World

Vision, Plan International, and ChildFund estimated that 4 million or 70% of children across the larger PICTs in Melanesia and Polynesia, and 2.8 million or 75% of children in PNG experience violent discipline at home (Suthanthiraraj, 2019) (see Fig. 3.5). The study also notes that the median rate of physical and sexual violence against adolescent girls (15–19 years) is 24.4% and 10.5%, respectively. Unfortunately, data on Micronesian and smaller Polynesian countries and territories is not available and, importantly, data on physical and sexual violence experienced by boys has not been documented. Other studies—such as that by Fulu et al. (2013), which includes data on PNG and Fiji—indicate that boys experience both physical and sexual violence at high levels and this contributes to a cycle of violence as boys mature into adulthood. Experiences of violent discipline in homes—especially in the context of changing family and communal structures of living in urban contexts, persistent socioeconomic inequality, and a lack of mental health and other needed social services—have meant that young people are being drawn into substance abuse, being victimised into further violence, and perpetrating violence as well. In Fiji, a study commissioned by the Ministry of Women, Children and Poverty Alleviation confirms that levels of neglect and violence experienced by both boys and girls across their childhood are high and severe (Meo-Sewabu, 2021).

The Pacific Youth Risk and Resilience Framework (Noble et al., 2011, p. 10) points to the importance of a looking at youth crime and delinquency holistically and developmentally. Many police officers emphasise that dealing with youth violence requires 'upstream' engagement with youth through multiple social actors, including social welfare officers, teachers, counsellors, community elders, leaders, and faith-based institutions. Meo-Sewabu (2021) also documents the need for a multi-stakeholder approach at different stages and spaces of youth development to address youth criminality and, in particular, the urgent need to deal with neglect of and violence against youth in their homes. Meo-Sewabu (2021) further emphasises the need to for cooperation and collaboration across the different agencies implicated in dealing with youth violence and violence against children.

Gender-Based Violence

Women, children, and sexual minorities continue to face regular and everyday forms of violence that are gendered in the Pacific. As Fig. 3.6 indicates, level surveys conducted between 2000 and 2018 on women's

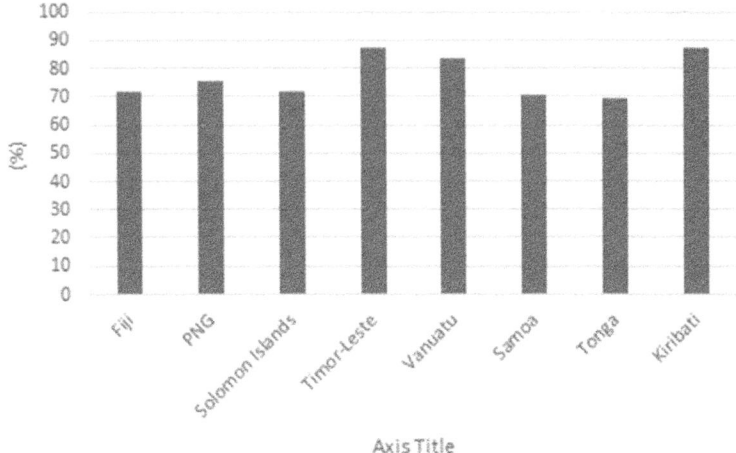

Fig. 3.5 Estimated percentage of children (1–14 years) experiencing violent discipline (psychological and physical) at home (*Source* Suthanthiraraj, 2019)

experience of violence, PICTs continue to have some of the highest rates of IPV in the world. Importantly, in the majority of PICTs, the violence experienced by women is perpetrated the most often by their partners; and when it is not their partners, it is often a family member or a teacher (kNOwVAWdata, 2020) (Table 3.1).

The surveys were conducted by various Women's Crisis Centres in partnership with the UNFPA.

In most PICTs, girls (aged 15 years and above) and women are more likely to experience physical violence from their partners than non-partners. In Cook Islands, Samoa, and Tonga, women are more likely to experience violence from non-partners: see Fig. 3.7. For sexual violence against females since age 15, rates of non-partner violence are lower compared to sexual violence by partner across PICTs except in Nauru, Palau, and Tuvalu (see Fig. 3.7).

The high rates of VAW in PICTs are produced through an intersection of cultural norms that rationalise and normalise violence against wives/female partners (see Amin et al., 2020; Eves, 2006; Heard et al., 2020); cultural and religious practices that make it difficult for women to report violence (Forster, 2010; Thaggard & Montayre, 2019); political dynamics and practices that both marginalise women and de-legitimise

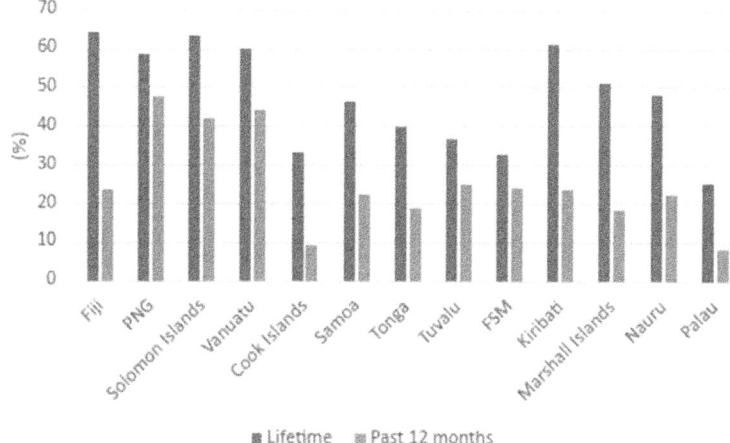

Fig. 3.6 Proportion of ever-partnered women disclosing experience of IPV (physical and/or sexual) (*Source* See Table 3.1)

Table 3.1 Years, survey methodologies, and age groups of IPV data in Figs. 3.6 and 3.7

	Year of data collection	Survey methodology	Age group
Fiji	2010	WHO	18–64
PNG	2016	DHS	15–49
Solomon Islands	2008	WHO	15–49
Vanuatu	2009	WHO	15–49
Cook Islands	2012	WHO	15–64
Samoa	2000	WHO	15–49
Tonga	2009	WHO	15–49
Tuvalu	2007	DHS	15–49
FSM	2014	WHO	15–64
Kiribati	2018	MICS-DHS	15–49
Marshall Islands	2012	WHO	15–64
Nauru	2013	WHO	15–64
Palau	2013	WHO	15–64

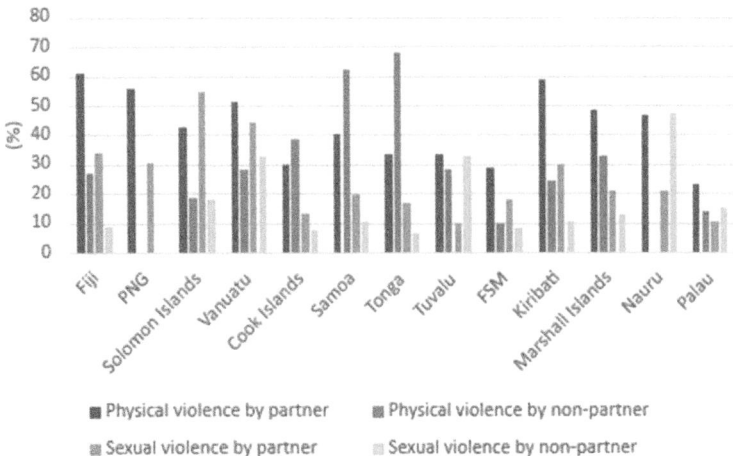

Fig. 3.7 Comparison of lifetime experience of women and girls since age 15 of physical and sexual violence by intimate partner vs. non-partner (*Source* See Table 3.1)

policing institutions (George, 2016); and socio-economic structures that exclude or subordinate women and constrain their ability to leave, change, or speak out against violent relationships (Macintyre, 2012). Additionally, in understanding dynamics of IPV, it is important to consider how (rapid) social changes have produced changes in gender relations, marital and sexual relations, and the ability to perform dominant masculinities (Eves, 2006). Related to the latter, a persistent failure of education systems and employment markets to socialise and integrate young people, especially young men, has led to a range of dynamics that further reinforce the use of violence as a way to 'solve problems', maintain (gendered) power, and assert control.

Therefore, while there has been a great deal of work by government ministries and civil society organisations with citizens, communities, and the police forces focused on raising awareness, gender training programs, and how to respond to VAW, some of the key problems of gendered inequalities in the state, in police institutions, in aid agencies, in the economy, and in cultural and religious institutions remain unaddressed.

As such, structures that reinforce gendered violence continue to be reproduced and thus limit the effectiveness of programs trying to reduce VAW (Eves, 2006; George, 2016; Macintyre, 2012).

The high prevalence of VAW is also linked to inter/transgenerational transmission of trauma and violence, in which children are subjected to violence. The boys often grow up to become perpetrators and the girls often grow up to become subjected to IPV. In addition, histories of colonial and other political forms of violence have been documented to produce inter/transgenerational trauma that becomes linked to high rates of violence (Carrington et al., 2018; Rose, 2014). More Pacific-focused research is needed on both inter/transgenerational trauma and the role of colonial histories in producing gender-based violence, including IPV in PICTs. Amin, Girard, and Calabrò write:

> The topic of trans-generational trauma should be dislodged from the niche it still occupies, to consider both how boys and men re-enact their own trauma and how colonial violence has been internalised and absorbed in PICTs. The impact of the interactions between masculinities and large-scale processes like globalisation equally deserves more attention. (2022, n.p.)

Important ethnographic work that has attempted to do this includes the work on men, masculinities, and violence in PNG (Eves, 2006) and some work in Fiji (see e.g., Romanos, 2005). The use of some PICTs as military bases by foreign powers, authoritarian governments, hierarchies that exclude participatory processes of decision-making, and exploitative labour structures in local and international economies are all important in understanding how Pacific masculinities are shifting and their links to dynamics of IPV and VAW (Biersack, 2016).

IPV and VAW are recognised in many contexts as a public health issue and, as such, the place of policing and the judicial system in this approach needs to be considered carefully to avoid the kind of 'securitised' responses to IPV that increase state power without addressing the structural inequalities that produce IPV, sexual violence, and gender-based violence (Kapur, 2014). Relatedly, research on IPV, sexual and domestic violence among young people in PICTs makes clear that there is a change in perspectives related to what intimate relationships should look like and a desire for more egalitarian relationships. However, research shows that 'intersections of identities related to gender, age, religion and

Table 3.2 Criminalisation of homosexuality in PICTs

PICTs where homosexuality is not criminalised (as of 2020)	PICTs that continue to criminalise homosexuality (as of 2020)
Fiji	PNG
Vanuatu	Solomon Islands
FSM	Cook Islands
Marshall Islands	Samoa
Nauru	Tonga
Palau	Tuvalu
	Kiribati

Source ILGA World (2020)

sexuality, with social gender expectations that support male leadership and hierarchical social systems' (Heard, 2018, p. ii), continue to produce not only violence but also mental health issues and self-harm, including contributing to risks of suicide.

While IPV has been the major focus of policy discourse in relation to VAW across PICTs, other gendered violent crimes against persons include those associated with sorcery accusations (primarily in PNG and other parts of Melanesia) (Forsyth & Eves, 2015) and those against the LGBTQA+ communities (Amin & Girard, 2020; Amin et al., 2020; George, 2008; Kanemasu & Molnar, 2017). In relation to the latter, the continued criminalisation of homosexuality in some PICTs (see Table 3.2) continues to reinforce the risk of violence by both community and state against LGBTQA+ individuals (ILGA World, 2020). Moreover, among PICTs, only Samoa has hate crime legislation (ILGA World, 2020). At the same time, while most PICTs have not enforced these laws and some have legislation that prevents discrimination by sexual orientation in employment and other spheres (e.g., Kiribati), they create an environment of insecurity for LGBTQA+ communities and continue to reinforce stigmatisation, marginalisation, and physical violence against sexual minorities by families, publics, and even the police.

ORGANISED AND TRANSNATIONAL CRIME

While organised and transnational crime are not necessarily linked, in PICTs as elsewhere many aspects of organised crime have transnational dimensions. Rapid economic globalisation and the location of PICTs as part of major transport routes connecting metropoles in Asia, the Americas, Australia, and New Zealand, as well as the challenges of policing the vast area in which PICTs are located and often-weak institutional structures for crime prevention have made them vulnerable to both organised and transnational crime and 'progressively transnationalise crime' (Walton & Dinnen, 2019, p. 426). Schloenhardt summarises organised crime in PICTs as follows:

> there is general consensus that organised crime can be found throughout the Pacific Islands and the Police Commissioner of New Zealand has been quoted saying 'that criminal enterprises in the Islands account for $300 billion annually'. Among the most significant types of organised crime in the South Pacific are narcotrafficking, migrant smuggling, and firearms trafficking. Money laundering is another important phenomenon associated with organised crime and the Pacific Islands have gained some notoriety in that respect. Accordingly, this issue is comparatively well researched and documented elsewhere. Evidence about trafficking in persons, illegal gambling, tobacco smuggling, and electronic crime is so far only anecdotal. (2010, pp. 281–282)

Organised crime and transnational crime have become a major concern for some in the region, with the Pacific Transnational Crime Network identifying in 2019 that illicit drug trafficking and related crimes pose 'extreme risk' across Micronesia, Melanesia, and Polynesia. While the structure of criminal organisations is not fully understood, the Japanese *yakuza* and Chinese criminal gangs are considered to have significant influence (Schloenhardt, 2019). The *yakuza*'s influence and activities are mainly in Guam and former US territories of Micronesia, especially in relation to illegal gambling and the trafficking of illicit drugs and firearms (Schloenhardt, 2010).

Drug Trafficking

Ethnic Chinese gangs are understood to have increasing control over local drug markets in non-Melanesian PICTs, and narcotrafficking from South America to Australia via Melanesian PICTs—especially Fiji and Vanuatu—has been identified as a longstanding organised crime problem that has been amplified with the increase of globalised trade in PICTs (Broadhurst et al., 2013; Schloenhardt, 2010). For example, in 2004, a joint operation run by Fijian and Australian police, called Operation

Outrigger, broke up a methamphetamine warehouse in Suva, valued as a €500 million bust and believed to be run by an Asian gang aiming to ship the drug to Australia, New Zealand, Europe, and the United States of America (Boister, 2017). Since then, there have been many more drug seizures in Fiji, including in 2007 and 2015 (UNODC, 2013, 2016). There were also seizures in Port Vila (Vanuatu) of cocaine worth US$370 million in 2013 (Australian Associated Press, 2013). In addition, Tonga and Solomon Islands have become sites of these transnational drug-trafficking routes (Short, 2019). In 2018, cocaine (500 kg) was seized from a yacht in the Honiara marina in Solomon Islands. Like the 2004 raid in Fiji, the Vanuatu, and Solomon Islands seizures were the product of multi-agency transborder cooperation (Australian Associated Press, 2013; Short, 2019). Some PICTs have become bases for offshore money laundering and drug trafficking by criminal groups from other countries. For example, Michael (2014) reported that Port Moresby (PNG) has become a site for Australian bikie gangs to work with West African and Chinese criminal organisations for money laundering. Walton and Dinnen (2019) also point to how political elites in PNG are able to export illicit money into Australia through investing in property markets or via inflated invoices to lawyers that deposit money into Australian bank accounts. Further, some PICT governments have noted that the fishing industries and the decline in stocks in Palau, Solomon Islands, and Kiribati have become an opportunity for criminal networks to recruit fishermen and fisherwomen into drug and people trafficking (McVeigh, 2018).

One notable impact of transnational drug trafficking through PICTs is that some countries and territories are evolving from being 'just transit points' to becoming sites of drug production and distribution for local markets (Bohane, 2021; Lyons, 2019b). According to several different media sources, in Fiji, there has been a significant rise in 'busts' of methamphetamine that had been designated for local markets (from two cases in 2013 to 113 cases in 2018) (Boister, 2017; Lyons, 2019b; Sauvakacolo, 2020). On 25 February 2021, *The Fiji Times* reported that the Fiji Police Force had uncovered laboratories in the Western and Eastern Divisions producing methamphetamine (Vakasukawaqa, 2021). The transnational drug-trafficking routes have also created local drug markets in Tonga (Lyons, 2019b). In addition to methamphetamine and cocaine, other synthetic drugs such as Fentanyl have been identified as growing issues. For example, the Samoa Police Commissioner Fuiavailili Egon Keil at the Pacific Islands Chiefs of Police Conference in 2019 stated: 'We don't have the money, the resources, the funding. We don't have the equipment. Sometimes we don't have the training. For example, this new drug Fentanyl. It is a very dangerous, addictive drug' (Short, 2019). Pacific transnational crime expert Jose Luis Sousa-Santos warned in 2019 that while Samoa has not become yet a site of locally widespread use of ice, Tonga and Fiji should serve as warnings (Nataro, 2019). Local ice markets in Fiji, Tonga, and other PICTs are being served by local networks of criminal groups and are exploiting marginalised youth, increased social inequalities, and a lack of sufficient proactive responses from governments and civil society (Lyons, 2019b; Nataro, 2019). The importance of producing a holistic response to these security and crime threats early on, before they become law enforcement issues, has been emphasised by Sousa-Santos and Pacific border security scholar Tevita Tupou (Bohane, 2021; Nataro, 2019).

Human Trafficking

Human trafficking is understood to be part of the dynamics of organised and transnational crime in PICTs. In particular, human trafficking into the garment, agriculture, tourism/hospitality, fishing, logging, mining, construction, and sex industries have been documented. Human trafficking into these sectors in PICTs occurs from China, Vietnam, India, Bangladesh, Malaysia, Indonesia, and the Philippines, as well as from within PICTs (Joshua, 2019; Lindley & Beacroft, 2011; Reuters, 2019; Talebulal-Nuku & Kumar, 2021; US Department of State, 2020). In addition to the shared pattern of (sex) trafficking of women and girls (Pacific and non-Pacific) into the tourism and hospitality industries of PICTs, the US Department of State, 2020 *Trafficking in Persons Report* points to different forms of human trafficking:

- trafficking of individuals from Southeast and South Asia into construction industries in Vanuatu and the Republic of the Marshall Islands;
- trafficking of local and East Asian women and girls for forced childbearing as part of international fraudulent adoption schemes in the Republic of the Marshall Islands;
- foreign nationals from Southeast Asia under forced labour on fishing and sea vessels in Fiji, Vanuatu, the Republic of the Marshall Islands, and the FSM (see also Carreon, 2020);

- trafficking of individuals (including foreigners, locals, and children) into logging, fishing, and mining industries in PNG and Solomon Islands;
- trafficking of individuals through PICTs (especially PNG) as transit points for illegal migration to Australia, New Zealand, and Canada.

Data collection efforts on human trafficking have faced many challenges (Pacific Immigrant Development Community (PIDC), 2010). Reporting of trafficking cases to authorities is understood to be limited, especially in the case of women and girls, because trafficked women and girls also face additional stigmatisation linked to sexual violence (presumed or real). Moreover, local recruiters and brokers are often linked up to either local or national-level economic and political elites and thus continue to operate without much disruption from policing agencies (Chaudhry, 2020; US Department of State, 2020). In addition, the commodification, distortion, and/or exploitation of customary practices (such as bride price,[5] child swapping, and labour obligations) may be contributing to the increased risk of trafficking of both children and women in some PICTs, including Vanuatu and the Republic of the Marshall Islands. The use of *kastom* to justify practices also makes it difficult to investigate and prosecute elites (US Department of State, 2020). While the overall penetration of the cash economy and the associated exacerbation of socio-economic marginalisation and/or inequalities are understood to increase the risk and incidence of trafficking, environmental degradation-induced displacements in PICTs are also an important contributor.

Firearms Trafficking

Firearms trafficking has been identified as a longstanding problem in the Melanesian PICTs, especially PNG and Solomon Islands, and is understood to be occurring through organised crime at the domestic rather than transnational level (Koorey, 2016; McDowell, 2012). However, Koorey (2016) does note that the availability of at least 260,000 illicit firearms in Australia could become a problem due to a high demand for

---

[5] Bride price—also called bridewealth or bride token—is a practice in some PICTs where money, property, or another form of wealth is paid by the groom or his family to the bride or her family.

arms in PNG and existing routes of exchange and trafficking via Torres Strait. Moreover, the UNODC (2016) reports that there have been instances of groups trafficking material for methamphetamine production also trafficking firearms. Nevertheless, Koorey notes that:

> many illicit small arms – firearms essentially – are sourced from inside the country in which they are used, and recycled multiple times within it, and ... the security sector has been, or remains, both a source of supply and driver of demand. This is particularly so for the Royal Papua New Guinea constabulary. (2016, pp. 1–2)

While hard data on firearms possession is difficult to find, Alpers and Wilson (2014) note that rates of civilian-held firearms in Melanesia range from 0.35 guns per 100 people in Solomon Islands (equivalent to 1 gun per 600 people) in 2003 to 58.59 guns per 100 people in New Caledonia in 2013. These are the same numbers reported by the UNODC (2016) in its report on transnational crimes in Melanesia. In other parts of PICTs, the rates range from a high of 19.85 guns per 100 people in Niue to no privately owned firearms in Nauru or and Palau (UNODC, 2016). In PNG, while the overall rate is low, the number of civilian-held firearms was close to 71,000 in 2007 (UNODC, 2016). Alpers (2015) notes that Melanesia, with the exception of PNG, remains relatively gun free. Only New Caledonia and PNG allow registered handguns for self-defence, and firearms licences have been suspended in Solomon Islands (since 1999) and Fiji (since 2000) following the 'ethnic tensions' and the coup, respectively. While arms manufacturing is prohibited (as in PNG, Solomon Islands and Vanuatu) or prevented through not issuing manufacturing licences (as in Fiji), single-shot home-made guns are reported to be available in PNG, Fiji and Solomon Islands (Alpers & Twyford, 2003).

Raids of and thefts from police/military stockades—as well as, possibly, officers releasing arms in return for bribes—are considered to be the main mechanism through which trafficking in firearms is occurring (Schloenhardt, 2010). Koorey (2016) reiterates that the issue of illicit small arms in Melanesia should be understood as a problem linked to societal and governance problems and not a 'gun problem'.

Extractive Industries, Corruption, and the Politics–Crime Nexus

The role of governance problems noted above in relation to firearms trafficking also raises questions about another aspect of organised and transnational crime, related to corruption and the role of public officials in facilitating criminal activities. This is particularly evident in analyses of organised and transnational crime related to wildlife trafficking and illicit extraction of natural resources, especially in the logging, agriculture, and fishing sectors in PICTs. Walton and Dinnen suggest that 'the most significant organised crime in the region has involved the nexus between political elites and seemingly licit actors' (2019, p. 419). They further state that while transnational drug, human and wildlife trafficking have become important areas of concern for law enforcement agencies, civil society organisations, and governments, 'they pale in comparison – in terms of social and economic disruption – to other forms of "organised crime", which involve elite politicians, government officials, private sector elites and intermediaries' (Walton & Dinnen, 2019, p. 421).

Walton and Dinnen (2019) document the politics–crime nexus in PICTs in various resource industries, including logging and fishing. Human rights abuses of workers and landowners, illicit logging, and the corruption of public officials by technically legal and legitimate logging companies (often Asian) have been recorded in the logging industry in PNG and Solomon Islands. Similarly, the Australian company Getax has been accused of using different forms of inducements for the state of Nauru to gain access to and control over phosphate mining in the country, whereby local political elite and the Australian company profit at the expense of the public (Thomas, 2016 as cited in Walton & Dinnen, 2019).

Organised criminal behaviour involving politicians in the fishing sector, especially in the smaller PICTs, occurs in relation to obtaining fishing licensing and access agreements (Tsamenyi & Hanich, 2008). While governance of the fisheries has improved through regional cooperation that reduces incentives and opportunities for corruption and illegal activities (Walton & Dinnen, 2019). Keen et al. (2020) note that much more action is needed to increase transparency and efficiency around data collection, data sharing, data accessibility, and multi-sector, multi-agency cooperation to respond to the complex and sophisticated nature of transnational and organised crime in the maritime environment.

Deep sea or seabed mining (DSM) is another significant opportunity for criminal exploitation that is perhaps even harder to regulate than the logging and fisheries sector. Both climate change and the environmental impact of DSM, as well as the potential for illegal and illicit extraction, have been cited as major concerns in the 2021 Drawing the Pacific Blue Line campaign by the Pacific Network on Globalisation and other regional and national PICT non-governmental organisations, which calls for a complete ban on DSM (Pacific Blue Line, 2021).

The tourism industry, especially in relation to land development by foreign companies, is a site in which environmental harm is being produced through the lack of enforcement of different environmental laws. An example of this is the case in Fiji of Freesoul Real Estate, which has damaged and polluted a reef, disrupted traditional fisheries, and stopped other landowners from using the land (Tarai, 2020).

It is important to emphasise that many of the above dynamics are driven by unequal globalisation, increased precarity, a lack of local and participatory forms of decision-making about development and social change, and the politics–crime nexus discussed above. While Vanuatu, Palau, and even Solomon Islands have been able to create significant disruptions to and changes in the politics–crime nexus, Walton and Dinnen note:

> Available evidence suggests that the greatest challenge is often not the detection of offences, but the development of effective strategies to disrupt the growing number of offenders involved in financial crimes in countries such as PNG. This challenge is exacerbated by the limited resources available to specialist units, such as Financial Intelligence Units (FIUs), the slowness of judicial proceedings, and the limited capacities of law enforcement to investigate and prosecute such offences, thereby contributing to the high levels of impunity which enable this kind of offending to thrive. (2019, p. 427)

Cybercrime

Police across PICTs face a relatively new but growing threat related to cybercrime, which includes both violent and non-violent crime types. Information and communication technologies (ICTs) have enabled the 'transformation of crime beyond people, places and even identifiable crimes' (Findley, 1999, p. 2). While much cyber-offending extends the limits of existing offences such as fraud and scams, cybercrimes are unique in their scale and reach and, as such, cannot be simply understood as analogous to similar activities in the non-virtual/physical world (Jewkes, 2007; Lee, 2018).

Data on cybercrime is even more difficult to aggregate than data on other crime. However, available statistics suggest that international cybercrime rates may be very high, with organised money-laundering schemes via ICTs estimated to be at 2–5% of global GDP (Lee, 2018). Global North data suggests that it is the second most reported economic crime and often involves fraud and identity theft. In PICTs, cyber-offences have economic costs due to the 'clogging' of networks in already limited-bandwidth countries and territories. Given the reliance of many PICTs on ICTs, they also pose a risk for disaster management and recovery.

In PICTs, police forces have had to respond to different forms of cybercrime. Most PICTs do not have strong formal institutions to address cybercrimes and only some PICTs have established cybercrime units in police departments, which sometimes consist of just one or two people. It is important to understand that some aspects of cybercrimes may not even be legislated under criminal laws (Ahmadu, 2006; Angelo, 2009). Legislation specifically defining crime related to ICTs has been slowly put into place since 2003 in PICTs but there continue to be gaps (Kshetri, 2013). The relatively underregulated financial systems in some PICTs (e.g., Nauru) make them a attractive sites for online money laundering.

Money laundering, credit card and other financial fraud, malware/ransomware, and data breaches are all potential sources of cybercrime in the Pacific landscape and perpetrators are not typically PICT residents (Kshetri, 2013). The availability of free domain names, and cheap or free web addresses from some PICTs, make PICTs an ideal environment for cybercrime. For example, Pitcairn Island, Niue, and Tokelau were noted in 2008 to be the top three economies generating spam and phishing per capita. The Tokelau domain (.tk) was the second most used domain for malicious registrations, with fake websites created to advertise teaching jobs for which applicants had to pay visa fees. Finau, Samuwai, and Prasad (2013) note that Cook Islands lost US$100,000 through a 2007 telephone hijacking incident, while in 2008 companies and the government in the Republic of the Marshall Islands faced large losses in a two-day denial of service attack. In 2019, the Samoan Central Bank announced that the cryptocurrency OneCoin had compromised

Samoa's financial system, implicating Samoan businesses churches and individuals (Smith, 2019).

Cybercrime committed by PICT residents includes 'sextortion', use of social media to recruit young people (including children) for organised paedophilia rings (e.g., in Fiji: see Tabureguci, 2007 as cited in Kshetri, 2013) and production of child pornographic sites (e.g., in Tonga: see Sager et al., 2002 as cited in Kshetri, 2013). Cyberbullying, cyber-stalking, and/or social media crimes leading to violence, self-harm, and/or suicide are important issues, and revenge porn and extortion via social media have also been noted as problems. For example, in 2017, 900 nude images of women from Fiji (mainly students from the University of the South Pacific and Fiji National University) were being sold and/or used for extortion (Chanel, 2017). There have been also instances of social media being used for pyramid schemes where Indigenous conceptions of gifting have been exploited to target victims.

There have been increased efforts by PICT governments to regulate cyberspace to prevent cyber-offences, as well as increased cooperation between agencies. However, there is also concern that fears about cybercrimes are being used to regulate political opposition. For example, Nauru, Samoa, Solomon Islands, PNG, and Fiji have either proposed or enforced very strict legislation limiting access to social media in the name of dealing with fake news, incitement of violence, and cases of suicide/violence linked to social media-based bullying and harassment (Watson, 2021a). These types of restrictive policies are often seen by the public as coinciding with political interests to maintain power and limit criticism of the government.

STATE CRIMES: EXCESSIVE USE OF FORCE BY POLICE

Finally, as legal and political processes have placed state and police actions under greater media, activist, and citizen scrutiny (especially with the availability of internet and social media), PICT police forces have also had to deal with questions of use of excessive force, corruption, and abuse of power (Brimacombe et al., 2018). Cases of criminal use of force by police in Fiji have reached international media, including acts that have resulted in deaths in custody and one incident involving police throwing a man off a bridge (Anthony, 2020; RNZ, 2020). Anthony (2020) reports that Fiji police officers have been charged with 400 offences in a five-year period. Amnesty International has repeatedly noted that Fiji police and security forces are able to use excessive force with impunity, especially since the 2006 coup, and reports in 2016 suggest that this has continued even after the technical restoration of democracy (Amnesty International, 2016). Use of excessive violence has been reported by either victims or whistleblowers, and some officers have been charged and convicted in Tonga (RNZ, 2017, 2018), Samoa (Tupufia-Ah Tong, 2019), and Tuvalu (Amin, Watson, et al., 2022).

In understanding excessive use of force by police, it is important to consider the larger institutional and socio-political dynamics. The 'bad apple' argument is a problematic one. Instead, what is required is institutional review—not only examining how police structures and policing cultures produce violence, but also investigating how political authoritarianism, a culture of impunity of political and economic elites, and placing police in situations that require other services (e.g., social work or counselling) shape the relationship between police and communities and the use of excessive force by police.

Conclusion

This chapter has reviewed the trends in crime in PICTs, paying special attention to crime and violence related to young people and women, as well as noting the increasing concerns about substance-abuse-related crimes, and organised and transnational crimes. Most of the crime trends and dynamics discussed in the chapter are driven by persistent economic, socio-political, and gender inequalities in the region, as well as by political and decision-making structures that are often authoritarian, unequal, or exclusive. While local dynamics are important, the chapter has also shown that many dimensions of crime in PICTs have a global component. For example, global mobilities are having an impact on crime dynamics in the region, including the deportation of Pacific youth in the diaspora 'back' to the Pacific, and PICTs being transit points in trafficking of wildlife, drugs, and people. The intensification of extractive processes at the global level, despite advocacy in the region for environmental protection, has also produced 'opportunities' for organised criminal activity that are leaving PICT communities more vulnerable to displacement, being victimised by crime and being recruited into illicit activities. The chapter has also shown that advocacy impacts on responses to crime. Specifically, social mobilisation, civil society activism, and regional and international legal frameworks and conventions have led to the criminalisation of forms of violence against women and children and also created pressures on police to respond more—and respond better—to gender-based violence and violence against children.

The chapter has highlighted that there are important gaps in crime data and crime research. Increasing systematic data collection on crime, perception of crime, and victimisation would help to better inform policymaking and police action in reducing crime. Importantly, data analysis and policy responses require what Forsyth et al. (2020) call a 'Pacific people's criminology', in which criminological research and data collection: (a) become grounded in Indigenous methodologies and multi-stakeholder and interdisciplinary collaborations; and (b) directly engage with publics and policymakers in multiple forums to support advocacy and mobilisation for change and reform.

Forsyth et al. (2020) also argue that the focus on crime prevention (instead of crime control) would expand policy and action beyond police and judiciary systems. The socio-political dynamics noted in this chapter that are shaping crime and criminality require not only context-specific policing responses, but also holistic approaches that involve multiple stakeholders, locally and regionally. In the next three chapters, some of these different approaches are discussed in the context of plural policing, women in police and transnational policing.

References

Adinkrah, M. (1995). *Crime, deviance & delinquency in Fiji* (Vol. 10). Fiji Council of Social Services.

Ahmadu, M. L. (2006). The legal aspects of electronic government in Pacific Island Countries: A reflection. *Journal of South Pacific Law, 10*(1). http://www.paclii.org/journals/fJSPL/vol10/1.shtml

Al Jazeera. (2019, July 1). How has Fiji become a highway for drugs? *The Stream*. https://www.aljazeera.com/program/the-stream/2019/7/1/how-has-fiji-become-a-highway-for-drugs

Alpers, P. (2015, February 27). The Pacific region lives up to its name with disarming success. *The Conversation*.

Alpers, P., & Twyford, C. (2003). *Small arms in the Pacific* (Occasional Paper No. 8). The Small Arms Survey. https://www.smallarmssurvey.org/sites/default/files/resources/SAS-OP08-Pacific.pdf

Alpers, P., & Wilson, M. (2014). *Guns in Melanesia: Small arms policy, firearm injury and gun law*. Sydney School of Public Health, The University of Sydney. https://www.gunpolicy.org/firearms/region/melanesia

Amin, S. N., & Girard, C. (2020). Insecurities and strategies of the leiti (transgender) community in Tonga and the role of businesses and indigenous reconciliation practices. In S. N. Amin, D. Watson, & C. Girard (Eds.), *Mapping security in the Pacific: A focus on context, gender and organisational culture* (pp. 146–157). Routledge.

Amin, S. N., Watson, D., & Trussler, T. (2022). Policing and religion in Tuvalu: Perspectives on navigating tensions between multiple security actors. *Journal of Contemporary Criminal Justice, 38*(3), 330–345.

Amin, S. N., Trussler, T., Watson, D., & Niulakita, S. T. (2022). Serving God, the Community, and the State: Policing in Tuvalu. In Watson, Danielle, Amin, Sara N., Wallace, Wendell C., Akinlabi, Oluwagbenga (Michael), & Ruiz-Vásquez, Juan Carlos (Eds.) *Policing the Global South: Colonial Legacies, Pluralities, Partnerships, and Reform* (pp. 95–105). Routledge.

Amin, S. N., Girard, C., & Calabrò, D. G. (2022). Gender inequality and development pedagogy. In S. Kearrin, N. Banks, S. Engle, J. M. Hodge, N. Nakamura, J. Rigg, A. Salamanca, & P. Yeophantong (Eds.), *The Routledge handbook of global development* (pp. 418–430). Routledge.

Amin, S. N., Trussler, T., & Johnson, J. (2020). Rape myths and sexual prejudice. In S. N. Amin, D. Watson, & C. Girard (Eds.), *Mapping security in the Pacific: A focus on context, gender and organisational culture* (pp. 88–103). Routledge.

Amin, S. N., Trussler, T., Watson, D., & Niulakita, S. T. (forthcoming). Serving God, the community and the state: Policing in Tuvalu. In Watson, D., Wendall, W., de Cruz, R., Amin, S. N., & Oluwagbenga, A. (Eds). *Policing in the Global South*. London: Routledge.

Amin, S. N., Watson, D., & Trussler, T. (forthcoming). Religion and policing in the PICs: Perspectives on the roles of secular and non-secular institutions in policing in Tuvalu. *Journal of Contemporary Criminal Justice*.

Amnesty International. (2016, February 24). *Amnesty International report 2015/16—Fiji*. https://www.refworld.org/docid/56d05b5815.html

Angelo, A. H. (2009). Cyber security and legislation in the Pacific. *Télécommunications dans le Pacifique* (pp. 11–26). https://www.wgtn.ac.nz/law/research/publications/about-nzacl/publications/special-issues/hors-serie-volume-ix,-2009/Angelo,-Cyber.pdf

Anthony, K. (2020, November 10). Fiji death in custody reignites debate over police brutality. *The Guardian: The Pacific Project*. https://www.theguardian.com/world/2020/nov/11/fiji-death-in-custody-reignites-debate-over-police-brutality

Asian Development Bank. (2016). *Gender statistics: The Pacific and Timor-Leste*. https://www.adb.org/sites/default/files/publication/181270/gender-statistics-pacific-tim.pdf

Australian Associated Press. (2013, February 23). Cocaine worth $370m seized from luxury yacht in Vanuatu. *The Guardian*. https://www.theguardian.com/world/2013/aug/23/cocaine-seized-from-vanuatu-yacht

Biersack, A. (2016). Introduction: Emergent masculinities in the Pacific. *The Asia Pacific Journal of Anthropology, 17*(3–4), 197–212.

Blaustein, J., Pino, N. W., & Ellison, G. (2018). Crime and development in the Global South. In K. Carrington, R. Hogg, J. Scott, & M. Sozzo (Eds.), *The Palgrave handbook of criminology and the Global South* (pp. 205–221). Palgrave Macmillan.

Bohane, B. (2021, September 22). Pacific Wayfinder: The Pacific's transnational black markets. *Asia & the Pacific Policy Society: Policy Forum*. https://www.policyforum.net/pacific-wayfinder-the-pacifics-transnational-black-markets/

Boister, N. (2017). Regional cooperation in the suppression of transnational crime in the South Pacific. In G. Leane & B. Von Tigerstrom (Eds.), *International law issues in the South Pacific* (pp. 35–93). Routledge.

Brimacombe, T., Kant, R., Finau, G., Tarai, J., & Titifanue, J. (2018). A new frontier in digital activism: An exploration of digital feminism in Fiji. *Asia & the Pacific Policy Studies, 5*(3), 508–521.

Broadhurst, R., Lauchs, M., & Lohrisch, S. (2013). Transnational organized crime in Oceania. In J. Albagense & P. Reichel (Eds.), *Transnational organized crime: An overview from six continents* (pp. 141–162). Sage.

Cain, T. N. (2001). An overview of crime, law and justice in the South Pacific Islands. *Criminal Justice Matters (CJM), 45*, 35–36.

Carrabine, E. (2017). *Crime and social theory*. Macmillan International Higher Education.

Carreon, B. (2020, December 15). Tiny Pacific nation of Palau details 'illegal' Chinese fishing vessel. *The Guardian*. https://www.theguardian.com/world/2020/dec/15/pacific-nation-of-palau-detains-chinese-fishing-crew

Carrington, K., Hogg, R., Scott, J., & Sozzo, M. (2018). Criminology, southern theory and cognitive justice. In K. Carrington, R. Hogg, J. Scott, & M. Sozzo (Eds.), *The Palgrave handbook of criminology and the Global South* (pp. 3–17). Palgrave Macmillan.

Chanel, S. (2017, September 23). Nudes for cash in car park exchange claim. *Fiji Sun*. https://fijisun.com.fj/2017/09/23/nudes-for-cash-in-car-park-exchange-claim/

Chaudhry, M. (2020, October 10). Human trafficking. *The Fiji Times*. https://www.fijitimes.com/human-trafficking-2/

Cunneen, C. (2011). Postcolonial perspectives for criminology. In M. Bosworth & C. Hoyle (Eds.), *What is criminology?* Oxford University Press.

Devaney, M. L., Reid, G., & Baldwin, S. (2006). Prevalence of illicit drug use in Asia and the Pacific. *Drug and Alcohol Review, 26*(1), 97–102.

DiCristina, B. (2016). Durkheim's theory of anomie and crime: A clarification and elaboration. *Australian & New Zealand Journal of Criminology*, 49(3), 311–331.
Dinnen, S. (2020). Insecurity, policing and marketisation: Papua New Guinea's changing security landscape. In S. N. Amin, D. Watson, & C. Girard (Eds.), *Mapping Security in the Pacific: A focus on context, gender and organisational change* (pp. 186–198). Routledge.
Duncan, R., & Sharma, A. (2005). Private crime prevention expenditure in Fiji. *Agenda: A Journal of Policy Analysis and Reform*, 12(1), 47–56.
Eves, R. (2006). *Exploring the role of men and masculinities in Papua New Guinea in the 21st century: How to address violence in ways that generate empowerment for both men and women*. Caritas Australia.
Fa'avae, D., Otunuku, M. A., Robyns, R., & Siale, L. I. (2017). *School related gender based violence: A case study in Tonga*. Tonga (Professional and Technical Reports for UNESCO) Bangkok, Thailand) (Unpublished). http://repository.usp.ac.fj/10815/1/SRGBV_Final_Report_23_August_2017_Final2_IOE_v2.pdf
Fiji Bureau of Statistics. (2013). *Crimes—Offences*. https://www.statsfiji.gov.fj/statistics/other-statistics/crimes-offences.html
Fiji Women's Crisis Centre. (2013). *Somebody's life, everybody's business! National Research on Women's Health and Life Experiences in Fiji (2010/2011): A survey exploring the prevalence, incidence and attitudes to intimate partner violence in Fiji*. Fiji Women's Crisis Centre.
Finau, G., Samuwai, J., & Prasad, A. (2013, March). Cybercrime and its implications to the Pacific. *The Accountant: The Journal of the Fiji Institute of Accountants*, 15–16.
Findley, M. (1999). *Governing through globalised crime: Futures for international criminal justice*. Routledge.
Forster, C. (2010). Ending domestic violence in Pacific Island countries: The critical role of law. *Asian-Pacific Law and Policy Journal*, 12, 123.
Forsyth, M. (2009). *A bird that flies with two wings: Kastom and state justice systems in Vanuatu*. ANU Press.
Forsyth, M., Dinnen, S., & Hukula, F. (2020). A case for a public Pacific criminology? In K. Henne & R. Shah (Eds.), *Routledge handbook of public criminologies* (pp. 163–178). Routledge.
Forsyth, M., & Eves, R. (Eds.). (2015). *Talking it through: Responses to sorcery and witchcraft beliefs and practices in Melanesia*. ANU Press. http://www.jstor.org/stable/j.ctt169wd7b
Fulu, E., Warner, X., Miedema, S., Jewkes, R., Roselli, T., & Lang, J. (2013). *Why do some men use violence against women and how can we prevent it? Quantitative findings from the United Nations multi-country study on men and violence in Asia and the Pacific*. UNDP, UNFPA, UN Women & UNV.

George, N. (2008). Contending masculinities and the limits of tolerance: Sexual minorities in Fiji. *The Contemporary Pacific, 20*(1), 163–189.

George, N. (2016). 'Lost in translation': Gender violence, human rights and women's capabilities in Fiji. In A. Biersack, M. Jolly, & M. Macintyre (Eds.), *Gender violence and human rights: Seeking justice in Fiji, Papua New Guinea and Vanuatu* (pp. 81–125). ANU E-Press.

Global Burden of Disease Collaborative Network. (2018). *Global burden of disease study 2017: Results*. Institute for Health Metrics and Evaluation (IHME).

Goddard, M. (2005). *Unseen city: Anthropological perspectives on Port Moresby, Papua New Guinea*. Pansanus Books.

Guam Police Department. (2015). *Citizen centric report*. https://www.opaguam.org/sites/default/files/gpd_ccr14.pdf

Guam Police Department. (2020). *Citizen centric report*. https://www.opaguam.org/sites/default/files/gpd_ccr19.pdf

Heard, E. (2018). *Using drama-based research and practice to understand intimate partner violence with young people in Samoa: Exploring an intersectionality informed approach to health promotion* [Ph.D. Dissertation]. School of Public Health, University of Queensland.

Heard, E., Fitzgerald, L., Whittaker, M., Va'ai, S., & Mutch, A. (2020). Exploring intimate partner violence in Polynesia: A scoping review. *Trauma, Violence, & Abuse, 21*(4), 769–778.

Heiskanen, M. (2010). Trends in police-recorded crime. *International Statistics of Crime and Justice, 64*, 21–48. https://www.unodc.org/documents/data-and-analysis/Crime-statistics/International_Statistics_on_Crime_and_Justice.pdf

Hipp, J. R. (2013). Assessing crime as a problem: The relationship between residents' perception of crime and official crime rates over 25 years. *Crime & Delinquency, 59*(4), 616–648.

Howes, L. M., Watson, D., & Newett, L. (2021). Police as knowledge brokers and keepers of the peace: Perceptions of community policing in Tuvalu. *Police Practice and Research, 22*(1), 745–762.

ILGA World. (2020). *State-sponsored homophobia: Global legislation overview update*. ILGA World. https://ilga.org/downloads/ILGA_World_State_Sponsored_Homophobia_report_global_legislation_overview_update_December_2020.pdf

Jewkes, Y. (2007). *Crime online*. Routledge.

Joshua, J. (2019, May 14). Repatriation efforts underway for Bangladeshis trafficked to Vanuatu. *Daily Post*. https://dailypost.vu/news/repatriation-efforts-underway-for-bangladeshis-trafficked-to-vanuatu/article_a1e795c3-3df9-5a4a-bb7a-98ace8021a32.html

Kanemasu, Y., & Molnar, G. (2017). Double-trouble: Negotiating gender and sexuality in post-colonial women's rugby in Fiji. *International Review for the Sociology of Sport, 52*(4), 430–446.

Kapur, R. (2014). Gender, sovereignty and the rise of a sexual security regime in international law and postcolonial India. *Melbourne Journal of International Law, 14*(2), 1–30.

Keen, M., Hanich, Q., & Walton, G. (2020, July 1). Fishing for a future: Transparency challenges in the Pacific Island tuna fisheries: Can states cooperate to save sustainable fishing? *Asia and the Pacific Policy Society: Policy Forum.* https://www.policyforum.net/fishing-for-a-future-transparency-challenges-in-pacific-island-tuna-fisheries/

Kessaram, T., McKenzie, J., Girin, N., Roth, A., Vivili, P., Williams, G., & Hoy, D. (2016). Alcohol use in the Pacific region: Results from the STEPwise approach to surveillance, Global School-Based Student Health Survey and Youth Risk Behavior Surveillance System. *Drug and Alcohol Review, 35*(4), 412–423.

kNOwVAWdata. (2020). *Violence against women—Regional snapshot.* United Nations Population Fund. https://asiapacific.unfpa.org/en/resources/violence-against-women-regional-snapshot-2020-knowvawdata

Koloto, A. H., & Fowles, J. B. (2012). *2011 Community perceptions survey & police staff survey: Final report.* University of the South Pacific Tonga Campus. https://repository.usp.ac.fj/5551/1/Final_Report_2011_Tonga_Police_Community_Perception_Survey.pdf

Koorey, S. (2016). Illicit small arms in the Pacific. *Civil-Military Occasional Papers.* Australian Civil-Military Centre, Australian Government. https://www.acmc.gov.au/sites/default/files/2018-11/Illicit_Small_Arms_in_the_Pacific.pdf

Kraemer, D. (2013). *Planting roots, making place: An ethnography of young men in Port Vila, Vanuatu* [Doctoral dissertation]. The London School of Economics and Political Science (LSE). http://etheses.lse.ac.uk/825/1/Kraemer_roots_place_ethnography_young_men_Vanuatu_(publilc).pdf

Kshetri, N. (2013). *Cybercrime and cybersecurity in the Global South.* Macmillan.

Lakhani, S., & Willman, A. M. (2014). *Trends in crime and violence in Papua New Guinea* (Research and dialogue series: no. 1). World Bank Group. http://documents.worldbank.org/curated/en/992741468287127441/Trends-in-crime-and-violence-in-Papua-New-Guinea

Lee, H. (2017). Overseas-born youth in Tongan high schools: Learning the hard life. In J. Taylor & H. Lee (Eds.), *Mobilities of return: Pacific perspectives* (pp. 75–98). http://press-files.anu.edu.au/downloads/press/n4043/pdf/ch04.pdf

Lee, H., & Craney, A. (2019). Pacific youth, local and global. In H. Lee (Ed.), *Pacific youth: Local and global futures* (pp. 1–31). ANU Press. http://pressfiles.anu.edu.au/downloads/press/n6024/pdf/ch01.pdf

Lee, M. (2018). Crime and the cyber periphery: Criminological theory beyond time and space. In K. Carrington, R. Hogg, J. Scott, & M. Sozzo (Eds.), *The Palgrave handbook of criminology and the Global South* (pp. 223–244). Palgrave Macmillan.

Lindley, J., & Beacroft, L. (2011). Vulnerabilities to trafficking in persons in the Pacific Islands. *Trends and Issues in Crime and Criminal Justice, 428*, 1–7. https://www.aic.gov.au/sites/default/files/2020-05/tandi428.pdf

Lyons, K. (2019a, June 23). The new drug highway: Pacific Islands at centre of cocaine trafficking boom, *The Guardian*. https://www.theguardian.com/world/2019/jun/24/the-new-drug-highway-pacific-islands-at-centre-of-cocaine-trafficking-boom

Lyons, K. (2019b, June 24). 'I've seen terrible, terrible violence': Cocaine and meth fuel crime and chaos in Fiji. *The Guardian*. https://www.theguardian.com/global-development/2019/jun/24/ive-seen-terrible-terrible-violence-cocaine-and-meth-fuel-and-chaos-in-fiji

Ma'a Fafine mo e Famili. (2012). *National study on domestic violence against women in Tonga*. Ma'a Fafine mo e Famili.

Macintyre, M. (2012). Gender violence in Melanesia and the problem of Millennium Development Goal No. 3. In M. Jolly & C. Stewart (Eds.), *Engendering violence in Papua New Guinea* (pp. 239–266). ANU E-press.

Maguire, M., & McVie, S. (2017). Crime data and criminal statistics: A critical reflection. In A. Liebling, S. Maruna, & L. McAra (Eds.), *The Oxford handbook of criminology* (6th ed., Vol. 1, pp. 163–189). Oxford University Press.

McDowell, S. (2012). The threat of small arms to regional security in the Pacific. *Canterbury Law Review, 18*, 41–61.

McMurray, C. (2014). *Pacific police development program: Tuvalu survey*. Australian Demographic and Social Research Institute, Australian National University.

McVeigh, K. (2018, October 16). Drug trafficking at sea is devastating island states, ministers say. *The Guardian*. https://www.theguardian.com/environment/2018/oct/16/drug-trafficking-at-sea-is-devastating-island-states-ministers-say

Meo-Sewabu, L. (2021). *Child violence in Fiji*. Ministry of Women, Children and Poverty Alleviation.

Michael, P. (2014, May 2). Queensland bikies and Nigeria crime syndicates team up to run drugs out of PNG. *The Courier Mail*. https://www.cou riermail.com.au/news/queensland/queensland-bikies-and-nigerian-crime-syn dicates-team-up-to-run-drugs-out-of-png/news-story/37b96409ed770427ba a46690d06adf7a

Nataro, I. (2019, August 23). Expert warns Samoa about hard drugs. *Samoa Observer*. https://www.samoaobserver.ws/category/samoa/47914

Neimila, N. (2019). *Crime rate drops despite illegal activities*. Fiji Government. https://www.fiji.gov.fj/Media-Centre/News/Feature-Stories/Crime-Rate-Drops-Despite-Illegal-Activities

Nichols, P., Toomey, L., Besley, M., Pakoasong, B., & Hagan, P. (2019). *Stretem Rod blong Jastis mo Sefti 2017–2020 (Vanuatu–Australia Policing and Justice Program): Evaluation Report*. https://www.dfat.gov.au/sites/default/files/vapjp-evaluation-report_05022020.pdf

Noble, C., Pereira, N., & Saune, N. (2011). *Urban youth in the Pacific: Increasing resilience and reducing risk for involvement in crime and violence*. United Nations Development Programme Pacific Centre. https://www.youthpolicy.org/wp-content/uploads/library/2011_U rban_Youth_Pacific_Eng.pdf

Pacific Blue Line. (2021). *Deep sea mining is not needed, not wanted, not consented!* https://www.pacificblueline.org/pacific-blue-line-statement

Pacific Immigrant Development Community (PIDC). (2010). *Understanding human trafficking and people smuggling* (Policy brief: No. 2). PIDC. https://www.pidcsec.org/UserFiles/PidcSec/File/Policy/20100924-Policy-brief%202-Human-Trafficking-and-People-Smuggling.pdf

Plange, N. (2000). *Generation in transition. Volume 1: Pacific youth and the crisis of change in the late twentieth century*. Fiji Institute of Applied Studies and Department of Sociology, University of South Pacific.

Pratt, J., & Melei, T. (2018). One of the smallest prison populations in the world under threat: The case of Tuvalu. In K. Carrington, R. Hogg, J. Scott, & M. Sozzo (Eds.), *The Palgrave handbook of criminology and the Global South* (pp. 729–750). Palgrave Macmillan.

Putt, J., & Dinnen, S. (2020). *Reporting, investigating and prosecuting family and sexual violence offences in Papua New Guinea*. Department of Pacific Affairs and Australian National University. https://openresearch-repository. anu.edu.au/bitstream/1885/205549/7/DPA%20FSV%20report%202020% 207%20July%20smallfile.pdf

Reuters. (2019, March 26). Dozens of Bangladeshi migrants trafficked to Vanuatu stuck in limbo. *The Fiji Times*. https://www.fijitimes.com/dozens-of-bangladesh-migrants-trafficked-to-vanuatu-stuck-in-limbo/

RNZ. (2017, July 22). Another Tongan Police officer suspended. *RNZ*. https://www.rnz.co.nz/international/pacific-news/335587/another-tongan-police-officer-suspended

RNZ. (2018, June 26). Tonga police investigate alleged police brutality. *RNZ*. https://www.rnz.co.nz/international/pacific-news/360429/tonga-police-investigate-alleged-police-brutality

RNZ. (2020, June 18). Five Fiji police officers charged over bridge assault. *RNZ*. https://www.rnz.co.nz/international/pacific-news/419318/five-fiji-police-officers-charged-over-bridge-assault

Romanos, A. (2005). *Working with boys and men for a change: Lessons from Fiji*. A thesis presented in partial fulfilment of the requirements for the degree of Master of Philosophy in Developmental Studies. Massey University.

Rose, S. D. (2014). *Challenging global gender violence: The global clothesline project*. Palgrave Pivot.

Roser, M., & Ritchie, H. (2013). *Homicides*. Our World in Data. https://ourworldindata.org/homicides

Royal Solomon Islands Police Force. (2013). *Annual report 2013*. https://www.rsipf.gov.sb/sites/default/files/download%20%2813%29.pdf

Royal Solomon Islands Police Force. (2014). *Annual report 2014*. https://www.rsipf.gov.sb/sites/default/files/download%20%2814%29.pdf

Royal Solomon Islands Police Force. (2015). *Annual report 2015*. https://www.rsipf.gov.sb/sites/default/files/download%20%2817%29.pdf

Royal Solomon Islands Police Force. (2016). *Annual report 2016*. https://www.rsipf.gov.sb/sites/default/files/Annual%20Report%20-2016.pdf

Royal Solomon Islands Police Force. (2017). *Annual report 2017*. https://www.rsipf.gov.sb/sites/default/files/Annual%20Report%20-2017.pdf

Royal Solomon Islands Police Force. (2018). *Annual report 2018*. https://www.rsipf.gov.sb/sites/default/files/Annual%20Report%20-2018.pdf

Samoa Bureau of Statistics. (2013). *Report of the Community Perception Survey*. Samoa Bureau of Statistics.

Samoa Office of the Ombudsman and National Human Rights Institution (NHRI). (2018). *State of human rights report: National public inquiry into family violence in Samoa*. Samoa Office of the Ombudsman & NHRI.

Sauvakacolo, S. (2020, June 28). Seruiratu: Increase in methamphetamine busts. *The Fiji Times*. https://www.fijitimes.com/seruiratu-increase-in-methamphetamine-busts/

Schloenhardt, A. (2010). *Palermo in the Pacific: Organised crime offences in the Asia Pacific Region*. Brill-Nijhoff.

Schloenhardt, A. (2019). Smugglers and Samaritans: Criminalising the smuggling of migrants in international and Australian law. In P. Billings (Ed.), *Crimmigration in Australia* (pp. 253–273). Springer.

Secretariat of the Pacific Community (SPC). (2009a). *Kiribati Family Health and Support Study: A study on violence against women and children*. Report prepared by the Secretariat of the Pacific Community for the Ministry of Internal and Social Affairs, and the Statistics Division, Ministry of Finance and Economic Development, Republic of Kiribati. SPC.

Secretariat of the Pacific Community (SPC). (2009b). *Solomon Islands family health and safety study: A study on violence against women and children*. Report prepared by the Secretariat of the Pacific Community for the Solomon Islands Ministry of Women, Youth and Children's Affairs, and the National Statistics Office, Ministry of Finance and Treasury, National Reform and Planning. SPC.

Secretariat of the Pacific Community (SPC). (2009c). *Tuvalu demographic and health survey 2007*. SPC. https://sdd.spc.int/digital_library/tuvalu-demogr aphic-and-health-survey-dhs-report-2007

Short, F. (2019, August 27). Pacific transnational crime and specifically drug smuggling demands ever tighter surveillance, networking and intelligence sharing. *LinkedIn*. https://www.linkedin.com/pulse/pacific-transnati onal-crime-specifically-drug-smuggling-frank-short

Smith, M. (2019, May 1). Samoa probes cryptocurrency-linked churches. *RNZ*. https://www.rnz.co.nz/international/pacific-news/388161/samoa-probes-cryptocurrency-linked-churches

Stern, M. (2017). Is music a 'safe place'? The creative and reactive construction of urban youth through reggae music (Port Vila, Vanuatu). *Journal De La Société Des Océanistes, 144–145*, 117–130.

Sumner, C. (1982). *Crime, justice and underdevelopment*. Heinemann.

Suthanthiraraj, K. (2019). *Unseen, unsafe: The underinvestment in ending violence against children in the Pacific and Timor-Leste*. Melbourne: Save the Children (Australia), Plan International, World Vision Australia, ChildFund Australia. https://apo.org.au/node/250406

Talebulal-Nuku, W., & Kumar, A. (2021, February 16). Prober after expat worker claim: 49 Bangladeshi nationals claim they were scammed. *The Fiji Sun*. https://fijisun.com.fj/2021/02/16/probe-after-expat-worker-claim/

Tarai, J. (2020). Fiji. *The Contemporary Pacific, 32*(2), 554–570.

Thaggard, S., & Montayre, J. (2019). 'There was no-one I could turn to because I was ashamed': Shame in the narratives of women affected by IPV. *Women's Studies International Forum, 74*, 218–223.

Tonga Police. (2014). *Annual report 2013/2014*. Tonga Police.

Tonga Police. (2019). *Annual report 2018/2019*. Tonga Police.

Tsamenyi, M., & Hanich, Q. (2008). *Addressing corruption in Pacific Island fisheries*. Report prepared for the IUCN Profish Law Enforcement, Corruption and Fisheries Project. https://www.iucn.org/sites/dev/files/import/downlo ads/addressing_corruption_tsumenyi.pdf

Tupufia-Ah Tong, L. T. (2019, December 18). Court condemns 'police brutality, abuse of power'. *Samoa Observer.* https://www.samoaobserver.ws/category/samoa/54928

United Nations Children Fund (UNICEF). (2017). *Situation analysis of children in the Pacific Island Countries.* UNICEF Pacific.

United Nations Office on Drugs and Crime (UNODC). (2013). *World drug report.* UNODC. https://www.unodc.org/unodc/secured/wdr/wdr2013/World_Drug_Report_2013.pdf

United Nations Office on Drugs and Crime (UNODC). (2016). *Transnational crime in the Pacific: A threat assessment.* Bangkok: Regional Office for Southeast Asia and the Pacific, UNODC & Pacific Islands Forum Secretariat. https://www.unodc.org/documents/southeastasiaandpacific/Publications/2016/2016.09.16_TOCTA_Pacific_web.pdf

United Nations Office on Drugs and Crime (UNODC). (2019). *Global study on homicide: Homicide, development and the Sustainable Development Goals.* UNODC. https://www.unodc.org/documents/data-and-analysis/gsh/Booklet_4.pdf

United Nations Populations Fund (UNFPA). (2006). *The Samoa family health and safety study.* SPC. https://pacific.unfpa.org/en/publications/samoa-family-health-safety-study

United Nations Populations Fund (UNFPA). (2019). *Violence against women—Regional snapshot.* kNOwVAWdata. https://asiapacific.unfpa.org/sites/default/files/resource-pdf/2019_knowvawdata_regional_vaw_map_-_v2_updated_31_july_2020.pdf

US Department of State. (2020). *Trafficking in persons report.* US Department of State. https://www.state.gov/wp-content/uploads/2020/06/2020-TIP-Report-Complete-062420-FINAL.pdf

Vakasukawaqa, A. (2021, February 25). Police find drugs more lethal than meth. *The Fiji Times.* https://www.fijitimes.com/police-find-drugs-more-lethal-than-meth/

Vanuatu Women's Centre (VWC). (2011). *Vanuatu national survey on women's lives and family relationships.* VWC.

Wacquant, L. J. (2009). *Prisons of poverty* (Vol. 23). University of Minnesota Press.

Walton, G. W., & Dinnen, S. (2019). The Pacific Islands: Politics, organised crime and corruption. In F. Allum & S. Gilmour (Eds.), *Handbook of organised crime and politics* (pp. 418–435). Edward Elgar Publishing.

Watson, A. H. A. (2021a). Are telecommunications in the Pacific at risk? *Asia and the Pacific Policy Society.* https://www.policyforum.net/are-telecommunications-in-the-pacific-at-risk/

Watson, A. H. A. (2021b). Telecommunication security in the Pacific region. *Development Bulletin, 82,* 131–135.

Watson, D. (2017). *Tuvalu Police stakeholder perceptions study*. University of the South Pacific.

Watson, D., & Dinnen, S. (2020). Contextualising policing in Melanesia: History, adaptation and adoption problematised. In S. N. Amin, D. Watson, & C. Girard (Eds.), *Mapping security in the Pacific: A focus on context, gender and organisational culture* (pp. 161–173). Routledge.

Watson, D., Rivera, J., & McNinch, R. (2019). *Stakeholder perceptions about Guam Police*. University of the South Pacific.

Watson, D., Sousa-Santos, J. L., & Howes, L. M. (2021). Transnational and organised crime in Pacific Island countries and territories: Police capacity to respond to the emerging security threat. *Development Bulletin, 82*, 151–155.

World Health Organization (WHO). (2013). Global and regional estimates of violence against women: Prevalence and health effects of intimate partner violence and non-partner sexual violence. WHO. https://www.who.int/publications/i/item/9789241564625

World Health Organization (WHO). (2021). *Global, regional and national estimates for intimate partner violence against women and global and regional estimates for non-partner sexual violence against women*. WHO.

Open Access This chapter is licensed under the terms of the Creative Commons Attribution 4.0 International License (http://creativecommons.org/licenses/by/4.0/), which permits use, sharing, adaptation, distribution and reproduction in any medium or format, as long as you give appropriate credit to the original author(s) and the source, provide a link to the Creative Commons license and indicate if changes were made.

The images or other third party material in this chapter are included in the chapter's Creative Commons license, unless indicated otherwise in a credit line to the material. If material is not included in the chapter's Creative Commons license and your intended use is not permitted by statutory regulation or exceeds the permitted use, you will need to obtain permission directly from the copyright holder.

CHAPTER 4

Plural Policing in the Pacific

Abstract Plural policing has become a key focus in critical policing and security scholarship, with growing acknowledgement that policing practices involve multiple actors and diverse institutional forms. While much of the recent interest in plural policing has been prompted by the global growth of private security, plural policing in the Pacific Islands has long been evident in the co-existence of state-based police organisations operating nationally, and traditional or customary policing forms operating at local levels in most of these countries and territories. This chapter examines the plural character of Pacific policing in the context of historical and more recent processes of pluralisation, including the expanding domains of private and transnational policing, highlighting the deepening entanglement and interdependency between these various policing forms. The geographic focus is on the independent Melanesian countries, the region's most populous, socially diverse, and challenging policing environments.

Keywords Policing pluralisation · Melanesia · Colonialism · Institutional modernisation · Policing beyond the state

Introduction

While policing is still equated with the work of public police organisations, scholars increasingly acknowledge its plural character in practice. Plural policing denotes the provision of policing services by multiple actors and diverse institutional arrangements, rather than being the monopoly of a single provider. Recent interest in the plural nature of policing has been prompted by the expansion of private security, with a proliferation of commercial entities offering many similar services to the public police. Economic liberalisation has been a key driver of this growth across the globe (Ellison & Pino, 2012). Scholars have also noted the corporatisation of public police organisations (Loader, 1999), the increase in other government regulatory and investigatory agencies involved in policing (Jones & Newburn, 2006), and the rise in citizen- and community-led policing initiatives (Bayley & Shearing, 2001).

Growing scholarly interest in plural policing has been accompanied by a shift in focus from the police as a discrete institutional form to policing as a social process directed at maintaining a given social order (Diphoorn, 2016). This broader conceptualisation of policing goes beyond a narrow focus on the work of the public police and, instead, encompasses a wide range of actors and practices. For Jones and Newburn, policing comprises any 'organised forms of order maintenance, peacekeeping, rule or law enforcement, crime investigation and prevention and other forms of investigation and associated information-brokering undertaken by individuals or organisations' (1998, pp. 18–19). Baker includes '[a]ny organised activity, whether by the state or civil groups, that seeks to ensure the maintenance of communal order, security and peace through elements of prevention, deterrence, investigation of breaches, resolution and punishment' (2008, p. 22). A plural policing lens unsettles long-standing assumptions about the centrality of governments (and states) in the authorising and exercise of power. As Loader has put it, '[w]hat we might call a shift from *police* to *policing* has seen the sovereign state – hitherto considered focal to both provision and accountability in this field – reconfigured as but one node of a broader, more diverse "network of power"' (2000, p. 323, emphasis in original). In addition to what public police organisations do, policing extends 'to private policing forms secured *through* government; to transnational police arrangements taking place *above* government; to markets in policing and security services unfolding beyond government; and to policing activities engaged in by citizens *below* government' (2000, p. 324, emphasis in original).

Plural policing is particularly useful for considering policing provision in the complex and fragmented social settings found in many post-colonial and conflict-affected parts of the world. The workings of the public police in such places often bear little resemblance to the ideals of democratic and service-oriented policing that inform depictions of modern police organisations. On the contrary, popular perceptions of the police might be shaped by well-founded beliefs about the latter's politically compromised or corrupt character. These perceptions might attest to practical difficulties in accessing scarce public police resources in areas of limited statehood, or lack of confidence in the technical capabilities of the police, or, in some places, they might signify fear and distrust of an organisation with a reputation for brutality and human rights abuses. They might also reflect the existence of an extensive array of alternative (non-state) providers whose services can be drawn upon for different policing needs. Baker provides a flavour of non-state policing actors in sub-Saharan Africa, such as 'customary leaders, religious organisations, ethnic associations, youth groups, work-based associations, community police forums, conflict resolution nongovernmental organisations (NGOs), the lowest or informal levels of local government, and entrepreneurs' (2010, p. 10).

Plural policing scholars have sought to highlight and investigate the interactions between different policing actors operating within broader policing or security webs (Albrecht & Kyed, 2015). Terms such as 'security networks' (Dupont, 2004), 'nodal governance' (Wood & Shearing, 2007), and 'security assemblages' (Abrahamsen & Williams, 2011) have been used to describe these fluid configurations and the interplay between their constituent parts. Relational frameworks enable a more nuanced understanding of the dynamic and fragmented character of policing provision found in many such settings. With their emphasis on the intersections and overlap between providers, they also steer us away from familiar but unhelpful binaries between public/private and state/non-state domains.

These frameworks help us explore the messy realities of policing provision in the contemporary Pacific, where public police organisations typically co-exist and intermingle with Indigenous forms of self-regulation that preceded the imposition of colonial states and continue to influence everyday order-making. This is especially so in the Melanesian sub-region, well known for the diversity and versatility of its local social orders and the relative fragility of its state institutions (Hirsch & Rollason, 2019). While interactions between state and local socio-legal orders have long preoccupied scholars of legal pluralism (Scaglion, 2004), the social foundations of policing practice in the Pacific have attracted less attention, with some notable exceptions (see e.g., Forsyth, 2021).

This chapter examines the plural character of policing and security in the contemporary Pacific, including the factors that have animated historical and ongoing processes of pluralisation, as well as the deepening entanglement between different policing providers resulting from these processes. Given extensive variations across the region, illustrations will be drawn primarily from the independent Melanesian states, notably Papua New Guinea (PNG), Solomon Islands and Vanuatu. These countries are where most of the region's population live and are well known for their internal diversity and the fragility of their government sectors. Relative to their neighbours, they have also experienced the most serious problems of crime, violence, and insecurity that have, in turn, prompted a range of policing responses at national, transnational, and local levels. The first part of the chapter provides a short review of the distinct trajectory of policing pluralisation in the Melanesian Pacific—an important dimension of the larger story of colonisation, state-building, and globalisation in this region. Following a broad historical chronology, this part is arranged around two key junctures: first, colonisation; and second, decolonisation and modern state-building. The second part of the chapter provides a sketch of plural policing in post-colonial Melanesia, including the growing challenges facing fragile public police organisations. This entails an examination of four intersecting layers or scales of policing provision, namely public policing (*policing through the state*), transnational policing (*policing above the state*), private policing (*policing beyond the state*), and locally driven policing (*policing beneath the state*). The chapter concludes with some broad observations.

Colonial Administration and the Pluralisation of Policing in Melanesia

The history of the public police is closely entwined with that of European colonialism, as indicated in Chapter 2. Scholars have documented the relationship between early police development in metropolitan and colonial settings, showing how the need to maintain order in colonial territories influenced the establishment and development of public police organisations back in the metropolitan centres (Sinclair & Williams, 2007).

Colonisation was a major source of legal and policing pluralisation as imperial powers introduced colonial law and police into territories already possessing diverse local forms of social order and regulation (Tamanaha, 2012). The origin of the public police as a key instrument of external domination has also had a significant influence on their subsequent development in many parts of the post-colonial world (Comaroff & Comaroff, 2006).

Official colonisation in the Southwest Pacific commenced, for the most part, in the second half of the nineteenth century, as European powers competed with each other to extend their presence across much of the region. In the Melanesian territories, the first police organisations were integral parts of small and underresourced colonial administrations on the periphery of the empire. The initial members of the 'native police' in these newly created colonial entities often came from more settled neighbouring colonies. For example, Fijians and Fijian-based Solomon Islanders provided the original recruits in the armed constabulary in British New Guinea (Dutton, 1985, p. 63). Fijians were also the first policemen in the British Protectorate of Solomon Islands (Bennett, 2002). Vanuatu was a colonial oddity with separate British and French police divisions, each dealing with their own citizens under English or French law, and both dealing with locals under a separate 'native code'. A senior British official described Australia's administration in the much larger territories of Papua and New Guinea as a 'benevolent type of police rule' (Lord Hailey as cited in Mair, 1948, p. 45). The police were a critical instrument for extending and consolidating government influence in both territories—a slow and uneven process that had barely been completed in some areas by the time of PNG's independence in 1975.

Rather than being a neutral law enforcement agency operating independently of government, colonial police were active agents of pacification and 'native administration'. European field staff typically commanded small units of armed 'native constabularies', spending much of their time patrolling on foot or by boat to visit widely dispersed local populations. Early policing work included suppressing resistance to colonial incursion, ending fighting and raiding between local groups, safeguarding Europeans, adjudicating infringements of 'native regulations', and collecting the head taxes that were introduced in most territories to compel a labour force for European-owned plantations. Initial encounters with Indigenous populations were often violent, entailing extensive resort to punitive expeditions against recalcitrant local groups (Ballard & Douglas, 2017).

In Solomon Islands, most of the areas where European commercial activities took place had been secured by the 1920s (Bennett, 1987, p. 112) and by 1922 the armed constabulary had a strength of 153 men (Boutilier, 1984, p. 45). PNG's size and extraordinarily challenging topography resulted in a distinct style of frontier policing. Patrols of armed police led by Australian patrol officers, known as *kiaps*, provided the most visible face of colonial government. By 1930 there were around 1000 Indigenous police (Kituai, 1988). Government by patrol was low intensity, involving visits whose regularity depended on local geography and distance from administrative centres. The *kiap* would inspect villages, collect head taxes, complete the census forms, and hear minor cases relating to breaches of 'native regulations' (Dinnen & Braithwaite, 2009). The primary concern of colonial policing was with maintaining some semblance of order rather than preventing and investigating crime. Unless perceived as direct threats to colonial authority or the security of Europeans, most local disputes and infractions were left to community leaders and other local mechanisms for resolution. Policing practice was different in the small European-dominated urban enclaves and was provided by a handful of police with a focus on crime control, as with their counterparts in towns across colonial Australia.

The modest resources available to colonial authorities tasked with policing widely dispersed local populations led to the adoption of various forms of indirect rule. These accentuated pluralisation by introducing a variety of other policing actors alongside colonial police forces. They included the appointment of village-based officials—village constables in Papua and *luluais* (local leaders appointed to represent the administration at village level) and *tultuls* (their interpreters) in New Guinea—to liaise with the visiting *kiap* and contribute to order maintenance and dispute resolution during his absence. In Solomon Islands, district headmen, village headmen, and village constables were appointed and worked under the supervision of European district officials, although the regularity of such supervision varied from place to place (Dinnen & Allen, 2016). In practice, the effectiveness of these local police actors largely depended on their standing in their own societies.

Colonial authority and policing in Melanesia, as in most parts of the colonial world, were not simply imposed on passive subject populations but were actively mediated through the agency of local actors, including 'native police' (Kituai, 1998). Although inevitably impacted by colonialism, Indigenous forms of policing and regulation were not displaced by these larger transformations. Given the limited reach of the colonial state and its shallow penetration of local societies, most people continued to rely on customary mechanisms for their everyday policing and security needs. These mechanisms adapted over time through their interactions with the newer policing forms introduced by colonialism. While colonial order could always draw on superior firepower when needed, it also depended on high levels of local acquiescence. An important factor behind the relative success of *kiap*-style policing in rural PNG and Solomon Islands was the negotiated character of its engagements with local leadership and policing forms (Dinnen & Braithwaite, 2009). Thus, while colonial and Indigenous forms of policing could and did come into conflict, at other times they could complement and even strengthen each other (Gordon, 1983).

Decolonisation and the Centralisation of Policing

As political independence approached, police forces across the colonial world were restructured and modernised, often acquiring centralised command systems and specialist units, as well as increasing in size (Anderson & Killingray, 1992, p. ix). In the Melanesian territories, decolonisation entailed an intense and prolonged period of state-building as colonial administrative systems were dismantled and incrementally replaced by the institutional framework of modern statehood, particularly in the two decades prior to independence. These institutional transformations were premised on the doctrines of the separation of powers and rule of law. They included major police reform aimed at establishing a professional and politically neutral law enforcement organisation. Rather than serving the political and economic interests of the colonial order, the police were now to serve the needs of an independent citizenry. This has proved to be a challenging transition to realise, with legacies of colonial policing remaining, including a proclivity for 'rough justice', the underfunded and uneven distribution of police resources, and the continuing reliance on informal (non-state) policing and justice practices by a substantial portion of the local population.

Police reform started in Solomon Islands in the 1950s, when the newly renamed Royal Solomon Islands Police (RSIP) began to be 'trained as a civilian force to help and protect rather than to repress' (RSIP, 1981, p. 5). British police officers were recruited to oversee the professionalisation of the RSIP. New infrastructure was established, including a new police headquarters and training school in the capital, Honiara. A specialised field force was created to reinforce district police and serve as a riot squad in public order situations. In Vanuatu, the French and British divisions of the police were officially integrated before independence but continued to operate separately in the context of disagreement between the two colonial powers over the timing of independence and the outbreak of the short-lived Santo rebellion.

From a plural policing perspective, decolonisation represented a concerted push to centralise and consolidate policing power into a single institutional form. This involved moving away from the plural policing auspices of indirect rule involving village-based policing actors, such as village constables, serving as intermediaries between state-based and local (non-state) social orders. It also heralded the demise of *kiap*-style policing in PNG. The multi-functional character of the *kiap*—combining roles of police officer, magistrate, and gaoler—was viewed as incompatible with the separation of powers. In 1961 the PNG police were separated from the old Department of Native Affairs and became a standalone agency with a high degree of operational autonomy. Mobile squads were established to manage public order and inter-group conflict, while new urban police stations were built (Gordon & Meggitt, 1985). Institutional modernisation was an uneven and incremental process. Although the aspiration was for a centralised and uniform system of public policing, accomplishing it in practice has proved to be more difficult than anticipated.

Contemporary Dimensions of Plural Policing: Public Policing (*Policing Through the State*)

The most serious issues of crime and disorder have been experienced in the independent Melanesian states of PNG, Solomon Islands, and Vanuatu—in part a reflection of their larger size, the fragility of their state institutions and a range of complex development challenges. More fundamental questions have also been raised periodically around the fitness for purpose of the models of state policing and justice inherited at independence. These factors have contributed to a growing crisis of public policing in post-colonial Melanesia. The evolution and character of this crisis in policing through the state is outlined in the following two sections.

Papua New Guinea

Decolonisation in PNG was accompanied by a variety of emergent social order problems. Some related to the accentuation of longstanding antagonisms between local groups that had been suppressed, albeit temporarily, for much of the colonial period, while others arose from stresses of more recent origin. The most serious included micro-nationalist movements in some of the more developed regions, notably Bougainville and East New Britain (May, 1982), the revival of inter-group conflict in parts of the Highlands (so-called 'tribal fighting'), and a growing moral panic around rising levels of urban crime.

For some observers, the resumption of inter-group conflict was attributed to the withdrawal of state from rural areas following the dismantling of the old colonial system of district administration in which *kiap*-style policing played a key role (Oram, 1973). This was combined with what many locals viewed as the weakness of the modern justice system as a way of settling disputes and preventing conflict (Strathern, 1972). Older forms of violent self-help such as tribal fighting reappeared, while in recent years increasing use of high-powered weapons and military-style tactics have contributed to rising casualties, as well as to widespread destruction of property and displacement of local populations (Hallak, 2019).

Anxieties around crime and personal safety accompanied the rapid growth of the national capital, Port Moresby, in the 1960s and 1970s. With the lifting of colonial restrictions over the movement of local people, young migrants flocked to town in search of better opportunities, and levels of recorded crime increased (Biles, 1976). Local crime outbreaks were typically followed by suppressive policing measures, often involving heavy-handed raids of the informal settlements that were viewed as incubators of the city's notorious *raskol* gangs (Dinnen, 2001). Pervasive insecurity among town residents is today manifested in fortifications, razor wire, and the ubiquitous presence of private security across the urban landscape. The incidence of family and sexual violence also appears to be endemic. According to Human Rights Watch (HRW), PNG is one of the most dangerous countries in the world for women (HRW, 2017). At the same time, relatively few crimes are ever reported to, or recorded by, the police, resulting in an absence of reliable crime data. Although media reports, surveys and anecdotal evidence indicate that victimisation rates are high by global standards, other data suggests some stabilisation in the incidence of violent crime (Lakhani & Wilman, 2014b).

PNG's policing environment would test the most capable and proficient of police organisations, let alone one that has become progressively more dysfunctional over the years. The size of the Royal Papua New Guinea Constabulary (RPNGC) has failed to keep apace with population growth and the organisation continues to have a limited presence and reach in many areas. At PNG's independence in 1975, police responsibility was estimated to cover only 10% of the country's total land area and 40% of its population (Dorney, 2000, p. 304), and the organisation at that time was largely staffed by inexperienced and untrained personnel. Since then, the size of the RPNGC has increased by only around 30% while the population has more than tripled and the scale of PNG's law-and-order problems has continued to grow. Estimates put the size of the force at around 7383 personnel in 2020, while the national population is now about 9 million people (Deloitte, 2020, p. 19). The current police-to-population ratio of 1:1145 is significantly lower than the United Nations recommended ratio of 1:450, and with RPNGC resources concentrated in the urban centres, accessing police remains a challenge for many citizens, 87% of whom live in rural areas (Bourke & Allen, 2021). Police numbers have been supplemented by the deployment of defence force and correctional service personnel during special policing operations, and also by auxiliary and reserve police drawn from the wider community. However, serious abuses by these often poorly supervised volunteer police have led to their regular disbandment by police authorities in the face of public pressure (Post-Courier, 2020).

Government pledges to increase the size of the force are unlikely to be realised any time soon given severe fiscal constraints accentuated by economic fallout from the COVID-19 crisis. According to a 2020 report, the RPNGC faces a recurrent funding gap of K126 million per annum and would need a one-off injection of around K3.9 billion to enable it to deliver its service mandate (Deloitte, 2020, p. 5). Lack of funds to buy fuel for vehicles is a common reason provided for failure to respond to requests for assistance. Flat-lined budgets fund salaries but leave little to cover operational expenses. This leads to rent-seeking behaviour on the part of some police, including demands for payment for attendance and the imposition of unlawful on-the-spot fines at roadblocks. It also renders the police susceptible to reliance on wealthy patrons, including political and business actors, with the accompanying risks this poses to professional integrity.

Over the years, the travails of the RPNGC (and the larger justice system) have provoked two broad sets of critiques. The more common is a technical one focused on organisational deficiencies, such as training, management systems, budgeting, operational skills, leadership, and professionalism. This has been the dominant framing of successive donor-funded institutional-strengthening and capacity-building programs since the late 1980s. The other critique raises more fundamental issues around the 'fit' of existing police and justice models in the local context—ones that cannot be adequately addressed by reliance on technical or administrative solutions and tweaked delivery modalities (Peake & Dinnen, 2014). The clearest articulation of this more radical critique was made in the 1984 *Clifford Report*, a comprehensive review of the national law and justice system and a compelling indictment of its limited traction in PNG's diverse and plural social settings (Clifford et al., 1984). At its core was the perceived overreliance on a fragile formal (state) system and the weak linkages between that system and the community-based mechanisms that most citizens relied upon for their daily justice and security needs. In the words of the report:

> [T]he possibility that existing services may be defective or inefficient – not because they are starved of resources but because they are either irrelevant to the situation in Papua New Guinea or refusing to work with communities – does not seem to have detained people long. (Clifford et al., 1984, p. 125)

Despite the prescience of its insights, the *Clifford Report* was quickly overtaken by more pressing political concerns about responding to law-and-order problems in Port Moresby and other urban centres. Reliance on reactive and militarised policing responses became the familiar pattern of crisis management adopted by successive governments in the 1980s and 1990s. The more radical implications of the report, premised on its recognition of the plural reality of policing (and justice) provision in

PNG, were seemingly not palatable to members of the legal, judicial, and policing establishment. They were also largely ignored by donors at the time, who remained focused on propping up the country's formal police and justice organisations.

Solomon Islands and Vanuatu

While neither country has experienced crime or public order problems on the scale and intensity of PNG, many of the same plural policing issues arise in neighbouring Solomon Islands and Vanuatu. Both countries are considerably smaller in terms of population and land mass, but share similar colonial histories and many of the same social and demographic characteristics as PNG. The latter include internal diversity and fragmentation, predominantly rural-based populations dependent on subsistence agriculture and cash-cropping, and a small formal government sector whose reach is circumscribed by geography and fiscal constraints. As is the case in PNG, most Ni-Vanuatu and Solomon Islanders identify not so much as individual citizens of a state or nation, but as relational members of collectivities such as clans, extended families, cultural and linguistic groups, islands, or regions. Both countries are archipelagos with small populations scattered across numerous islands, presenting major challenges for centralised administrative systems and the delivery of essential services, as noted in Chapter 2.

Solomon Islands had an estimated population of 640,000 in 2019 (Department of Foreign Affairs and Trade [DFAT], 2021a), with around 1400 employees in the Royal Solomon Islands Police Force (RSIPF, 2018), while Vanuatu, with a population of approximately 300,000 (DFAT, 2021b), had about 500 personnel in the Vanuatu Police Force (VPF) in 2021 (Radio New Zealand, 2021). In addition to the VPF, there is a separate paramilitary Vanuatu Mobile Force (VMF). Relations between these two branches of the police have been characterised by intense rivalry over the years (McLeod & Morgan, 2007), with the VMF implicated in several periods of political instability (Rio, 2011). Police resources tend to be concentrated in the national capital and several provincial centres, with a smattering of smaller police posts in rural areas. Most people rely on local mechanisms and informal approaches to manage disputes and routine security needs, often involving extended families and community leaders or chiefs. Police visits to the remote rural areas may be rare and largely confined to responding to the most serious crimes (such as homicide) and making occasional patrols to undertake awareness raising or gather information. The police and the national justice system operate predominantly in Vanuatu's two main islands of Efate and Santo, leaving only a small number of police and magistrates dispersed across other islands, many of which have no permanent police or state justice presence (Forsyth, 2009). In such places, resort to local non-state mechanisms is often the only available option for addressing everyday justice or security needs.

As in Vanuatu, the bulk of everyday disputes and security issues in Solomon Islands continue to be managed informally in most rural, and many urban, communities, with little resort to the RSIPF. The prevalence and variety of these local approaches—policing and justice provision beneath the state—was documented in research undertaken across five island provinces on behalf of the Solomon Islands Ministry of Justice and Legal Affairs (Allen et al., 2013). Research into perceptions of access to justice in 2019 confirms the continuing importance of non-state policing and justice approaches for many Solomon Islanders, although also noting a growing demand among women and young people for better access to the RSIPF (Sloan et al., 2021). Like the RPNGC and the VPF, the RSIPF has long faced chronic resource shortages, including severe understaffing of rural posts, limiting its ability to extend its reach across the country (Gouy & Harding, 2011).

Solomon Islands' ethnic tensions (1998–2003) (see Chapter 5) led to the breakdown of government authority. Divided loyalties within the RSIPF resulted in the effective collapse of the organisation, with some of its members implicated in serious crimes of violence and intimidation (Amnesty International, 2000). The tensions left a profound legacy of lack of public trust and confidence in the RSIPF. While the factors behind the crisis were complex (Allen, 2013), it is worth noting that the initial outbreak of violence on Guadalcanal coincided with the abolition of area councils. These councils were a legacy of indirect rule under the British. Their abolition in the late 1990s also signalled the demise of area constables—officials who were empowered to assist in the enforcement of by-laws and local court decisions. These officials had acted as critical intermediaries between the most local levels of governance and regulation and the state justice system, including referring serious matters to the police and court hierarchy. As locally based officials working closely with community leaders, they practised a form of hybrid policing that combined the authority of both local *kastom* and state law. The abrupt removal of this layer of government contributed to what some rural Solomon Islanders experienced as a withdrawal of state (Dinnen & Allen, 2013). This, in turn, had implications for the management of disputes and security in rural areas. According to one observer, the demise 'of the local policing and justice systems removed restraints on anti-social behaviour that were formerly available' (Scales, 2003, p. 9). In short, these changes meant that disputes and grievances that might once have been successfully managed locally were, instead, allowed to fester and escalate.

TRANSNATIONAL POLICING (POLICING ABOVE THE STATE)

The challenges facing Pacific Island police organisations have prompted substantial levels of policing assistance from international development partners. Australia, the region's largest bilateral donor and, along with New Zealand, the dominant metropolitan power, has been the main provider of this kind of assistance to the independent Melanesian states. Building effective police and justice capabilities has long been viewed by international development and security actors as a prerequisite for long-term stability and economic prosperity in developing countries.[1] Police-building also became a prominent feature in the spate of liberal peace interventions in conflict-affected countries in the early years of the new millennium, as in the case of the Regional Assistance Mission to Solomon Islands (RAMSI) (Allen & Dinnen, 2010; Barbara, 2008). International or transnational policing, which is examined in greater detail in Chapter 5, is an increasingly important additional layer of policing in the Pacific Islands and one that, drawing on Loader's (2000) formulation (see 'Introduction', above), takes place above the state.

As well as capacity-building programs with Pacific police organisations undertaken on a bilateral basis, these transnational policing engagements have included regional initiatives supporting a range of police development activities across the region, such as the Pacific Police Development Program. This kind of policing has sometimes involved the deployment of external police acting in an executive policing capacity, as with RAMSI in Solomon Islands and the short-lived Enhanced Cooperation Program (ECP) in PNG (see Chapter 5). One of the most significant

---

[1] This is currently recognised in Goal 16 of the United Nations Sustainable Development Goals: Peace, justice and strong institutions: https://www.un.org/sustainabledevelopment/peace-justice/.

areas of expansion in recent years has been in response to perceptions of growing transnational threats posed by organised crime, terrorism and resource-poaching to small states with porous borders and constrained enforcement capabilities (Watson et al., 2021). This has led to the development of a complex regional security architecture in which Australian and New Zealand agencies, including the Australian Federal Police and the New Zealand Police, play a leading role (Wallis et al., 2021). The architecture and role of transnational policing actors continue to evolve in the broader geostrategic context of intensifying great power competition between the United States of America and China that is playing out across the region (Fry, 2019, pp. 250–253).

International policing assistance has provided external actors with considerable influence in the shaping of police development in Pacific Island countries and territories where, as we have seen, domestic governments have limited resources and, in some cases, little interest in police reform. What is perhaps more surprising is the continued promotion of elaborate capacity-building programs when the tangible outcomes from such endeavours appear to be so modest (Peake & Dinnen, 2014). A review of Australian law and justice assistance in 2012 identified a number of possible reasons for the patchy results from capacity-building that might equally apply in the case of police-building engagements (AusAID, 2012). In the first place, lack of capacity is not always the most binding constraint on institutional performance. Other more immediate factors include the dense network of informal institutions and practices that often overlay the police and the formal justice system in pluralistic social settings such as Melanesia. Second, capacity-building programs are often overambitious in scope and there may be extremely limited ability to implement them in these fragile settings. Finally, capacity-building approaches often work towards best international practice and imported models, which are often a poor fit in the local environment.

The issue of institutional transfer and 'fit', discussed earlier in relation to the RPNGC, is also salient when considering this domain of policing practice. International policing assistance has ultimately served to reinforce a state-centric view of policing through its focus on a single institutional form. This orientation reflects what some critical policing scholars view as the international community's 'ideological commitment to statebuilding' (Baker, 2010, p. 587). However, focusing narrowly on public police organisations ignores the plural reality of policing for most citizens in the Melanesian countries and the many ways in which they manage their everyday dispute resolution and security needs (Dinnen & McLeod, 2009). It also neglects the increasingly prominent role of private policing actors, which is discussed in the following section.

PRIVATE POLICING (POLICING BEYOND THE STATE)

While consistent with global trends, the expansion of private security in the Pacific Islands has attracted relatively little attention from scholars, domestic policymakers, or international donors. Occurring largely beyond the state, industry growth has been most dramatic in PNG, reflecting several intersecting currents (Dinnen, 2020). These include high levels of insecurity and the manifest shortcomings of that country's public police organisation, the RPNGC. Rising investment in private security companies and services in recent years has occurred against the backdrop of a mining and gas boom that saw robust growth in the national economy and increased demand from corporate clients for more effective security services. Other specific factors include Australia's controversial offshore processing centre for asylum seekers on Manus Island, which has provided lucrative contracts for a succession of local and international security companies, while PNG's hosting of the Asia–Pacific Economic Cooperation (APEC) summit in 2018 provided another, albeit temporary, boost for the industry.

The corporate and business sector has been a major driver of industry growth, both as consumers and suppliers of private security services. Law-and-order issues have consistently been identified as among the top constraints to doing business in PNG. World Bank research in 2014 indicated that concerns with crime and violence among the PNG business community was more than four times the regional average in East Asia and the Pacific, and was comparable with countries such as El Salvador, Venezuela, and the Democratic Republic of the Congo (Lakhani & Wilman, 2014a). The same research showed that business investment in security personnel and infrastructure was significantly higher in PNG than the average for each of the East Asia and Pacific, sub-Saharan, and Latin American regions.

Private security services are now routinely used by a wide range of clients including government departments, schools, and universities, hospitals, banks, hotels, shopping centres, embassies, and NGOs, as well as by some households and individuals. Companies vary in terms of size, the services offered, and the geographic spread of their operations. They range from small-scale local companies with one car and a few employees through to major multinational companies, such as G4S, with global reach. Most are based in the main towns, but some also operate in rural areas where large resource projects are located. As well as static protection, services include escorting mobile assets, close personal protection, security training and assessments, emergency evacuations, rapid response capabilities, and, increasingly, the supply, installation, and monitoring of sophisticated electronic surveillance and satellite tracking systems.

Evidence of the rapid growth of the industry in PNG is found in the figures provided by the industry regulator, the Security Industries Authority (SIA), which issues licences to security companies and permits to their personnel. The number of licensed security companies grew from 174 in 2006 to 566 in 2018 (see Fig. 4.1), while the number of security guards with permits increased from 12,396 in 2006 to 30,279 in 2018. According to senior SIA officials, the significant increase in licensed security companies between 2013 and 2014 resulted in part from the authority's own efforts to track down unlicensed companies.[2] The SIA figures are, however, extremely conservative and do not include what is widely believed to be a very substantial number of unlicensed companies and personnel operating in different parts of the country. Even if we confine ourselves to the official data, the number of guards with permits is still well over three times that of serving police officers and exceeds the combined strength of PNG's three disciplined services (the police, defence force, and correctional service). By any account, the private security industry is both a significant employer and a major provider of security services in PNG.

Although PNG's private and public security sectors are still commonly viewed as discrete players in the security and policing landscape, there is considerable overlap and interdependency between them in practice. Larger companies are involved in many of the same kinds of policing activities as their RPNGC colleagues, including crime prevention, investigations, and responding to incidents. Strong informal networks exist

---

[2] This section draws on empirical research into PNG's private security industry undertaken in 2018–2019. The research, which included in-country fieldwork and interviews, was supported by a grant from the Australian Civil Military Centre (ACMC), an Australian government body that supports best practice approaches to civil–military–police engagements in conflict and disaster management activities.

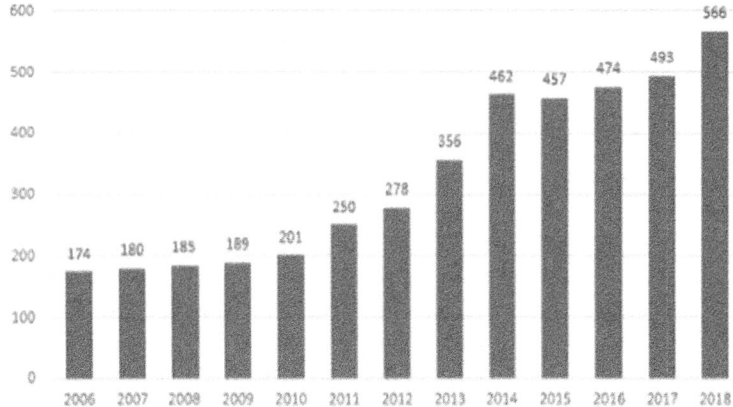

Fig. 4.1 Growth of licensed security companies, PNG (*Source* Adapted from Isari [2019], p. 4)

between the two, with many security companies started and staffed by ex-police officers. Some private security personnel also serve as reserve police officers. Building and sustaining these links is understood as mutually beneficial. For security company operatives, maintaining good relationships with the police is important to their business practice. For example, it enables them to call on police assistance in the case of violent incidents or to conduct background checks on potential employees. Private operators can also be an important source of material support to cash-strapped public police. For example, some companies provide the police with food, help buy uniforms, supply fuel and maintenance for police vehicles, and, sometimes, pay allowances when working together. Informal networks facilitate critical intelligence sharing. Superior resources available to high-end private operators include communications, surveillance, and tracking systems that are simply unavailable to the police. Support to the police is not simply an act of philanthropy—it is an important way of sustaining reciprocal relationships and the benefits that these provide to all parties.

Concerns have been raised about the potentially adverse implications of the growing industry for public security. For example, PNG's *National Security Policy* warns of the proliferation of foreign-owned companies engaging 'in areas designed for PNG state agencies' and undermining 'the state's ability and authority to deliver public safety and security' (Government of Papua New Guinea, 2013, p. 37). While these and other concerns about the private security sector may be valid, the rapid growth of the industry in PNG appears to be as much a response to the state's inability to 'deliver public safety and security' as a cause of it. Extensive interaction between public and private security providers indicates how, in some respects, private security is helping to augment the country's fragile public policing services, thereby contributing to public security rather than undermining it. In a similar vein, one can surmise that if private security were to suddenly disappear, PNG's security situation would be even worse than it already is. Just as it is important to acknowledge that there has been a privatisation of the public, it is also important to recognise that there has been a publicisation of the private (Freeman, 2003). Rather than being a temporary gap-filler until such time as the RPNGC is capable of fulfilling the policing needs of all citizens, evidence suggests that private security is here to stay and, moreover, that the delineation between public and private is becoming increasingly indistinct in PNG, as it has in many other parts of the world.

Locally Driven Policing (*Policing Beneath the State*)

Recalling Loader's (2000) conception of policing as a 'network of power' (see 'Introduction', above), we see public and private policing in the Pacific Islands occurring through and beyond the state, as well as transnational policing happening above the state. However, the most common form of policing experienced by most Pacific Islanders historically has been policing beneath the state. This remains the case in many places today—especially in the Melanesian countries, given the constrained capacities and reach of public police organisations and the resilience of local policing approaches.

The diversity of local policing forms makes it difficult to generalise, as does their limited visibility from the vantage point of government agencies and donors based in distant national capitals. In some countries, such as Vanuatu, local policing continues to revolve around appeals to traditional authority or *kastom*, with chiefs and other local leaders performing key policing roles within and between different communities (Forsyth, 2009). Elsewhere, there is considerable variation in the strengths of *kastom*. Although the dynamism of local social orders has made it remarkably adaptable, its authority has eroded in many places in light of ongoing globalisation.

Local policing and justice practices often have a distinctly hybrid character, involving a variety of institutional arrangements drawing on different sources of authority and legitimacy. For example, research in rural areas of Solomon Islands shows how villagers navigate between three broad and overlapping systems of rules based on different sources of authority—namely, state, *kastom,* and church (Allen et al., 2013). Each was viewed as having a core sphere of operation. Thus, the state system, associated with the enforcement powers of state police, was seen as the best way of dealing with serious crimes and disputes. *Kastom*, associated with the exercise of traditional authority by local chiefs, was preferred in the case of socially embedded disputes, such as those over land where genealogical knowledge was crucial to resolution. Church-based approaches were preferred in the case of marital and family disputes, especially by women.

This Solomon Islands research also highlighted the increasing stresses on these local approaches in many rural areas (Allen et al., 2013). New forms of contestation have emerged—for example, around commercial logging projects—which local approaches struggle to manage. Despite this growing fragility—or, perhaps, because of it—there was also evidence of extensive local experimentation as community leaders sought to adjust and strengthen their coping strategies. This often involved attempts to revitalise community governance structures, including through elaborate committee systems and, in some cases, through resort to unofficial 'community laws' targeting anti-social behaviour such as substance abuse, fighting, and swearing. Community law making as a response to security problems in areas of limited statehood has been noted throughout Melanesia, including in Vanuatu, Solomon Islands, and PNG (Forsyth, 2014).

Contrary to what tends to be perceived as the insular and circumscribed character of customary forms of regulation, these local initiatives are often actively seeking out connections and engagement with external actors and agencies. Rather than representing a rejection or turning away from the state, they usually entail significant efforts to strengthen linkages with relevant parts of the state, including the police or courts. Locally driven attempts to forge greater engagement with the state are frequently combined with a desire to retain high levels of local autonomy. Rather than being contradictory, the dual wishes for improved state engagement and for local autonomy are quite compatible. They represent local attempts to imbricate the local with the state and vice versa, with the ultimate aim of enhancing the authority and legitimacy of each in places where both have become extremely fragile (Dinnen & Allen, 2016). Similar observations have been made in different parts Melanesia (Higgins, 2020; Schwoerer, 2018).

Related activities appear to be going on in many urban contexts. For example, in PNG's sprawling urban settlements, *komitis* (committees) and local leadership networks play a crucial role in forging and sustaining linkages with external actors, such as police officers, magistrates, private security companies, or NGOs. According to a 2018 study, the potential value of these *komitis* lies in their convening power, which enables them to 'combine the authority of leaders and ethnic groups inside the blok[3] and also draw in individual with connections to the state, police, or others whose power and respect is derived from a range of sources physically external to the settlement' (Craig & Porter, 2018, p. 5).

In recognising extensive policing activity taking place beneath the state, it is also important to acknowledge its limitations and potential risks. Practices carried out under the auspices of tradition, *kastom* or other forms of local autonomy can be oppressive and discriminatory. They can conceal profound imbalances of power within communal social orders—not least in respect of gender, given the patriarchal character of traditional societies. Local policing forms often lack the most basic kind of accountability, rendering them susceptible to capture and abuse by more powerful individuals and groups. However, such inequitable outcomes are not inevitable. Some local policing can be respectful and empowering. Indeed, many of the same concerns are regularly raised in respect of the public police and provide the basis for remedial interventions.

Rather than being static relics of a bygone era, there is evidence of the inherent dynamism of these local forms of regulation and their capacity to adapt to change. Evidence of this dynamism includes shifting attitudes resulting from awareness campaigns and other forms of engagement by government, donor, and civil society actors that are aimed at challenging and transforming prevailing norms and practices. In this respect, we noted earlier (see 'Contemporary Dimensions of Plural Policing: Public Policing (Policing Through the State)') how women and young people are demanding better access to the RSIPF in Solomon Islands, which may well reflect growing dissatisfaction among these groups with the authority

---

[3] Larger settlements in PNG typically consist of a number of locally identified zones or *bloks* (the Tok Pisin term for 'blocks') (Craig & Porter, 2018).

and decision-making of older men, as well as enhanced awareness of their legal rights under national or state law (Sloan et al., 2021).

Security and order-making in the Pacific Islands have always been heavily dependent on local policing and justice practices. As we have seen, small and underresourced colonial administrations were incapable on their own of maintaining order over their scattered local subjects. That they were able to do so was, in large part, due to the role of local forms of policing and order maintenance. The same applies today in many parts of post-colonial Melanesia, where these local forms continue to bear the burden of everyday policing, albeit under mounting stress in many places. Forsyth points out that, in Vanuatu:

> [t]he *kastom* system … relieves the burden on the police to an enormous extent by dealing with a large percentage of criminal cases – minor and serious. It is clear that if the *kastom* system stopped operating, the VPF, stretched as it already is, could not possibly meet the law-and-order needs of the community. (2009, p. 155)

Insecurity experienced in countries such as PNG, Solomon Islands, and Vanuatu would likely be considerably worse without the largely invisible layers of local policing occurring beneath the state.

Conclusion

This chapter has provided an overview of the plural character of policing and security provision in the independent Melanesian countries of the Southwest Pacific. Policing pluralism has been integrally connected to broader historical transformations including colonisation, modern state-building and, more recently, the impacts of economic liberalism animating contemporary globalisation. A relatively consistent driver of pluralisation in the Melanesian Pacific has been the fragility of centralised (state) institutions, including the public police, and their constrained reach in each country. This has been combined with the resilience of older forms of self-regulation or self-policing at local levels and their capacity to adapt to changing circumstances.

The many challenges facing Melanesian police organisations have become increasingly evident in the post-independence period—and nowhere more so than in PNG, the region's largest and most challenging nation. Given the limitations of small, underresourced, and urban-based police organisations in these overwhelmingly rural countries, most citizens continue to rely on local forms of policing and justice provision, just as they did during colonial times. However, while the authority of *kastom* and traditional leadership remains strong in some places, it has broken down or been seriously eroded in many others.

Lack of accessible and capable public police, in combination with the weakening of older policing forms, has had dire consequences in the most affected areas. The worse impacts in terms of crime and conflict can be seen today in parts of PNG's Highlands. However, growing levels of insecurity have also been a catalyst for locally driven policing experimentation in some places, much of which, as we have seen, is hybrid and networked in character. The growing prominence of transnational and private policing is another important dimension to contemporary patterns of policing pluralisation.

Adopting a plural policing perspective allows us to see the fuller spectrum of actors involved in policing and security services in the Southwest Pacific, and the diverse ways in which these individuals and entities interact across time and space as part of larger security assemblages or networks. Highlighting the networked quality of policing practice in contemporary Melanesia also serves to remind policymakers and researchers to place more attention on ways of building and enhancing productive relationships across different domains of policing provision that can ultimately improve security outcomes for all citizens. This requires a widening of our conceptualisation of policing and security beyond a single and discrete institutional form, and, instead, to see the encompassing network of power and regulation comprising multiple actors and forms.

REFERENCES

Abrahamsen, R., & Williams, M. C. (2011). *Security beyond the state: Private security in international politics*. Cambridge University Press.

Albrecht, P., & Kyed, H. M. (Eds.). (2015). *Policing and the politics of order-making*. Routledge.

Allen, M. G. (2013). *Greed and grievance: Ex-militants' perspectives on the conflict in Solomon Islands 1998–2003*. University of Hawai'i Press.

Allen, M., & Dinnen, S. (2010). The North down under: Antinomies of conflict and intervention in Solomon Islands. *Conflict, Security & Development, 10*(3), 299–327.

Allen, M., Dinnen, S., Evans D., & Monson, R. (2013, August). *Justice delivered locally: Systems, challenges and innovations in Solomon Islands*. World Bank, Justice for the Poor, Research Report.
Amnesty International. (2000). *Solomon Islands: A forgotten conflict* (Report ASA 43/005/2000).
Anderson, D., & Killingray, D. (Eds.). (1992). *Policing and decolonisation: Politics, nationalism and the police*. Manchester University Press.
AusAID. (2012). *Building on local strengths: Evaluation of Australian law and justice assistance*. AusAID.
Baker, B. (2008). *Multi-choice policing in Africa*. Nordiska Afrikainstituter.
Baker, B. (2010). *Security in post-conflict Africa: The role of nonstate policing*. CRC Press.
Ballard, C., & Douglas, B. (2017). 'Rough justice': Punitive expeditions in Oceania. *Journal of Colonialism and Colonial History*, 18(1). https://doi.org/10.1353/cch.2017.0018
Barbara, J. (2008). Antipodean statebuilding: The Regional Assistance Mission to Solomon Islands and Australian intervention in the South Pacific. *Journal of Intervention and Statebuilding*, 2(2), 123–149.
Bayley, D., & Shearing, C. (2001). *The new structure of policing: Conceptualization and research agenda*. National Institute of Justice.
Bennett, J. A. (1987). *Wealth of the Solomons. A history of a Pacific archipelago, 1800–1978*. University of Hawai'i Press.
Bennett, J. A. (2002). Roots of conflict in Solomon Islands. *Though much is taken, much abides: Legacies of tradition and colonialism* (pp. 1–16). Australian National University, State, Society and Governance in Melanesia Discussion Paper 2002/5.
Biles, D. (1976). *Crime in Papua New Guinea*. Australian Institute of Criminology.
Bourke, M., & Allen, B. (2021, February 2). *What is the population of Papua New Guinea?* Development Policy Centre, Australian National University, DEVPOLICYBLOG. https://devpolicy.org/what-is-the-population-of-papua-new-guinea-20210202-1/
Boutilier, J. A. (1984). *The law of England has come: The application of British and Custom Law in the British Solomon Islands Protectorate, 1893–1942*. Paper presented at the Association for Social Anthropology in Oceania Annual Conference, Molokai, Hawai'i, 28 February to 3 March.
Clifford, W., Morauta, L., & Stuart, B. (1984). *Law and order in Papua New Guinea* (Vol. 1). Institute of National Affairs and Institute of Applied Social and Economic Research.
Comaroff, J., & Comaroff, J. L. (Eds.). (2006). *Law and disorder in the postcolony*. University of Chicago Press.

Craig, D., & Porter, D. (2018). *Learning about leadership, regulation and security from Papua New Guinea's urban settlements*. World Bank. http://documents1.worldbank.org/curated/en/391621530276694395/pdf/Learning-about-Leadership-Regulation-and-Security-from-Papua-New-Guinea-s-Urban-Settlements.pdf

Deloitte. (2020, January). *True cost of policing services in PNG* (Final report).

Department of Foreign Affairs and Trade (DFAT). (2021a). *Solomon Islands*. Fact sheet. https://www.dfat.gov.au/sites/default/files/solo-cef.pdf

Department of Foreign Affairs and Trade (DFAT). (2021b). *Vanuatu country brief*. https://www.dfat.gov.au/geo/vanuatu/vanuatu-country-brief

Dinnen, S. (2001). *Law and order in a weak state: Crime and politics in Papua New Guinea*. University of Hawai'i Press.

Dinnen, S. (2020). Insecurity, policing and marketisation: Papua New Guinea's changing security landscape. In S. N. Amin, D. Watson & C. Girard (Eds.), *Mapping security in the Pacific. A focus on context, gender and organisational culture* (pp. 186–198). Routledge.

Dinnen, S., & Allen, M. (2013). Paradoxes of police-building in post-colonial societies: Solomon Islands. *Policing & Society, 23*(2), 222–242.

Dinnen, S., & Allen, M. (2016). State absence and state formation in Solomon Islands: Reflections on agency, scale and hybridity. *Development and Change, 47*(1), 76–97.

Dinnen, S., & Braithwaite, J. (2009). Reinventing policing through the prism of the colonial state. *Policing & Society, 19*(2), 161–173.

Dinnen, S., & McLeod, A. (2009). Policing Melanesia: International expectations and local realities. *Policing & Society, 19*(4), 333–353.

Diphoorn, T. (2016). *Twilight policing: Private security and violence in urban South Africa*. University of California Press.

Dorney, S. (2000). *Papua New Guinea: People, politics and history since 1975*. ABC Books.

Dupont, B. (2004). Security in the age of networks. *Policing and Society, 14*(1), 76–91.

Dutton, T. (1985). *Police Motu: Iena sivarai*. University of Papua New Guinea Press.

Ellison, G., & Pino, N. W. (2012). *Globalization, police reform and development: Doing it the Western way?* Palgrave Macmillan.

Forsyth, M. (2009). *A bird that flies with two wings: Kastom and state justice systems in Vanuatu*. ANU Press.

Forsyth, M. (2014). *The writing of community by-laws and constitutions in Melanesia: Who? Why? How?* Department of Pacific Affairs, Australian National University, In Brief 2014/53. http://dpa.bellschool.anu.edu.au/sites/default/files/publications/attachments/2015-12/IB-2014-53-Forsyth-ONLINE_0.pdf

Forsyth, M. (2021). Policing in a relational state: The case of sorcery accusation-related violence in Papua New Guinea. *Policing and Society*. https://doi.org/10.1080/10439463.2021.1953026

Freeman, J. (2003). Extending public law norms through privatization. *Harvard Law Review*, 116(5), 1285–1352.

Fry, G. (2019). *Framing the islands: Power and diplomatic agency in Pacific regionalism*. ANU Press.

Gordon, R. J. (1983). The decline of the Kiapdom and the resurgence of 'tribal fighting' in Enga. *Oceania, 53*, 205–223.

Gordon, R. J., & Meggitt, M. (1985). *Law and order in the New Guinea Highlands*. University Press of New England.

Gouy, J., & Harding, M. (2011, March 9). 'True cost' of policing in the Solomon Islands: Identifying policing and security expenditures and costs borne by external agencies (Final report).

Government of Papua New Guinea (GoPNG). (2013). *Papua New Guinea national security policy*. Government Printer.

Hallak, A. (2019, October 29). *In the fight: The challenge of tribal conflict in Papua New Guinea*. Australian Institute of International Affairs, Australian Outlook. https://www.internationalaffairs.org.au/australianoutlook/in-the-fight-the-challenge-of-tribal-conflict-in-papua-new-guinea/

Higgins, K. (2020). Place, peace and security in Solomon Islands. *Cooperation and Conflict, 55*(4), 442–460.

Hirsch, E., & Rollason, W. (Eds.). (2019). *The Melanesian world*. Routledge.

Human Rights Watch (HRW). (2017). *World report 2017. Papua New Guinea: Events of 2016*. https://www.hrw.org/world-report/2017/country-chapters/papua-new-guinea

Isari, P. K. (2019, July 15). *How the security industries authority (SIA) is supporting the security companies address law and order issues in PNG*. Presentation to Consultative Implementation and Monitoring Council conference, Popondetta, Papua New Guinea.

Jones, T., & Newburn, T. (1998). *Private security and public policing*. Clarendon Press.

Jones, T., & Newburn, T. (2006). Understanding plural policing. In T. Jones & T. Newburn (Eds.), *Plural policing. A comparative perspective* (pp. 1–11). Routledge.

Kituai, A. (1988). Innovation and intrusion: Villagers and policemen in Papua New Guinea. *Journal of Pacific History, 23*(2), 156–166.

Kituai, A. (1998). *My gun, my brother: The world of Papua New Guinea colonial police 1920–1960*. University of Hawai'i Press.

Lakhani, S., & Willman, A. (2014a). *Gates, hired guns and mistrust: Business as unusual*. World Bank.

Lakhani, S., & Willman, A. (2014b). *Trends in crime and violence in Papua New Guinea*. World Bank.

Loader, I. (1999). Consumer culture and the commodification of policing and security. *Sociology, 33*(2), 373–392.

Loader, I. (2000). Plural policing and democratic governance. *Social & Legal Studies, 9*(3), 323–345.

Mair, L. P. (1948). *Australia in New Guinea*. Christophers.

May, R. J. (1982). *Micronationalist movements in Papua New Guinea* (Political and social change monograph 1). Australian National University.

McLeod, A., & Morgan, M. (2007). An incomplete arc: Analysing the potential for violent conflict in the republic of Vanuatu. *Pacific Affairs, 80*(1), 67–86.

Oram, N. (1973). Law and order: Maximum participation at all levels. *New Guinea, 7*(3), 4–22.

Peake, G., & Dinnen, S. (2014). Police development in Papua New Guinea: The need for innovation. *Security Challenges, 10*(2), 33–51.

Post-Courier. (2020, September 10). Manning to rid constabulary of 'criminals in uniform'. *Post-Courier online*. https://postcourier.com.pg/manning-to-rid-constabulary-of-criminals-in-uniform/

Radio New Zealand (RNZ). (2021). In brief: News from around the Pacific. 7.20 pm on 28 June. https://www.rnz.co.nz/international/pacific-news/445687/in-brief-news-from-around-the-pacific

Rio, K. M. (2011). Policing the holy nation: The state and righteous violence in Vanuatu. *Oceania, 81*(1), 51–71.

Royal Solomon Islands Police (RSIP). (1981, May 30). *The Royal Solomon Islands Police*. Booklet prepared for the information of officers from the Australian Joint Services Staff College undertaking an Overseas Study Tour to Solomon Islands.

Royal Solomon Islands Police Force (RSIPF). (2018). *Royal Solomon Islands police force annual report 2018*. http://www.rsipf.gov.sb/?q=reports

Scaglion, R. (2004). Legal pluralism in Pacific Island societies. In V. Lockwood (Ed.), *Globalization and culture change in the Pacific Islands* (pp. 86–101). Prentice Hall.

Scales, I. (2003). *The flourishing of local level governance after the coup in Solomon Islands: Lessons for reform of the state*. Paper presented at the symposium on Governance in Pacific States: Reassessing roles and remedies. Australian National University, 30 September to 2 October.

Schwoerer, T. (2018). Mipela Makim Gavman: Unofficial village courts and local perceptions of order in the Eastern Highlands of Papua New Guinea. *Anthropological Forum, 28*(4), 342–358.

Sinclair, G., & Williams, C. A. (2007). 'Home and away': The cross-fertilisation between 'colonial' and 'British' policing, 1921–1985. *Journal of Imperial and Commonwealth History, 35*(2), 221–238.

Sloan, T., Dinnen, S., & Rowe, M. (2021). *Access to justice in post-RAMSI Solomon Islands. Part 2: Perceptions of access to justice*. Department of Pacific Affairs, Australian National University, In Brief 2021/26. https://openresea rch-repository.anu.edu.au/handle/1885/247815

Strathern, M. (1972). Official and unofficial courts: Legal assumptions and expectations in a Highlands community. *New Guinea Research Unit, Bulletin, 47*, 1–166.

Tamanaha, B. Z. (2012). The rule of law and legal pluralism in development. In B. Z. Tamanaha, C. Sage, & M. Woolcock (Eds.), *Legal pluralism and development* (pp. 34–49). Cambridge University Press.

Wallis, J., McNeill, H., Batley, J., & Powles, A. (2021). *Mapping security cooperation in the Pacific Islands*. Department of Pacific Affairs, Australian National University, Research report. http://dpa.bellschool.anu.edu.au/exp erts-publications/publications/8060/mapping-security-cooperation-pacific-isl ands-research-report

Watson, D., Sousa-Santos, J. L., & Howes, L. (2021, February). Transnational and organised crime in Pacific Island countries and territories: Police capacity to respond to the emerging security threat. *Development Bulletin, 82*, 151–155.

Wood, J., & Shearing, C. (2007). *Imagining security*. Willan Publishing.

Open Access This chapter is licensed under the terms of the Creative Commons Attribution 4.0 International License (http://creativecommons.org/licenses/by/4.0/), which permits use, sharing, adaptation, distribution and reproduction in any medium or format, as long as you give appropriate credit to the original author(s) and the source, provide a link to the Creative Commons license and indicate if changes were made.

The images or other third party material in this chapter are included in the chapter's Creative Commons license, unless indicated otherwise in a credit line to the material. If material is not included in the chapter's Creative Commons license and your intended use is not permitted by statutory regulation or exceeds the permitted use, you will need to obtain permission directly from the copyright holder.

CHAPTER 5

The International Policing Agenda in the Pacific

Abstract International policing is a complex and non-neutral endeavour, which encompasses a diverse range of activities such as peace operations, capacity development, cross-border partnerships to combat transnational crime, and disaster assistance. In the Pacific region, while partnerships have long been part of the development and security landscapes, they entail various expectations and obligations, influenced by the historical relationships between countries and their relative status as aid donors or recipients. This chapter outlines the nature and development of international policing in the Pacific context. It then provides examples of international policing in the region, where many Pacific Islands countries have been involved both as host nations for—and contributors to—these efforts. The chapter highlights the complexities of partnerships in the Pacific region, and the challenges and benefits involved.

Keywords Police capacity development · Cross-border cooperation · Disaster assistance · International policing · Transnational policing

Introduction

International policing involves the deployment of police officers from one or more countries to assist in another country. The scope of activities includes not only training, technical assistance, and working together to address transnational crime, but also activities that were traditionally outside the ambit of policing (Greener, 2011a; Harris, 2010). Police involvement has extended to a role in peace operations, police reform, and capacity development, often as part of broader state-building agendas that promote the maintenance of peace and sustainable development. These new roles for police have been dubbed 'new international policing' (Greener, 2009). Some scholars refer to these activities as 'transnational policing', with the emphasis on transcending or traversing national boundaries (Bowling & Sheptycki, 2012, 2015). Others define transnational policing more narrowly to refer to cross-border responses to transnational crime, such as the trafficking of people, wildlife, and illicit goods (Boister, 2003; Perras, 2017). Similarly, international policing can be defined narrowly, referring to instances when international law is invoked. Although war crimes, genocide, and crimes against humanity do not necessarily involve the crossing of borders, they impact the global community and require a collective (or international) response due to the scale of suffering involved (Perras, 2017). However, while these narrower definitions may be useful if the intention is to focus on relevant areas of law, international policing in its broadest sense is most fitting for the present focus on policing in the Pacific.

International policing is an inherently political process (Goldsmith & Dinnen, 2007). The Honiara Declaration on Law Enforcement Cooperation, which was made by the South Pacific Forum (1992), recognised that for sustainable development to occur, it was first necessary to establish the rule of law. This necessity has since been supported empirically (see e.g., Murney et al., 2011). However, a lack of international consensus about best practices in policing raises questions about whose ideas of policing should be used in the international sphere. Police use law in non-neutral ways to achieve objectives, as is highlighted by the concept of 'rule *with* law' (Bowling & Sheptycki, 2015, p. 142). Reaching a consensus on international policing seems an unlikely prospect due to the range of policing practices used in different countries and within different cultural contexts, and guided by different values and norms—including ideas about the appropriate use of force (Hills, 2009). Despite a lack of consensus, the United Nations (UN) has promoted liberal democratic ideals of policing, which are drawn from developed countries of the global North (Bayley, 2005; Hills, 2009). Consequently, policing is often conceptualised as a centralised institution of the state, which has a monopoly on the legitimate use of force, and a democratic policing ethos. It is associated with the ideals of gender equality, human rights, transparency and accountability, and community policing partnerships (Dinnen & McLeod, 2009).

For the countries of the global South, including Pacific Islands countries (PICs), it is reasonable to question how the same kind of policing model can be applied. The Pacific has been described as one of the most aid-reliant regions worldwide (Dornan & Pryke, 2017). Many PICs are typically categorised as small island developing states, with several additionally categorised as least developed countries (see Chapter 2). These classifications reflect a range of challenges and constraints for PICs in terms of small populations, vast expanses of ocean, remoteness and limited access to resources, as well as vulnerability to climate change and disasters. Additionally, some PICs have been described at different times as 'weak', 'fragile', or 'failed' states (Fraenkel, 2015, p. 400). In such contexts, concerns exist about the potential for international policing to act as a neo-colonial force. During the colonial period in PICs, the police were instrumental in enforcing and sustaining colonial orders. In many of these countries, now independent, the legacy of colonisation is evident in the existence of hybrid systems—including in the justice sector, where there exists a blend of state institutions, and non-state or customary ways and locally developed initiatives (Dinnen & McLeod, 2009). Interventions that support only state policing institutions are unlikely to be effective if other justice service providers receive only minimal attention (see Chapter 4). Indeed, the presence of non-state service providers reflects the strength and resilience (or tenacity: McDougall, 2015) of local communities, and opportunities to engage in culturally meaningful ways (Dinnen & McLeod, 2009).

Despite the challenges and ambiguities of international policing, PICs have been involved in the full range of these efforts, including peace operations, police reform as a component of state-building, targeted training and technical assistance, partnerships to prevent transnational crime, and disaster assistance. Their involvement has been both as host countries and contributors within and beyond the region.

This chapter provides a brief overview of how international policing has developed in the Pacific context, with a focus on the roles of Australia and New Zealand as long-term partners in the policing, security, and development space. It then explores examples of different types of international policing in the Pacific region, highlighting the challenges inherent within them and the benefits achieved. The chapter suggests that international policing is an integral part of policing in the Pacific for all countries involved. It shapes and is shaped by domestic, regional, and international politics, and historical relationships, as well as evolving nuances in the development and security agendas.

HISTORICAL DEVELOPMENT OF INTERNATIONAL POLICING

International policing evolved out of various types of military operations (Sismanidis, 1997). These included multinational military action against the Barbary pirates in the nineteenth century, colonial interventions (Goldsmith & Sheptycki, 2007), US occupational military forces in Germany and Japan after World War II (Greener, 2009), and disaster assistance and riot control (Sismanidis, 1997). Some of these military operations even contained elements of civilian policing (Sismanidis, 1997). Sometimes police were deployed to countries within the Pacific region to support policing, as with New Zealand's involvement in the Cook Islands from 1909 and Niue from 1951 (Brennan, 2015). However, the advent of international policing as it is now understood is largely associated with the UN. In 1960 'civilian police', as they were known at the time, were first deployed under the UN banner—to the UN Operation in the Congo (Department of Peacekeeping Operations [DPKO], 2011a). This was followed by the UN Peacekeeping Force in Cyprus in 1964, which included police from Australia and New Zealand.

The Cold War period saw police and military interventions by both the United States of America and the Soviet Union (USSR) in affiliated states (Goldsmith & Sheptycki, 2007). For the Pacific, concerns arose about a potential threat to trade routes if the United States and the USSR began to compete for influence in the region. In Australia, fears about foreign powers—which were heightened during World War II as PICs became battle sites—continued to influence foreign policy (Dibb, 2012). The period was also characterised by a post-colonial turn; former colonies of large powers gradually gained independence (Goldsmith & Sheptycki, 2007). Australia had been the colonial administrator in Papua

New Guinea (PNG) and Nauru, and New Zealand had been the colonial administrator in Samoa. These twentieth-century colonial relationships reflected anxiety about foreign interests in the region and the consequent desire for a 'British Oceania' (Lawson, 2017).

The Pacific Islands Forum was established in 1971, with independent PICs as members, along with Australia and New Zealand (Lawson, 2017). The inclusion of Australia and New Zealand has been contentious at times—in recent years because of their slowness to act on climate change, and previously because of their early dominance of the forum and colonial history in the Pacific region (Fry, 2019; Lawson, 2017). As PICs gained independence, Australia and New Zealand continued to maintain interest in the region through programs that have provided substantial aid, with a strong focus on promoting and strengthening good governance (Dziedzic, 2018; Lowy Institute, 2019).[1] Australian and New Zealand influence in policing in the Pacific was primarily through bilateral development assistance (McLeod & Dinnen, 2007).

Following the unexpected collapse of the USSR in 1989, fears of anarchy within post-colonial states and former Soviet satellites paved the way for greater urgency in international policing. Stabilisation of 'collapsed', 'failing', and 'fragile' states was on the agenda (Goldsmith & Sheptycki, 2007, p. 9). This perception of urgency was felt in the Pacific region. In Australian political circles, the Pacific region was described as an 'arc of instability' (Dibb, 2012; Dobell, 2012). Following a series of incidents, including two coups in Fiji in 1987 and growing instability in other Melanesian countries (Dinnen & McLeod, 2009), the focus shifted to the potential for weak states to pose a threat to regional stability (Dibb, 2012). In 1989, despite instability within the country, Fiji began sending

---

[1] Australia provides the largest amount of aid to the Pacific region (Dziedzic, 2018; Lowy Institute, 2019). The contributions of Japan, China, and the United States reflect similar US dollar figures to New Zealand's contribution (Dziedzic, 2018). Other key donors include the Asian Development Bank, the World Bank, the European Union, the UN, and Taiwan (Lowy Institute, 2019). Australia's policing contributions are funded through the Australian Federal Police (AFP), with broader justice initiatives funded by Australian Aid (AusAID) and coordinated through Australia's Department of Foreign Affairs and Trade (DFAT). New Zealand Police contributions are funded by New Zealand Aid (NZAID) and coordinated through the Ministry of Foreign Affairs and Trade (MFAT).

police officers on UN peacekeeping missions,[2] having begun contributing military troops to such missions in 1978 (Wyeth, 2018).

The 1990s saw a rise in UN Police numbers as civilian police were increasingly included in peacekeeping missions. Specifically, the number of UN Police deployed grew from 1600 in 1994 to 4600 by the end of the decade (UN Police, 2017). The role of UN Police in peace operations was largely to support policing that promoted human rights. The relevant activities were summarised by the acronym 'SMART', which referred to supporting human rights, monitoring performance of local law enforcement agencies, advising local police on humane effective law enforcement, reporting on incidents to the UN, and training local police in best practices and human rights (Hartz, 1999, p. 31). However, UN Police came to adopt more active roles, such as executive policing and police reform, when local governance mechanisms had ceased to function (Greener, 2009). In 1999, the first UN peacekeeping mission took place in East Timor (now known as Timor-Leste). Among the participants were police officers from Samoa, Vanuatu, Australia, and New Zealand, and military personnel from Fiji, Australia, and New Zealand.

Since the 1990s, the Australian Government has increasingly perceived a responsibility to contribute to the stability of the Pacific (Dobell, 2012). Australian and New Zealand Governments have aligned increasingly in their explicit focus on the Pacific region, although they have adopted a generally cautious stance on intervention in independent countries. A turning point occurred in response to the attacks in the United States on 11 September 2001. Since then, a new security agenda—namely, the war on terror—has been witnessed in many countries of the global North. For Australia, the Bali bombings in 2002 and Jakarta bombings in 2003 and 2004 contributed to this agenda (Dinnen, 2004/2005; 2012). Further, it has been argued that failed states can become a haven for international criminal and terrorist groups with a destabilising effect on a region (McDougall, 2004; Wainwright, 2003). This argument provided a powerful rationale for intervention. Australia's international engagement with its Pacific Island neighbours shifted in ways described as 'the new interventionism' (Dinnen & McLeod, 2008, p. 25).

---

[2] Since beginning to contribute military troops to international missions in 1978, Fiji's military has grown large relative to its size. This military growth has provided financial opportunities for the government and service personnel (Wyeth, 2018), but has also played a role in the country's political coups (Baledrokadroka, 2012).

A range of UN-based and non-UN-based international police missions commenced during the 2000s. Many PICs not only hosted international policing efforts, but also contributed to contingents during the Regional Assistance Mission to Solomon Islands (RAMSI) between 2003 and 2017, as discussed below: see 'Peace Operations in Solomon Islands—RAMSI'. Acting on the recommendations of a report by the Panel of UN Peace Operations (2000), known as the *Brahimi Report*, in 2004 the Australian Federal Police (AFP) established the International Deployment Group. The International Deployment Group involved a standing force, comprising members of the AFP and of Australian state and territory police organisations, which could be deployed as needed.[3] The AFP also established a purpose-built training facility in Canberra to meet the demand for international deployment and training to the relevant UN doctrine and standards (Bellamy, 2009). Similarly, in 2005 New Zealand established the International Service Group. Its aim was to facilitate communication between the agencies involved in international operations, and to coordinate New Zealand Police staff involved in deployments (Greener, 2011b). These efforts to support police deployment reflected the compatibility of international policing with whole-of-government policies in Australia and New Zealand (Greener, 2008, 2011b; Hameiri, 2009).

The number of deployed UN Police reached almost 14,000 in 2010 (DPKO, 2011b) and decreased to approximately 11,000 in 2018 (DPKO, 2018a). To help achieve consistency of policing under its banner, the DPKO has published manuals, frameworks, and guidelines (e.g., DPKO, 2018b). One of its most prominent initiatives, launched in 2009, is the global effort to increase the participation of female police officers in both national policing organisations and UN peace operations (DPKO, 2011c; UN Police, 2015). The largest contingents of international police are now primarily from countries of the global South in Africa and Asia (DPKO, 2018a), for whom the remuneration is most attractive. Inequities exist in deployment contributions, with developed countries focusing on financial contributions and deploying only small numbers of police officers to provide leadership and expertise (see e.g., Bellamy, 2012; Durch & Ker, 2013; Greener, 2017).

---

[3] The AFP's international component underwent a significant restructure in 2015 (Hornung, 2020). International deployments from Australia are now under the AFP's International Operations banner.

Despite the influence of the UN, international policing deployments in the Pacific region have not typically been UN-affiliated missions (although such missions have taken place in Timor-Leste). Instead, they have long been based on bilateral, trilateral, multilateral, or regional agreements, and have varied in their legal basis and levels of formality (Watson et al., 2011). In recent years, the focus of emerging threats has been the influence of globalisation, connectivity, and transnational crime. This is set against a backdrop of both renewed commitment to Pacific regionalism and geopolitical posturing in the region, with increased interest from China.[4] What is clear is that the nature and emphasis of international policing—and its particular forms in the Pacific region—continue to evolve.

Examples of International Policing in the Pacific

International policing in the Pacific region aims to address a broad range of needs and interests. Table 5.1 outlines the main categories of international policing and the types of activities that they encompass. Given the complexity of international policing, the boundaries between categories are not always clear and overlaps occur in practice.

Peace Operations and Stabilisation Missions

Several peace operations and stabilisation missions have been undertaken in the Pacific region. These include peacekeeping missions to Bougainville (1997–2000) and a stabilisation mission to Tonga following riots in 2006. These operations typically involve larger numbers of military than police personnel, both with important roles. While peace operations have often been linked explicitly with attempts to achieve and implement a peace agreement, stabilisation missions aim to restore and maintain order in the absence of a peace agreement through various means, including using

---

[4] One example of increasing Chinese influence is via its flagship Belt and Road Initiative. While some regard this increased interest as an opportunity for the Pacific, low-cost loans and conspicuous infrastructure projects have raised concerns about a lack of associated governance. The risk of future debt traps for PICs has been highlighted (Rajah et al., 2019). Additionally, under its 'One China' policy, Beijing has aimed to influence Pacific nations that have diplomatic relations with Taiwan to shift their allegiance. Despite Pacific regionalism, the Pacific Islands Forum has acknowledged that some PICs recognise China while others recognise Taiwan (Dziedzic, 2019).

Table 5.1 Broad categories and roles of international policing

Category	Role
Peace operations and stabilisation missions	• After a conflict, military and police personnel are involved to disarm combatants, protect civilians, promote human rights, and restore the rule of law • Peacekeeping missions support the implementation of a peace agreement • If the local police organisation has collapsed, is untrustworthy, or lacks the capacity to perform necessary policing functions, international police may have an executive policing role to perform local policing duties until the local police organisation is re-established
Long-term police capacity development projects (in conflict-affected countries and developing countries)	• Large-scale police capacity development (or capacity building) programs involve the building or rebuilding, restructuring, or reform of a local police organisation. This may occur as part of a broader state-building process that involves contributions from government and non-governmental organisations and private companies • In a conflict-affected country, this work necessitates long-term engagement to re-establish the local police organisation, and to recruit, train, and mentor staff. Similarly, in a developing country, engagement is long-term and multi-faceted. Whether in a conflict-affected or developing country, international police officers may be embedded within the organisation temporarily • International deployments are gradually decreased once the requisite competencies have been achieved sustainably (i.e., they can be maintained)

(continued)

Table 5.1 (continued)

Category	Role
Discrete police capacity development initiatives	• Discrete police capacity development initiatives in partnership with developing countries are designed to strengthen the rule of law and specific areas of policing capacity. They involve deploying a small number of police officers to the host country, and focus on training, technical assistance, and mentoring • In addition to in-country programs, personnel can be offered opportunities to participate in training in the region or in a provider country. Alternatively, selected personnel may participate in a secondment or an exchange program, in which they spend time observing or serving in another country
Cross-border cooperation	• In response to transnational crime, different forms of cross-border partnerships have evolved. Joint operations may be undertaken to target transnational crime, such as drug trafficking • Additionally, various policing networks have developed to promote cooperation and share information and intelligence to prevent transnational crime. Police liaison officers who are posted overseas can act as a first point of contact for communication between the policing organisations of partner countries and can facilitate the exchange of information

Category	Role
Post-disaster assistance	• In the aftermath of a disaster, a wide range of international assistance can be called upon. This can include the provision of generalist and specialist personnel from medical and health services, emergency services (e.g., fire, search, and rescue), policing organisations (including forensic science), and military organisations • Depending on the available skills and resources of the sending country and the needs of the receiving country, police assistance may include victim support, disaster victim identification, technical assistance, mentoring, training, investigative support, restoring safety, and rebuilding

force, and political and developmental means (to address the perceived causes of conflict and instability). The language used to describe these missions shifts in response to changes in thinking and policy. RAMSI, which consisted of peace operations followed by capacity building, was a classic 'liberal peace' intervention within the region from 2003 (Allen & Dinnen, 2010; Barbara, 2008). It formally concluded in 2017.

RAMSI not only provides a key example of peace operations, but also is important for understanding the relationships in the region and the context in which the Solomon Islands Government requested assistance in 2021 following unrest in the island of Malaita, the largest of the nine provinces. In November 2021, riots were triggered in the capital of Honiara by a shift in diplomatic relations from Taiwan to China among other issues, such as concerns about corruption, poor service delivery, and associated differences in opinion on centralised versus decentralised governance (Newton Cain, 2021; Ride, 2021). Pacific Islands Forum countries—notably Australia, New Zealand, Fiji, and PNG—responded by deploying police officers and military troops. The Australian Government emphasised that the focus of the operation was policing support.

Peace Operations in Solomon Islands—RAMSI

RAMSI arose in response to conflict in Solomon Islands in 2000, the circumstances of which were complex (Fraenkel, 2004). Corruption among members of the government was an ongoing concern, particularly in relation to the timber industry (McDougall, 2004). People from Malaita had increasingly relocated to the island of Guadalcanal, which is home to Honiara. Resentment grew because of the perception that people from Malaita had benefited economically at the expense of those from Guadalcanal, with a belief that compensation was due. Militant forces emerged, forcing approximately 25,000 Malaitan people out of Guadalcanal (McDougall, 2004). Policing became increasingly compromised as violence escalated, and lines blurred between police and militia. While many police joined militia groups, others fled. The Royal Solomon Islands Police (RSIP) collapsed. Widespread criminality followed, with events culminating in a coup in June 2000. A small contingent of armed ex-militants, including police and corrupt leaders, paralysed the state (Peake & Brown, 2005).

The Prime Minister of Solomon Islands made a request for assistance, supported by the parliament (McDougall, 2004). Australia and

New Zealand had initially declined a request to become involved prior to the coup. However, following a ceasefire in August 2000, they facilitated the signing of the Townsville Peace Agreement in October, contributed to the International Peace Monitoring Team (along with personnel from Cook Islands, Tonga and Vanuatu) and kept a police presence in Solomon Islands until mid-2002 (McDougall, 2004). Influenced by concern over a failing state, high-profile murders in the country, and the realisation that due to Solomon Islands' recognition of Taiwan, China would likely block UN involvement, it was agreed that a regional mission would be undertaken if the Pacific Islands Forum was supportive (McDougall, 2004). The Australian Strategic Policy Institute published a rationale and blueprint for an Australian-led intervention, which aimed to build on previous experience (Wainwright, 2003). RAMSI proceeded with the support of the Pacific Islands Forum under the auspices of the Biketawa Declaration on Mutual Assistance (Pacific Islands Forum, 2000). It was known in Solomon Islands pidgin as *Helpem Fren* (Helping a Friend).

The need to establish law and order was a driving element of the preliminary phase of the mission, which was police-led with military support (Peake & Brown, 2005). The Participating Police Force (PPF) consisted of around 250 police officers and was drawn from Australia (70%), New Zealand (11.8%) and 13 PICs (18.2%) (Putt et al., 2018). Specifically, the Pacific Islands contingent was drawn from the Cook Islands, the Federated States of Micronesia, Fiji, Kiribati, the Republic of the Marshall Islands, Nauru, Niue, Palau, PNG, Samoa, Tonga, Tuvalu, and Vanuatu (Putt et al., 2018). Military personnel from Australia, New Zealand, Fiji, PNG, and Tonga were also involved.

The first contingent of the PPF arrived in Solomon Islands in July 2003 to begin the restoration of law and order. Local people were reported that they were pleased to have the international police presence and felt safer (Peake & Brown, 2005). Security was restored in Honiara and a police presence was extended to other parts of the country. Weapons were confiscated, hundreds of members of militia groups were arrested, and criminal and corrupt police officers were removed from the RSIP (Dinnen, 2012). The mission encountered little resistance, and many members of the military contingent were able to return home (Fraenkel, 2015). With executive policing in place and efforts made to mentor and assist the RSIP, the first phase of RAMSI was generally regarded as successful (McDougall, 2004).

Peace operations can sometimes achieve the stabilisation of law and order relatively quickly, giving a perception of success. This occurred in Solomon Islands, and in Timor-Leste from 1999. However, peace operations do not address the underlying issues that led to the initial conflict (Peake & Brown, 2005). Without long-term work to develop the conditions for sustainable peace and development, conflict and riots can reoccur—as happened in both Solomon Islands in 2006 and Timor-Leste in 2007. As a liberal peace approach suggests, it was essential that the initial phase to establish suitable conditions was followed by the long-term and more challenging phase of state-building and the associated police capacity development.

Long-Term Police Capacity Development Projects

Numerous long-term police capacity development projects have been undertaken in PICs as part of broader state-building interventions. Two examples are particularly important to consider first: the capacity development phase of RAMSI and the Enhanced Cooperation Program (ECP) in PNG. In both cases, the prevailing circumstances for local police included poor funding and lack of government support, poor working conditions, and a presence that was limited to specific (mostly urban) areas, leaving most of the population without access to state police (Dinnen & McLeod, 2009). Both countries had the institutional framework of the British Westminster system as a legacy of colonisation alongside the non-state local and customary approaches to governance and justice.

The Regional Assistance Mission to Solomon Islands

The capacity development phase of RAMSI was backed by the Pacific Islands Forum and characterised by multinational deployments (see 'Peace Operations in Solomon Islands—RAMSI', above). Following the initial response aimed at stabilising law and order, the priorities in Solomon Islands shifted to the far more difficult and long-term task of reconstruction and development. This included a focus on the ministries of police, justice, and finance (Fraenkel, 2015). For the police, the crucial task was to rebuild the RSIP. Because many members of the RSIP had been dismissed and charged with crimes under RAMSI, there was a need to recruit and train new police officers, as well as prosecute those charged (Fraenkel, 2015).

Following a period of institutional strengthening, then one of capacity development amid political volatility, efforts turned to working in partnership with Solomon Islands Government towards transition (Putt et al., 2018). From 2013, when the remaining military contingent left, RAMSI became a police assistance and capacity development mission. The Solomon Islands police, now known as the Royal Solomon Islands Police Force (RSIPF), had responsibility for policing as RAMSI moved towards the drawdown in 2017 (Putt et al., 2018).

As RAMSI's exit strategy was considered, a shift in narrative occurred, highlighting that the RSIPF had developed capacity throughout the mission (Dinnen & Allen, 2013). For example, the RSIPF and the PPF provided security for general elections in 2010 and 2014, which went ahead without incident (AFP, 2011, 2015). When flash flooding in Guadalcanal province in 2014 caused 22 deaths and the displacement of approximately 52,000 people, the RSIPF led the response—including establishing a temporary disaster victim identification centre—demonstrating its capacity to manage a major operation (AFP, 2014). Ultimately, by the time that the drawdown of RAMSI was complete, arrangements had been made to continue police capacity development through bilateral agreements (Putt et al., 2018). The RSIPF later oversaw the 2019 election, which built confidence both within the country and in the region about its effectiveness (AFP, 2019).

RAMSI was characterised by its capacity to adapt and change (Braithwaite et al., 2010; Dinnen, 2012; Dinnen & McLeod, 2009). While at the outset of the mission Solomon Islands was viewed through an external security lens, over time it came to be viewed from a more context-specific developmental perspective (Dinnen, 2012). Initially, the selection and pre-deployment training of those involved in capacity development did not ensure the right level of expertise and cultural awareness (Auditor-General, 2007). This evolved in response to feedback. For example, it came to include greater cultural training and input from Solomon Islanders, as well as training on how to mentor the local police rather than doing the job oneself (Putt et al., 2018)—a challenge exacerbated by the PPF's periodic and non-linear switching from executive to advisory roles. Although at first the duration of deployments was too short to build the necessary relationships of trust, later in the mission the time spent in one role and location was increased (Goldsmith & Harris, 2012). Initially, each new advisor within the Learning and Development Group wanted to change the curriculum. Once this problem was recognised, a full review was undertaken to develop curriculum for future requirements (Den Heyer, 2010, p. 222). Further changes occurred in response to the needs of the Pacific Islands contingent. These included the development of designated leadership and wellbeing roles staffed by members of the contingent (Putt et al., 2018).

One of the great strengths of the mission was the inclusion of police officers from Pacific Islands jurisdictions. First, at the international level, this multilateral regional approach provided far greater legitimacy to such an intervention. Second, the inclusion of Pacific police officers was extremely beneficial for practical reasons (Peake & Brown, 2005; Putt et al., 2018). Members of the Pacific Islands contingent from various countries often understood the challenges of working in hybrid systems of justice. Those from PNG and Vanuatu were able to communicate effectively with Solomon Islands locals given the similarities in Melanesian cultural context and the use of variations of pidgin language (Putt et al., 2018). The value of the Pacific Islands contingent's contribution is also evident in that Solomon Islands' leaders often requested that officers assigned for their protection be Pacific members. In addition, Australian members reflected favourably on the contribution of the Pacific Islands contingent (Putt et al., 2018).

However, the mission was not without critique. It was less ambitious in scope than initially intended. As an exercise in state-building, it was narrow, in that it only affected police, justice, and finance, while 21 other government ministries were not included (Fraenkel, 2015). It may be regarded as an exercise in strengthening the existing institutional frameworks rather than one in broader police reform (Dinnen & McLeod, 2009). Many of the changes achieved within the RSIPF were due to a new generation of police officers in the police organisation (Fraenkel, 2015). Further concerns included that RAMSI may have generated overreliance on external support (Dinnen, 2012). One of the paradoxes of having a highly professional and well-resourced PPF involved in policing was the stark contrast that it presented to the RSIPF. Solomon Islanders' confidence in the RSIPF was inadvertently undermined (Dinnen & Allen, 2013).

Ultimately, while RAMSI is often regarded as largely successful, police capacity building on its own will not ensure that the justice system, including the customary and local aspects, is functional and sustainable in the longer term (Dinnen & McLeod, 2009; Peake & Brown, 2005). Police officers are unlikely to know the range of options that exist for development, and therefore work to build police organisations and officers in their own images. To be most effective, police capacity development must be part of broader state-building and therefore requires partnerships beyond policing (Peake & Brown, 2005). Since the conclusion of RAMSI in June 2017, the Solomon Islands Police Development Program has been in place to continue to support the RSIPF (AFP, 2017a, 2019). This suggests a narrative of continuity rather than rupture following the RAMSI intervention.

The Enhanced Cooperation Program
The ECP was conceptualised in 2003 following the early success of RAMSI and provides a relevant contrast. The Australian Government was concerned that PNG was facing a period of instability and corruption and could become a failing state. Although PNG was not a country in a post-conflict scenario, addressing the challenges was viewed as a more difficult prospect than in Solomon Islands (Hawksley, 2005; McLeod & Dinnen, 2007). Envisaged as a five-year whole-of-government program, the ECP would involve placing 64 technical and specialist advisors—from law and justice; economic, finance and planning; and border control—in central governmental agencies in PNG to strengthen institutions. It would include a police-led intervention involving 210 Australian police known as the Australian Assisting Police (AAP), comprised of generalist and specialist police members drawn from the AFP and Australian state and territory police jurisdictions. The ECP would contribute A$800 million to PNG, in addition to $300 million from AusAID. When PNG gained independence in 1975 after a history of German and British claims followed by 70 years of Australian colonial administration (Ferns, 2015), Australia had promised to continue to provide substantial aid.

Even though the discourse surrounding Pacific aid at the time already included important elements such as mutual obligations and key performance indicators, the ECP was a heavy-handed approach by the Australian Government (Hawksley, 2005). Part of the plan for the AAP was that they would engage in executive policing. The police officers would hold line positions in the Royal Papua New Guinea Constabulary (RPNGC) but maintain a parallel command structure. They would have the power to arrest people, and—as is standard practice under peacekeeping deployments—they would have full immunity under PNG law (but not under Australian law). This arrangement was contentious in PNG—it was an affront to many members of the political elite. The legal foundations of the arrangement were challenged by PNG's Governor of Morobe, Luther Wenge, who was a former judge of PNG's National and Supreme Courts (Hameiri, 2009). AAP members had already been deployed to Port Moresby and Bougainville and were largely welcomed by the public, with reports of increased feelings of safety (McLeod, 2009). However, on 13 May 2005, the PNG Supreme Court ruled against the PNG legislation that had enabled the ECP, deeming it unconstitutional. Consequently, the AAP were withdrawn from PNG (May, 2012). Importantly, while most of the public servants remained, they did so as advisors rather than in-line officials in the agencies concerned. This reduced their potency.

Although the ECP was just beginning to be rolled out at the time of its demise in 2005—and thus was never fully implemented—it has provided fertile ground for analysis and critique. For example, while it was reportedly extremely popular among many ordinary Papua New Guinean people, including members of the RPNGC, the view among the political elite was that the program was too interventionist—it did not adequately respect the sovereignty of PNG (Hawksley, 2005). It was true that support was needed in PNG, but the approach to providing it had fallen short. In other words, because the program was *not* a humanitarian intervention and the Australian police contingent were *not* peacekeepers, Australia should have treated PNG as a sovereign state rather than a collapsed one (Hawksley, 2005, p. 37). Additional criticisms of the program were made based on its projected economic costs and benefits, which did not appear to offer the same value for money as those of health and education programs (Sugden, 2004). The previous aid project, a 15-year RPNGC Development Project (1989–2005), had been criticised because it lacked adequate mechanisms to measure achievements (Dinnen & McLeod, 2009), yet the ECP also lacked a framework for monitoring performance and accountability (Sugden, 2004).

Further, the aims, ethos, and values of the program were not sufficiently shared by its partners. Analysis of data from focus groups and interviews with ECP participants, including 100 members of the RPNGC and 33 members of the AAP, highlighted mismatches (McLeod, 2009). The premise of the ECP as a one-way transfer of skills or capacity development program was problematic. From the PNG perspective, recognition of two-way learning and knowledge exchange would have been more appropriate because, without sufficient understanding of the local context,

Australian advice and mentoring was unlikely to be meaningful (McLeod, 2009). In PNG, wisdom, knowledge, and experience are associated with age, the presence of grey hair, and the achievement of certain milestones in life, as well as significant relevant career experience. The fact that some AAP members had been deployed above their ordinary rank was not welcomed by PNG officers (McLeod, 2009). Stark contrasts in conditions, such as pay and accommodation, between the RPNGC and the AAP contributed to resentment. Further, differences in policing practices added complexity. For example, PNG officers reportedly regarded the use of force as an essential component of policing, due to a lack of resources and a perceived community desire for strong policing. For the AAP, however, the deterrence of police brutality was an important component of their role in building trust in local policing. Furthermore, the use of non-state dispute resolution processes, which focus on talk to resolve differences, often had widespread community and police support. The preference of PNG officers to resolve matters using community approaches posed a challenge for the AAP whose role was to help strengthen the state system (McLeod, 2009).

In short, the ECP did not reflect a true partnership, but a rather more domineering approach imposed by Australia. It lacked the legitimacy of a multilateral agreement (Patience, 2005). It did not have adequate accountability measures in place and it did not reflect adequate understanding of the PNG context.

In the aftermath of the program, efforts turned to a more suitable bilateral agreement to continue assisting the RPNGC and justice institutions. This meant abandoning the executive policing role and reverting to an advisory one. Since being re-established, a PNG–Australia Policing Partnership has been in place in various forms (AFP, 2019).

Follow-up research after international deployments for RAMSI and the ECP revealed that despite the many practical challenges and frustrations (Harris, 2010), both during deployment and when reintegrating at home (Auditor-General, 2007; Putt et al., 2018), participating police officers experienced several secondary benefits. For example, while it was challenging for Australian police to mentor local police rather than do the work themselves, they gained insights into other countries and cultures. Some were humbled by the way local colleagues demonstrated resilience in the face of extreme poverty and lack of resources (Harris, 2010). For a number of police officers, their international deployments had been life-changing experiences (Brennan, 2015).

Similarly, research with the Pacific Islands contingent after RAMSI revealed significant benefits. The month spent in pre-deployment training at Majura in Canberra was valuable not only for the mission itself but also for the members' roles in their home countries (Putt et al., 2018). The opportunities for confidence building and further development during the mission itself were wide-ranging. Informal networking and more formal efforts to institutionalise these connections were evident, for example, among female police officers in the Women's Advisory Network (Putt et al., 2018; see Chapter 6). Many participants reportedly used new skills in their roles, some achieved promotions, and others contributed to change in their organisations (Putt et al., 2018). In short, although the circumstances of deployment were challenging, the goodwill and personal connections developed may have benefits in the longer term if connections can be maintained.

Recent Capacity Development Programs
Many challenges associated with large-scale police capacity development programs also apply in projects of a smaller scale (e.g., in Nauru, Samoa, Tonga, Vanuatu, and Bougainville). Indeed, evidence from annual reports, evaluations, and program design suggests an ongoing challenge to ensure that programs respond to local needs and contexts and are well integrated into larger programs.

For example, the Tonga Police Development Programme is a trilateral agreement between Tonga, Australia, and New Zealand that grew out of a stabilisation mission after riots in 2006. Although an increase in skills in target areas has been achieved from the program, it does not appear to be part of a larger program to build capacity in the justice sector or state more broadly (Law and Development Partnership, 2013a). It was recommended that program partners engage in a planning session to identify needs, what will be done to meet them, and how outcomes will be monitored (Tennant & Bernklau, 2016). The importance of spending more time planning at each new phase of a project to identify and prioritise the needs, strategies, measurement, and reporting has been highlighted in regard to multiple capacity development programs (Law and Development Partnership, 2013a; Department of Foreign Affairs and Trade [DFAT], 2016).

In recent years, the Vanuatu–Australia Policing and Justice Program (*Stretem Rod blong Jastis mo Sefti*) has evolved. Prior to 2014, two separate programs for police and justice were operating simultaneously.

In response to earlier critique about the lack of communication, collaboration, and coordination of the programs, they were brought together to improve outcomes across the sector and its organisations and to undertake community-based pilot programs (DFAT, 2016). The design of the program explicitly recognises the role of traditional and community justice mechanisms. This shift acknowledges that sustainable reform in the justice sector requires a strong element of working with—rather than against—the grain (Cox et al., 2012). The program aims to build on policing, justice, and community services to enhance access to justice, especially for women and children who have experienced violence, in all parts of Vanuatu (DFAT, 2016).

Similarly, the Bougainville Community Policing Project aims to support the Bougainville Police Service and to integrate and support a strong and sustainable community auxiliary police program (Tennant & Cowley, 2019). It was established in 1998 after New Zealand's involvement in facilitating the peace declaration in 1997 between Bougainville leaders and PNG, and extends the reach of state police into previously isolated areas, enhancing access to justice. However, two evaluations highlighted that it could be better aligned with broader justice initiatives, including an Australian project that aims to strengthen criminal justice (Dinnen & Peake, 2013a; Law and Development Partnership, 2013a). This finding supported research in which stakeholders in PICs perceived that Australia and New Zealand could work together more effectively (Boswell, 2010; Dinnen & Peake, 2013b). Further, it was observed that planning should involve a long-term vision that fosters sustainability to avoid overreliance on hands-on support and funding. Working closely with other agencies is important so that police officers are not tasked with work that may be more appropriately undertaken by development professionals (Tennant & Cowley, 2019).

Discrete Police Capacity Development Initiatives

Discrete police capacity development initiatives aim to address local policing needs in generalist or specialist areas of policing, often through technical assistance or training. Many such initiatives exist in the Pacific region. One goal has been to support programs for the Pacific, by the Pacific (e.g., training on gender-based violence through the Women's Crisis Centre in Fiji) (AFP, 2015). Some examples of training 'by the Pacific' occurred following the Pacific Islands contingent's participation in RAMSI and the increased confidence its members developed. For example, Cook Islands Police delivered training on command and control to police from other PICs, and the RSIPF provided training on use of force and public order management to police in Nauru and Samoa (Putt et al., 2018). The Pacific Faculty of Policing, an initiative led by the AFP and the Australian Institute of Police Management (AIPM) aims to enhance leadership capabilities for the management of emerging regional security threats (AFP, 2019; AIPM, 2020). It is unclear the extent to which the training offered is also 'by the Pacific'.

Table 5.2 presents some examples of discrete initiatives, many of which have been offered in various forms over long periods of time with the support of the Pacific Islands Chiefs of Police (PICP).

The fact that many programs have received positive endorsements from the partner organisations and renewed funding in successive rounds may be encouraging to those involved, but is not an objective measure of success. Indeed, measuring the achievement of objectives has been notoriously difficult. While training and technical assistance may lead to increases in the skills of individual participants, these technical skills initiatives may fall short of meeting the needs of the police organisation in the host country (Law and Development Partnership, 2013b). Often, they may have limited impact on the organisation and the broader justice sector. To improve effectiveness and relevance, and to minimise duplication, overlap, and critical gaps, these initiatives must be undertaken within the context of a larger project design that recognises the local circumstances and needs (Law and Development Partnership, 2013b). On the one hand, evidence from evaluations suggests that stakeholders have made substantial efforts to improve offerings over time, listen to local stakeholders, and foster local ownership and leadership (see e.g., Allen & Clarke, 2017). However, such evidence also highlights that many of the same challenges are recurring and that initiatives must be connected in the broader context (Peake & Dinnen, 2014a). A further criticism has been that discrete initiatives often serve the needs of provider countries' interests in various ways, such as geostrategic positioning (e.g., in response to increased interest in the region from China) and improving the detection of transnational crime (McLeod, 2009).

Table 5.2 Examples of discrete police capacity development initiatives

Project	Activities	Partners
Preventing Family Violence in the Pacific Program (PDVPP)	• Aims to build capacity in host police organisations (including in the Cook Islands, Samoa, Tonga, Kiribati, and Vanuatu) to prevent and respond to domestic violence • Includes capturing data, developing action plans, raising awareness and changing social norms, establishing police domestic violence units, and supporting the broader justice sector response (Allen & Clarke, 2017; Law and Development Partnership, 2013b)	PICP New Zealand Police Ministry of Foreign Affairs and Trade (MFAT)
Partnership for Pacific Policing (3P)	• Offers targeted interventions, including training in specific areas of identified need, management support, and leadership mentoring (New Zealand Police, 2020) • Involves discussions about needs and priorities before country-specific programs are designed (Allen & Clarke, 2017) • Includes the Cook Islands, Kiribati, Niue, Tokelau, Tuvalu, Samoa, and Vanuatu (New Zealand Police, 2020)	New Zealand Police MFAT
Women's Advisory Network	• Offers conferences, secondments to the PICP head office in New Zealand, exchanges to other PICs, mentoring programs, leadership workshops, and driver training programs (PICP, 2019a)	PICP MFAT AFP

(continued)

Table 5.2 (continued)

Project	Activities	Partners
Pacific Police Development Program—Regional (PPDP-R)	• Includes multi-country programs and programs for countries without specific agreements (AFP, 2011) • Includes provision of police uniforms and equipment, investigation training, learning in generalist and specialist areas, and leadership development programs (AFP, 2015) • Provides support to regional organisations such as the PICP, the Pacific Police Training Advisory Group and the Pacific Police Policy Network (AFP, 2015)	AFP + others (depending on initiative)
Cyber Safety Pasifika (PPDP-R initiative)	• Aims to increase the police capability to enforce laws, and to investigate and prosecute relevant crimes (AFP, 2018) • Prepares police officers to act as trainers in cyber safety awareness, strengthens cybercrime legislation and policy in line with international standards, and increases police officers' skills in cybercrime investigations in conjunction with international experts from the FBI and Interpol (AFP, 2018; Cyber Safety Pasifika, 2019)	PICP AFP

Project	Activities	Partners
Pacific Forensic Working Group (PPDP-R initiative)	• Aims to enhance capacity to undertake forensic services work within policing • Includes refurbishing forensic laboratories (e.g., in Samoa, Tonga, and Cook Islands) and introducing the Pacific Automated Fingerprint Identification System (PAFIS) • Developed model provisions for forensic legislation that were approved by the PICP in 2015 • Offers fingerprint and crime scene examination courses and certification (AFP, 2018; PICP, 2019b) and reviewed the Pacific fingerprint training manual (AFP, 2018)	PICP AFP

Cross-Border Cooperation

Transnational crime is one of the key contemporary crime concerns associated with globalisation and technological connectivity (United Nations Office on Drugs and Crime [UNODC], 2016). Concerns arise in the Pacific region not only because weak or fragile states could become havens of criminal activity, but also because the borders of the Pacific are vast and porous. Existing data suggests that various PICs are affected by environmental crimes (especially illegal fishing and resource extraction), sex trafficking (associated with logging and resource extraction industries), and the trafficking of illicit drugs and their precursors (UNODC, 2016; see Chapter 3). News reports suggest that drug shipments from South America destined for the 'lucrative markets' of Australia and New Zealand have found their way into PICs (see e.g., Lyons, 2019). This 'spillover' presents a challenging social issue for PICs, even though they are the unintended recipients of supplies (UNODC, 2016).

The Governments of Australia and New Zealand (among others, such as the United States) have long been concerned about criminal enterprises transiting through the Pacific region. For many PICs, the primary focus of crime concerns has been internal security threats (see e.g., May, 2012). In the mid-2000s, it was considered unlikely that PICs would be able to address transnational crime—both for budget-related reasons (Mid-Term Review Team [MTRT], 2006) and because of the challenges of corruption of officials (McCusker, 2006). Most of the small PICs do not have separate military, prison, or maritime officers; the police fulfil many roles. Membership of various networks aimed at addressing transnational crime could burden staff and stretch resources due to the need to manage different information-sharing agreements and reporting requirements (MTRT, 2006). Nevertheless, donor partners expected Pacific police organisations to participate in training and capacity development initiatives designed to combat transnational crime. However, doing so has not always met local organisational priorities (McLeod, 2009; Peake & Dinnen, 2014b; Watson et al., 2021). Increasingly, a recognised need exists among PICs to document and address transnational crime in the Pacific (UNODC, 2016). This is supported by the Boe Declaration on Regional Security (Pacific Islands Forum, 2018), which explicitly endorsed an increased focus in the Pacific region on transnational crime.

A host of agencies within and beyond the Pacific region collaborate to address and prevent transnational crime. For example, some PICs are part of broader networks through their membership of Interpol. These are Fiji, Kiribati, the Republic of the Marshall Islands, Nauru, PNG, Samoa, Solomon Islands, Tonga, and Vanuatu. Additionally, the PICP is partnered with the International Association of Chiefs of Police and the UNODC (PICP, 2019c). Additionally, many PICs are members or observers of the Asia/Pacific Group on Money Laundering (APG). This autonomous regional body aims to prevent criminal entities from profiting from crime by addressing money laundering and associated crimes, and terrorist financing (APG, 2019).[5]

As shown in Table 5.3, partnerships include the Pacific Transnational Crime Network, which has grown since its establishment by the AFP in 2002, and the associated Pacific Transnational Crime Coordination Centre. The agreement by Fiji, Tonga, Australia, and New Zealand to form a transnational organised crime network—Transnational Serious and Organised Crime Pacific Taskforce—reflects the increased prominence of these types of crimes within PICs. Successful operations with Pacific partners targeting drug trafficking are routinely reported by the AFP (see e.g., AFP, 2017a). Australia and New Zealand also have police officers posted in the region as part of their international liaison officer networks. Specifically, the AFP has liaison officers in Fiji, PNG, and New Zealand (AFP, 2017b), while New Zealand Police has liaison officers in Samoa and Australia (New Zealand Police, 2020).

An explicitly Pacific regional focus is evident in other partnerships. In a complex arrangement of networks, the PICP partners with numerous regional stakeholder organisations (PICP, 2019c). For example, the Oceania Customs Organisation (OCO) is an intergovernmental organisation that aims to assist member countries in achieving international standards and best practices in border security (OCO, 2018). The Pacific Immigration Development Community is also aimed at protecting borders (PICP, 2019c). The Pacific Islands Law Officers Network (PILON) brings together judges and senior officials. Focus areas in recent years have included cybercrime, environmental crime, and corruption, with a focus on combating illegal fishing and illegal logging, and criminal activities and corruption associated with the resource extraction industries

---

[5] Notably, to promote effective functioning in their domains, each of the regional organisations and Interpol are involved in capacity development efforts at the regional and country levels, often with their counterparts in Australia and New Zealand and/or other providers, such as the UN.

Table 5.3 Pacific partnerships for addressing transnational crime

Partnership	Activities
Pacific Transnational Crime Network (PTCN)	The PTCN aims to work collaboratively to provide intelligence and investigative capability to combat transnational crime in the Pacific (PICP, n.d.). The network consists of 28 locally staffed transnational crime units (TCUs) in 20 Pacific Island countries and territories (AFP, 2019; PICP, n.d.). The first TCUs were established in 2002 in Fiji, Samoa, and Tonga, followed by Vanuatu and PNG, with funding from the AFP's Law Enforcement Cooperation Program (now PPDP-R)
Pacific Transnational Crime Coordination Centre (PTCCC)	The PTCCC is based in Apia, Samoa (having been established in Suva, Fiji in 2004 and relocated in 2008 following the coup of 2006). It coordinates, produces, manages, and disseminates intelligence products to PTCN member countries and territories and other international law enforcement partners (PICP, n.d.)
Transnational Serious and Organised Crime Pacific Taskforce (TSOC)	Established in 2019 by Fiji, Tonga, Australia and New Zealand, the aims of the TSOC are to enhance operations and information sharing through the PTCN and PTCCC. One of the focal concerns is crime facilitated by small craft in the region. It demonstrates commitment to effectiveness in multinational cooperation (AFP, 2019)

(PILON, 2016, 2019). The Pacific Islands Forum Fisheries Agency also collaborates to prevent fisheries crimes (PICP, 2019c).

The geography of the region makes it necessary to collaborate both within and between agencies and countries—a situation that is also evident in post-disaster assistance.

Post-Disaster Assistance

Although the Pacific region is well known for its geographical and geological vulnerability to natural disasters such as tropical cyclones, floods, tsunami, droughts, earthquakes, and volcanic activity, many PICs have limited access to local emergency assistance and resources for rebuilding (Noy, 2015). Examples in recent years of natural disasters in the region include volcanic activity in Vanuatu in 2017 and 2018, and Cyclone Harold, which impacted Fiji, Solomon Islands, Tonga, and Vanuatu in 2020. Due to climate change, the frequency and intensity of these disasters is expected to increase in the coming years (Gero et al., 2015). For many years, the Pacific Islands Forum was at an impasse on the issue of climate change due to inaction by Australia and New Zealand (Lawson, 2017). Thus, the Boe Declaration on Regional Security (Pacific Islands Forum, 2018)—which redefined security to recognise 'that climate change remains the single greatest threat to the livelihoods, security and wellbeing of the peoples of the Pacific' (article 1[i])—reflects an important step forward.

In terms of international policing, post-disaster assistance can include a deployment of generalist and specialist police officers; for example, to assist in community policing and support search and rescue (AFP, 2011). Family investigation liaison officers, forensic experts, and disaster victim identification experts can assist in cases of mass fatality. In instances of terrorist attacks, intelligence officers and investigative support can also be provided (AFP, 2019). For example, forensic specialists were deployed to Tonga to assist with investigation and the identification of five deceased persons following the 2006 Shoreline fire (AFP, 2008). Humanitarian forensic science is more complex than routine forensic science, and international deployments are therefore essential to provide the necessary skills and equipment (Cordner, 2018).

International humanitarian assistance in the wake of disasters is often a multidisciplinary and multi-agency endeavour (Gero et al., 2015). What is offered depends on the needs identified and requests made by the governments of affected countries, as well as the capacity and resources available in sending countries. The multifaceted nature of disaster assistance highlights the need for partnership approaches so that the activities of government agencies can be coordinated effectively with those of the private sector, non-governmental organisations, the UN, and other organisations and countries (Gero et al., 2015).

Disaster assistance has typically flowed from well-resourced countries of the global North, which have long-established partnerships in this regard. These include the FRANZ Arrangement of France, Australia, and New Zealand, and the Quadrilateral Defence Coordinating Group comprised of Australia, New Zealand, the United States, and France.[6] Other countries called upon to assist have included Canada and Singapore. However, the dominance of countries of the global North has begun to change, with greater prominence of relief efforts from PICs. In 2015, after Cyclone Pam in Vanuatu (among other PICs), Fiji contributed to international support through the provision of military engineers, health professionals, and supplies. The Royal New Zealand Air Force assisted with their transport needs (Greener & Powles, 2015).

Similarly, during Australia's unprecedented bushfires in the summer of 2019–2020, several PICs offered to assist (Wyeth, 2020). In response to the official Australian request, PNG sent 100 and Fiji sent 58 troops, most of whom were engineers. For PNG it was the largest overseas deployment to date. Additionally, Vanuatu donated funds to support fire services. Local people and small businesses in Fiji, PNG and Vanuatu collected donations (Ewart & Handley, 2020). The unexpected contribution from the Pacific region reflected warmth and reciprocity in Pacific partnerships (Wyeth, 2020). While there are striking differences in access to financial resources and specialist equipment between countries like Australia and PICs, these examples raised opportunities for renewed thinking and discussion about ways of working together. One suggestion is to extend the membership of existing groups such as the FRANZ Arrangement to PICs; another is for a regional body to coordinate disaster responses in such a way that leadership of the response need not be by those equipped with the greatest resources (Greener & Powles, 2015).

Conclusion

International policing is a multifaceted and political endeavour. This chapter has outlined the nature of international policing, providing an overview of its history in the Pacific and its association with objectives related both to security and development. It highlighted examples of international policing in the Pacific region. Collectively, these examples reflect motivations both of self-interest and of good global citizenship among the participating countries. However, while international policing in the Pacific has the potential to be mutually beneficial for those involved,

---

[6] It is unclear how these arrangements may be impacted by the Australian Government's withdrawal from a submarine-building agreement with France.

vast resourcing disparities are abundantly evident. Other critical disparities also exist. For example, Australia and New Zealand may benefit from gains in international reputation and their policing organisations may receive increased national government funding based on their international policing efforts. By contrast, policing in PICs often relies on a steady flow of aid funding for initiatives to continue effectively. Achieving tangible benefits in PICs requires appropriate planning and partnerships. While evidence suggests that there have been efforts to improve partnerships and program design over time, there is no room for complacency. These are not simple matters and remain ongoing challenges (Peake & Dinnen, 2014a).

Since its early beginnings, the story of international policing is one of learning to work with others. This has included the need for police to work with the military and police contingents from other countries. A substantial challenge exists for international police to understand the unique and specific cultural contexts of their Pacific deployments (Harris, 2010; McLeod, 2009). This need for understanding suggests the importance of adequate pre-deployment preparation, and the development and maintenance of relationships in the local context. More broadly, however, there is a clear need for communication and consultation across multiple agencies in provider and host countries at all phases of the process of international policing. One of the main characteristics of justice sectors in PICs is that they can be extremely broad, reflecting state, customary, and local community ways of providing justice (Dinnen & McLeod, 2009). The need to work within a broader programmatic framework for sustainable development that minimises gaps and overlaps has been a recurring theme of the chapter.

Importantly, despite the challenges associated with international policing, the mutual benefits of cooperation are apparent. The enduring relationships and partnerships are positive features of international policing in the Pacific. As PICs have contributed to international policing both within and beyond the region, police officers have experienced valuable professional development and cross-border relationships in the region, which have in turn benefited their organisations (Putt et al., 2018). Collaborative efforts to address security threats provide reason for optimism about the future of the region (Wallis, 2012, 2017), as does an increased focus on regionalism in the Pacific. The Boe Declaration on Regional Security (Pacific Islands Forum, 2018) is an important example—reflecting consensus on the need for regional security cooperation, and increased emphasis on both transnational crime and climate change as prominent security concerns. With continued efforts to work effectively in Pacific partnerships, this consensus has the potential to contribute to shaping international policing in new and as yet unknown ways in coming years.

REFERENCES

Allen & Clarke. (2017). *Evaluation of New Zealand's development cooperation in Tuvalu: Final report*. Allen & Clarke Policy and Regulatory Specialists Ltd.

Allen, M., & Dinnen, S. (2010). The North down under: Antinomies of conflict and intervention in Solomon Islands. *Conflict, Security and Development, 10*(3), 299–327.

Asia/Pacific Group on Money Laundering (APG). (2019). *APG terms of reference*. Asia/Pacific Group on Money Laundering.

Auditor-General. (2007). *Australian Federal Police overseas operations* (Audit Report No. 53, 2006–2007). Australian National Audit Office.

Australian Federal Police (AFP). (2008). *Annual report 2007–2008*. AFP.

Australian Federal Police (AFP). (2011). *Annual report 2010–2011*. AFP.

Australian Federal Police (AFP). (2014). *Annual report 2013–2014*. AFP.

Australian Federal Police (AFP). (2015). *Annual report 2014–2015*. AFP.

Australian Federal Police (AFP). (2017a). *Annual report 2016–2017*. AFP.

Australian Federal Police (AFP). (2017b). *International engagement: 2020 and beyond*. AFP.

Australian Federal Police (AFP). (2018). *Annual report 2017–2018*. AFP.

Australian Federal Police (AFP). (2019). *Annual report 2018–2019*. AFP.

Australian Institute of Police Management (AIPM). (2020). *Pacific programs*. https://www.aipm.gov.au/pacific-faculty/pacific-programs

Baledrokadroka, J. (2012). The unintended consequences of Fiji's international peacekeeping. *Security Challenges, 8*(4), 105–116.

Barbara, J. (2008). Antipodean statebuilding: The Regional Assistance Mission to Solomon Islands and Australian intervention in the South Pacific. *Journal of Intervention and Statebuilding, 2*(2), 123–149.

Bayley, D. (2005). *Changing the guard: Developing democratic police abroad*. Oxford University Press.

Bellamy, A. J. (2009). The international deployment group. In R. Broadhurst & S. E. Davies (Eds.), *Policing in context*. Oxford University Press.

Bellamy, A. J. (2012). *Contributor profile: Australia*. Providing for Peacekeeping. https://www.ipinst.org/wp-content/uploads/2020/05/ipi-pub-ppp-Australia.pdf

Boister, N. (2003). Transnational criminal law? *European Journal of International Law, 14*(5), 953–976.

Boswell, B. M. (2010). *The evolution of international policing in the Pacific: A critical analysis* [Master's thesis]. School of History, Philosophy, Political Science and International Relations, Victoria University of Wellington. https://researcharchive.vuw.ac.nz/handle/10063/1520

Bowling, B., & Sheptycki, J. (2012). *Global policing.* Sage.

Bowling, B., & Sheptycki, J. (2015). Global policing and transnational rule with law. *Transnational Legal Theory, 6*(1), 141–173.

Braithwaite, J., Dinnen, S., Allen, M., Braithwaite, V., & Charlesworth, H. (2010). *Pillars and shadows: Statebuilding as peacebuilding in Solomon Islands.* ANU Press.

Brennan, K. J. (2015). *A comparison of New Zealand Police officers' perceptions of development practice within New Zealand development programmes* [Master's thesis]. School of People, Environment and Planning, Massey University. https://mro.massey.ac.nz/handle/10179/10210

Cordner, S. (2018). Humanitarian forensic science. *Australian Journal of Forensic Sciences, 50*(6), 639–650.

Cox, M., Duituturaga, E., & Scheye, E. (2012). *Building on local strengths: Evaluation of Australian law and justice assistance.* Office of Development Effectiveness, AusAID.

Cyber Safety Pasifika. (2019). *About cyber safety Pasifika.* https://www.cybersafetypasifika.org/our-work/about-cyber-safety-pasifika

Den Heyer, G. (2010). Evaluating police reform in post-conflict nations: A Solomon Islands case study. *International Journal of Comparative and Applied Criminal Justice, 34*(1), 213–234.

Department of Foreign Affairs and Trade (DFAT). (2016). *Stretem rod blong jastis mo sefti (SRBJS) [Vanuatu–Australia policing and justice program] 2017–2020: Program design document.* DFAT.

Department of Peacekeeping Operations (DPKO). (2011a, January). Brief history of UN policing. *UN Police Magazine, 6,* 6–17.

Department of Peacekeeping Operations (DPKO). (2011b, January). Actual/authorized/female deployment of UN Police in peacekeeping and special political missions (December 2010). *UN Police Magazine, 6,* 24–25.

Department of Peacekeeping Operations (DPKO). (2011c, January). Power to empower. *UN Police Magazine, 6,* 36–46.

Department of Peacekeeping Operations (DPKO). (2018a). Actual/authorized/female deployment of UN Police in peacekeeping and special political missions (January 2018). *UN Police Magazine, 14,* 20–21.

Department of Peacekeeping Operations (DPKO). (2018b). *Community-oriented policing in United Nations peace operations* [Manual]. United Nations Headquarters.

Dibb, P. (2012). The importance of the inner arc to Australian defence policy and planning. *Security Challenges, 8*(4), 13–31.

Dinnen, S. (2004/2005). *Lending a fist? Australia's new interventionism in the Southwest Pacific* (Discussion paper). Research School of Pacific and Asian Studies, Australian National University.

Dinnen, S. (2012). The Solomon Islands—RAMSI, transition and future prospects. *Security Challenges, 8*(4), 61–71.

Dinnen, S., & Allen, M. (2013). Paradoxes of postcolonial police-building: Solomon Islands. *Policing and Society, 23*(2), 222–242.

Dinnen, S., & McLeod, A. (2008). The quest for integration: Australian approaches to security and development in the Pacific Islands. *Security Challenges, 4*(2), 23–43.

Dinnen, S., & McLeod, A. (2009). Policing Melanesia—International expectations and local realities. *Policing and Society, 19*(4), 333–353.

Dinnen, S., & Peake, G. (2013a, February). *Bougainville community policing project: Independent evaluation*. Ministry of Foreign Affairs and Trade.

Dinnen, S., & Peake, G. (2013b). More than just policing: Police reform in post-conflict Bougainville. *International Peacekeeping, 20*(3), 570–584.

Dobell, G. (2012). From 'arc of instability' to 'arc of responsibility.' *Security Challenges, 8*(4), 33–45.

Dornan, M., & Pryke, J. (2017). Foreign aid to the Pacific: Trends and developments in the twenty-first century. *Asia and the Pacific Policy Studies, 4*(3), 386–404.

Durch, W. J., & Ker, M. (2013, November). *Police in UN peacekeeping: Improving selection, recruitment, and deployment* (Providing for Peacekeeping No. 6). International Peace Institute.

Dziedzic, S. (2018). Which country gives the most aid to Pacific Island nations? The answer might surprise you. *ABC News*, August 9. https://www.abc.net.au/news/2018-08-09/aid-to-pacific-island-nations/10082702?nw=0

Dziedzic, S. (2019). Beijing intensifies lobbying to Pacific nations to recognise Taiwan as part of One China. *ABC News*, February 14. https://www.abc.net.au/news/2019-02-14/beijing-lobbying-pacific-nations-to-recognise-one-china-policy/10809412

Ewart, R., & Handley, E. (2020). Pacific nations Vanuatu and PNG pledge aid for Australia's bushfires. *ABC News*, January 6. https://www.abc.net.au/news/2020-01-06/pacific-nations-pledge-aid-for-australias-bushfires/11844008

Ferns, N. (2015). PNG marks 40 years of independence, still feeling the effects of Australian colonialism. *The Conversation*, September

16. https://theconversation.com/png-marks-40-years-of-independence-still-feeling-the-effects-of-australian-colonialism-47258

Fraenkel, J. (2004). *The manipulation of custom: From uprising to intervention in the Solomon Islands*. Victoria University Press.

Fraenkel, J. (2015). The teleology and romance of state-building in Solomon Islands. *The Journal of Pacific History, 50*(4), 398–418.

Fry, G. (2019). *Framing the islands: Power and diplomatic agency in Pacific regionalism*. ANU Press.

Gero, A., Fletcher, S., Rumsey, M., Thiessen, J., Kurrupu, N., Buchan, J., Daly, J., & Willets, J. (2015). Disasters and climate change in the Pacific: Adaptive capacity of humanitarian response organizations. *Climate and Development, 7*(1), 35–46.

Goldsmith, A., & Dinnen, S. (2007). Transnational police building: Critical lessons from Timor-Leste and Solomon Islands. *Third World Quarterly, 28*(6), 1091–1109.

Goldsmith, A., & Harris, V. (2012). Trust, trustworthiness and trust-building in international policing missions. *Australian and New Zealand Journal of Criminology, 45*(2), 231–254.

Goldsmith, A., & Sheptycki, J. (2007). Introduction. In A. Goldsmith & J. Sheptycki (Eds.), *Crafting international policing: Police capacity-building and global policing reform* (pp. 1–27). Hart Publishing.

Greener, B. K. (2008). New Zealand's military and policing efforts in the Pacific. *Australian Defence Force Journal, 117*, 73–84.

Greener, B. K. (2009). *The new international policing*. Palgrave Macmillan.

Greener, B. K. (2011a). The rise of policing in peace operations. *International Peacekeeping, 18*(2), 183–195.

Greener, B. K. (2011b). The diplomacy of international policing: A case study of the New Zealand experience. *Political Science, 63*(2), 219–319.

Greener, B. K. (2017). *Contributor profile: New Zealand*. Providing for Peacekeeping. https://www.ipinst.org/wp-content/uploads/2020/05/New-Zealand-profile.pdf

Greener, B., & Powles, A. (2015). Building natural disaster capacity in the Pacific. *The Strategist*, March 27. https://www.aspistrategist.org.au/building-natural-disaster-capacity-in-the-pacific/

Hameiri, S. (2009). Governing disorder: The Australian Federal Police and Australia's new regional frontier. *The Pacific Review, 22*(5), 549–574.

Harris, V. (2010). Building on sand? Australian police involvement in international police capacity building. *Policing and Society, 20*(1), 79–98.

Hartz, H. (1999). CIVPOL: The UN instrument for police reform. *International Peacekeeping, 6*(4), 27–42.

Hawksley, C. (2005). The intervention you have when you're not having an intervention: Australia, PNG and the Enhanced Cooperation Program. *Social Alternatives, 24*(3), 34–39.

Hills, A. (2009). The possibility of transnational policing. *Policing and Society, 19*(3), 300–317.

Hornung, J. (2020). How ready is Australia for peacekeeping operations? *The Strategist*, January 31. https://www.aspistrategist.org.au/how-ready-is-austra lia-for-peacekeeping-operations/

Law and Development Partnership. (2013a). *Strategic evaluation of police work funded under the New Zealand Aid Programme 2005–2011: Police work in fragile and conflict affected contexts*. Law and Development Partnership.

Law and Development Partnership. (2013b). *Strategic evaluation of police work funded under the New Zealand Aid Programme 2005–2011: Pacific regional report*. Ministry of Foreign Affairs and Trade.

Lawson, S. (2017). Australia, New Zealand and the Pacific Islands Forum: A critical review. *Commonwealth and Comparative Politics, 55*(2), 214–235.

Lowy Institute. (2019). *Pacific aid map* [interactive web resource]. Lowy Institute. https://pacificaidmap.lowyinstitute.org/

Lyons, K. (2019). The new drug highway: Pacific islands at the centre of cocaine trafficking boom. *The Guardian*, June 24. https://www.theguardian.com/world/2019/jun/24/the-new-drug-highway-pacific-islands-at-centre-of-cocaine-trafficking-boom

May, R. (2012). Papua New Guinea: Issues of external and internal security. *Security Challenges, 8*(4), 47–60.

McCusker, R. (2006). Transnational crime in the Pacific Islands: Real or apparent danger? In *Trends and Issues in Crime and Criminal Justice* (No. 308). Australian Institute of Criminology.

McDougall, D. (2004). Intervention in Solomon Islands. *The Round Table, 93*(374), 213–223.

McDougall, D. (2015). Customary authority and state withdrawal in Solomon Islands: Resilience or tenacity? *Journal of Pacific History, 50*(4), 1–23.

McLeod, A. (2009). Police capacity development in the Pacific: The challenge of local context. *Policing and Society, 19*(2), 147–160.

McLeod, A., & Dinnen, S. (2007). Police building in the Southwest Pacific—New directions in Australian regional policing. In A. Goldsmith & J. Scheptycki (Eds.), *Crafting transnational policing: Police capacity-building and global policing reform* (pp. 295–328). Hart Publishing.

Mid-Term Review Team (MTRT). (2006, October). *Mid-term review: Pacific Regional Policing Initiative* (Final report). Ministry of Foreign Affairs and Trade.

Murney, T., Carwford, S.-E., & Hlder, A. (2011). Transnational policing and international human development—A rule of law perspective. *Journal of International Peacekeeping*, 15, 39–71.

New Zealand Police. (2020). *ISG introduction*. https://www.police.govt.nz/about-us/programmes-initiatives/isg/introduction

Newton Cain, T. (2021). As Australia deploys troops and police, what now for Solomon Islands? *The Conversation*, November 26. https://theconversation.com/as-australia-deploys-troops-and-police-what-now-for-solomon-islands-172678

Noy, I. (2015). *Natural disasters and climate change in the Pacific island countries: New non-monetary measurements of impacts* (Working paper: 08/2015). School of Economics and Finance, Victoria University of Wellington.

Oceania Customs Organisation (OCO). (2018). *OCO annual report 2017–2018*. Oceania Customs Organisation Secretariat.

Pacific Islands Chiefs of Police (PICP). (2019a). *Women's advisory network*. https://picp.co.nz/our-work/wan/

Pacific Islands Chiefs of Police (PICP). (2019b). *Pacific Forensic Working Group*. https://picp.co.nz/our-work/#pfwg

Pacific Islands Chiefs of Police (PICP). (2019c). *We work with*. https://picp.co.nz/who-we-are/partners/

Pacific Islands Chiefs of Police (PICP). (n.d.). *Pacific Transnational Crime Network*. https://picp.co.nz/our-work/pacific-transnational-crime-network/

Pacific Islands Forum. (2000). *'Biketawa' Declaration*. https://www.forumsec.org/biketawa-declaration/

Pacific Islands Forum. (2018). *Boe Declaration on Regional Security*. https://www.forumsec.org/boe-declaration-on-regional-security/

Pacific Islands Law Officers Network (PILON). (2016). *Strategic plan 2016–2018*. PILON Secretariat. https://pilonsec.org/digital-library/corporate-governance-resources/

Pacific Islands Law Officers Network (PILON). (2019). *Strategic plan 2019–2021*. Apia, Samoa: PILON Secretariat. https://pilonsec.org/digital-library/corporate-governance-resources/

Panel on United Nations Peace Operations. (2000). *Report of the Panel on United Nations Peace Operations ('Brahimi Report')*. United Nations.

Patience, A. (2005). The ECP and Australia's middle power ambitions. In *State Society and Governance in Melanesia* (Discussion Paper 2005/4). Australian National University.

Peake, G., & Brown, K. S. (2005). Policebuilding: The international deployment group in the Solomon Islands. *International Peacekeeping*, 12(4), 520–532.

Peake, G., & Dinnen, S. (2014a). Police development in Papua New Guinea: The need for innovation. *Security Challenges*, 10(2), 33–51.

Peake, G., & Dinnen, S. (2014b). *Transnational crime in the Pacific—a conversation starter* (In Brief No. 16). State, Society and Governance in Melanesia Program, College of Asia and the Pacific, Australian National University.

Perras, C. (2017). Transnational policing and its contexts: Flexibility and (dis)trust. In S. Hufnagel & C. McCartney (Eds.), *Trust in international police and justice cooperation* (pp. 221–240). Hart Publishing.

Putt, J., Dinnen, S., Keen, M., & Batley, J. (2018). *The RAMSI legacy for policing in the Pacific region*. Department of Pacific Affairs and Australian National University.

Rajah, R., Dayant, A., & Pryke, J. (2019). *Ocean of debt? Belt and Road debt diplomacy in the Pacific*. Lowy Institute.

Ride, A. (2021). Honiara as the smoke subsides. *The Interpreter*, November 26. https://www.lowyinstitute.org/the-interpreter/honiara-smoke-subsides

Sismanidis, R. D. V. (1997). *Police functions in peace operations* (Report). United States Institute of Peace.

South Pacific Forum. (1992). *Declaration by the South Pacific Forum on law enforcement cooperation*. https://www.forumsec.org/declaration-by-the-south-pacific-forum-on-law-enforcement-cooperation/

Sugden, C. (2004). Putting the Enhanced Cooperation Package to the test. *Pacific Economic Bulletin, 19*(1), 55–75.

Tennant, S., & Bernklau, S. (2016, April). *Tonga Police Development Programme evaluation*. Ministry of Foreign Affairs and Trade.

Tennant, S., & Cowley, D. (2019, May). *Bougainville community policing programme: Evaluation report* (Final report). Ministry of Foreign Affairs and Trade.

United Nations Office on Drugs and Crime (UNODC). (2016). *Transnational organized crime in the Pacific: A threat assessment*. Regional Office for Southeast Asia and the Pacific, UNODC, and Pacific Islands Forum Secretariat.

United Nations Police (UN Police). (2015). *United Nations police gender toolkit: Standardised best practices on gender mainstreaming in peacekeeping* (Handbook). UN Police.

United Nations Police (UN Police). (2017). *Our history*. https://police.un.org/en/our-history

Wainwright, E. (2003). *Our failing neighbour: Australia and the future of Solomon Islands*. Australian Strategic Policy Institute.

Wallis, J. (2012). The Pacific: From 'arc of instability' to 'arc of responsibility' and then to 'arc of opportunity'? *Security Challenges, 8*(4), 1–12.

Wallis, J. (2017). *Pacific power? Australia's strategy in the Pacific Islands*. Melbourne University Press.

Watson, D., Sousa-Santos, J., & Howes, L. M. (2021). Transnational and organised crime in Pacific Island countries and territories: Police capacity to respond to the emerging security threat. *Development Bulletin, 82*, 151–155.

Watson, J., Fitzpatrick, M., & Ellis, J. (2011). The legal basis for bilateral and multilateral police deployments. *Journal of International Peacekeeping, 15*, 7–38.

Wyeth, G. (2018). Fiji: The peacekeepers. *The Diplomat*, September 27. https://thediplomat.com/2018/09/fiji-the-peacekeepers/

Wyeth, G. (2020). As Australia burns, Papua New Guinea and other Pacific states extend offers of assistance. *The Diplomat*, January 6. https://thediplomat.com/2020/01/as-australia-burns-papua-new-guinea-and-other-pacific-states-extend-offers-of-assistance/

Open Access This chapter is licensed under the terms of the Creative Commons Attribution 4.0 International License (http://creativecommons.org/licenses/by/4.0/), which permits use, sharing, adaptation, distribution and reproduction in any medium or format, as long as you give appropriate credit to the original author(s) and the source, provide a link to the Creative Commons license and indicate if changes were made.

The images or other third party material in this chapter are included in the chapter's Creative Commons license, unless indicated otherwise in a credit line to the material. If material is not included in the chapter's Creative Commons license and your intended use is not permitted by statutory regulation or exceeds the permitted use, you will need to obtain permission directly from the copyright holder.

CHAPTER 6

Women and the Institution of Policing in the Pacific

Abstract Gender equality has increasingly been a focus for governments of Pacific Islands countries (PICs) and the international, regional, and local organisations working with them. As the most visible arm of governance, police organisations have attracted significant attention in terms of the gender agenda due to their role in responding to issues affecting women. This shift can be attributed to increased recognition of gender inequality in PICs and its association with high rates of crimes against women. This chapter discusses the changing place of women in highly gendered policing organisations internationally and in the Pacific. It considers influences on gender in Pacific policing associated with international, regional, and national frameworks, policies, and agendas aimed at improving women's circumstances. The chapter then explores how regional instability and gender-based violence have shaped female officers' participation in policing and provides examples of the impacts of their involvement in regional initiatives.

Keywords Inclusivity · Gender balance · Gender mainstreaming · International frameworks · Gender-based violence

Introduction

Rooted in the gendered societies of nineteenth-century England and the United States of America, police organisations have been largely populated by men and characterised by strongly masculine cultures (Loftus, 2008; Prokos & Padavic, 2002). The pathway to equality (and equity) for female police officers has been difficult. The opposition to women's involvement in the previously male domain of policing has been evident in a range of countries and contexts, including Pacific Islands countries (PICs). In the closing decade of the twentieth century, however, the Western liberalists' view that gender, as a social process, has a strong impact upon women's (in)security and (dis)empowerment began to gain support (Curth & Evans, 2011). Women's empowerment and equal participation came to be viewed as integral to their engagement with social structures and the creation of social norms in a process of reordering gendered power relations. This view was expressed in various international governance frameworks, conventions, and agendas. These include the *Convention on the Elimination of All Forms of Discrimination Against Women* (CEDAW), the Beijing Declaration and Platform for Action, the United Nations Millennium Development Goals, and the 2030 Agenda for Sustainable Development. In the context of police or security sector reform, it has become widely accepted that women and girls experience crime and violence in particular ways because of gendered power structures, and that policing organisations should address this by striving for greater balance in the recruitment of women (Australian Federal Police [AFP], 2018; Department of Foreign Affairs and Trade [DFAT], 2016). This kind of violence and proposed response is evident in Pacific contexts where there is high dependency on international aid and the propensity to be guided by international and donor agendas.

The benefits of equity in policing encompass supporting the global mission to create genuine equality and independence for women (United Nations [UN], 2009). Policing can offer secure and stimulating work for women, with diverse career paths and increased opportunities for flexible employment. Additionally, there is a strong case that female victims should have access to female officers (Natarajan, 2008; National Center for Women & Policing, 2002). According to various UN-based bodies, women in policing can make a major contribution to improving security and prosperity in developing nations through participation in peacekeeping missions and as part of the professionalisation of Indigenous policing (UN Development Programme [UNDP], 2007; UN International Research and Training Institute for the Advancement of Women [UN-INSTRAW], 2007). It has been argued that female participation in policing will lead to reduced misconduct and complaints, and less reliance on the use of force (Corsianos, 2011; Lonsway et al., 2003; National Center for Women & Policing, 2002; Porter & Prenzler, 2017; Prenzler & Sinclair, 2013). However, policymakers need to guard against 'gender essentialism' and recognise variations in masculinities and femininities (Prenzler & Sinclair, 2013; Valenius, 2007). Equal opportunity should remain the primary rationale for promoting police careers to women.

In some contexts, improved numerical representation has been achieved through targeted recruitment campaigns, pre-application classes, career development courses, mentoring programs, gender-balanced selection panels, equity units, anti-harassment information and training, paid parental leave, flexible employment opportunities, childcare, and advisory and support services (Prenzler, 2002). While much has been done over recent decades to improve the gender ratio of law enforcement, women in policing in countries of the global North are still less likely to work in specialist roles, such as tactical response and drug squads (Curth & Evans, 2011). They are more likely to be restricted to particular roles, such as administrative, personnel, and communications units (Martin, 1990; Rabe-Hemp, 2008). Generally, women are poorly represented in senior police management (Guajardo, 2016; Prenzler et al., 2010). Researchers have documented how female police officers have been undermined by lack of support from colleagues, sexual harassment, and discrimination in deployment and promotion (Brown & Heidensohn, 2000; Elizabeth Broderick & Co., 2016; Hunt, 1990; South Australian Equal Opportunity Commission, 2016; Victorian Equal Opportunity and Human Rights Commission, 2015).

The challenges faced by women in policing are more starkly evident in strongly patriarchal societies, such as those associated with PICs. Limited research has focused specifically on women's involvement in policing in these countries, even though development assistance in the Pacific, including for justice and policing, is often linked with explicit gender equality initiatives (Dodge et al., 2011; Irving, 2009).

This chapter draws on published research, grey literature, and policing policy and strategy documents to sketch out a picture of the involvement of women in policing organisations across PICs. It begins by describing the social context that surrounds women's work as police officers, highlighting some of the challenges of this environment, before providing details on the numbers of women working in policing and their roles. The chapter then documents factors that have influenced the growth of women in policing in the Pacific, discussing international, regional, and national frameworks and organisational arrangements. It considers how addressing the challenges of regional instability and gender-based violence have contributed to supporting women's inclusion, providing examples of the benefits and the challenges associated with so doing in the Pacific context.

THE SOCIAL CONTEXT

Although many policing organisations across the globe acknowledge the need for improved gender representation of women, the drive for more female officers has often been met with organisational barriers and societal resistance (Martin & Jurik, 2006). The gendered division of labour and perceptions about gender-appropriate policing roles continue to inform officer assignment and task allocation (Miller, 1998). Thinking that equates policing with physicality contributes to negative symbolic representations of women as unsuited to policing roles, or as posing a threat to the performance and public perception of police officers' capabilities (Heidensohn, 1992; Prenzler & Sinclair, 2013). In largely male-dominated societies with strong patriarchal traditions and customary practices, like those characteristic of PICs, the promotion of a gender equality agenda challenges not only hegemonic masculinities, but also the longstanding and uncontested male domination of power over the maintenance of law and order (Connell, 2006; Heidensohn, 1992).

Policing organisations face challenges in recruiting women in sufficient numbers. For various reasons, women may be reluctant to take up law enforcement as a career. This is true in countries with well-developed state policing agencies, supportive human resourcing policies, and strong industrial relations frameworks of workforces (Prenzler & Sinclair, 2013). In PICs, the institutional accommodation of women in policing agencies, and their role in service delivery, is further complicated by the intersection of gender norms associated with professional policing and those that exist in cultures typically characterised by patriarchal power relationships. For example, McLeod (2007) identified problems experienced by female police officers in Papua New Guinea (PNG) where they became the target of broader social resentment regarding the changing role of women in society. Women's advancement in the organisation was undermined because husbands prevented their wives from engaging in work-related travel and female police officers were punished for career achievements (Curth & Evans, 2011). Research with Solomon Islands police identified similar gendered expectations and barriers for women in policing (Curth-Bibb, 2014).

In Pacific Island contexts, gender expectations embedded in alternative forms of regulatory authority that function alongside—and at times in competition with, or in the perceived or actual absence of—the rule of law in these countries add further complexity (Bull et al., 2019, 2021). Customary approaches to dispute settlement that are common in PICs, for example, tend to involve public meetings, known regionally as 'custom courts', where complainants present their grievances against alleged offenders before the community. The matter is then deliberated upon publicly, and local tribal chiefs or elders come to a consensus about the validity of the complaint and an appropriate form of customary punishment. In these forums, powerholders in the community are typically older men, who tend to dominate the decision-making processes, and the participation of women and youth can be limited. Male family members represent and speak on behalf of female relatives who have been victims of crime or are suspected of being involved in an unlawful act. This works against the interests of women (Garap, 2000).

These realities present an important backdrop for considering the potential for increasing the number of women in policing in PICs. They are also likely to impact perceptions about women in policing, and directly influence public views about appropriate policing roles and responsibilities for female police officers. Gender norms and gender bias, both within policing organisations and across society more broadly, might act as a barrier to increasing numbers of women in policing. Nevertheless, there is a commitment to improving gender equality across the Pacific region.

Proportions of Women in Policing in Pacific Island Countries

In PICs, most police services began to recruit women in the 1970s. For example, Eaton (2005) describes how the Tonga Police Force started to induct women at that time, reporting that the first eight female police officers were recruited in September of 1970. Faletau (2005 as cited in

Putt et al., 2018) estimated in 2005 that across the 19 island members of the Pacific Islands Chiefs of Police (PICP), approximately 10% of the then 1200 police officers were women, and the proportion of women in the police services ranged from 3% in the Federated States of Micronesia (FSM) to 20% in Tonga. Scant data currently exists on the numbers of women serving in policing organisations across the Pacific region. Figures are often not readily available in annual reports or other relevant administrative documentation. The Fijian Parliament's Standing Committee on Foreign Affairs and Defence (2019) review of the Fiji Police Force Annual Report for 2016–2017 noted that while female officers accounted for 20% of the force, no further detail or gender-disaggregated data was provided. Similarly, strategic initiatives such as the Tonga Police Development Program, while explicitly identifying improved gender equality through increasing participation by women as a goal, often do not include specific gender equality outcomes, indicators, or measures. This makes it difficult to monitor and evaluate any progress towards the development of gender-inclusive organisations and service delivery (Tennant & Bernklau, 2016).

Some indication of the numbers of women in Pacific Island policing organisations can be gleaned from various government and research reports. For example, Putt and colleagues' (2018) report on the legacy of the Regional Assistance Mission to Solomon Islands (RAMSI) for policing in the Pacific region helpfully details that in 2016 the percentage of women (including sworn and unsworn staff) in police services in the region ranged from 8% in FSM (of 266 officers) to 38% in Nauru (of 103). They list the proportions in larger police forces as Fiji 19% (of 3968), PNG 13% (of 6822), Samoa 23% (of 671), Solomon Islands 19% (of 1491, an increase from 14% in 2005), Tonga 24% (of 419), and Vanuatu 14% (of 675). In comparison, at that time, the proportions of female members in the New Zealand Police and the AFP were 31 and 35%, respectively. Both organisations had higher numbers of unsworn female staff than sworn female officers. This was not the case, however, for Pacific Islands organisations—where typically sworn female officers made up the majority of female staff (Putt et al., 2018), and even though many of these services were small they included women in the officer ranks.

According to the data available on the website of the Fiji Police Force, in 2012 there were 740 female officers (19% of 3875 officers)—28 female officers at Inspector rank, 35 at Sergeant rank, 65 at Corporal rank, and 612 at subordinate ranks (Prenzler & Sinclair, 2013). In addition,

69 female officers had been included in peacekeeping missions overseas. Earlier, Eaton (2005) reported that Tonga prided itself on leading the way with the highest proportion of women in policing in the Pacific region, with 36% of commissioned officers and 22% of the total sworn officers being women. In their evaluation of the Tonga Police Development Program, Tennant and Bernklau (2016) noted the high proportion of sworn officers—from a total of 419 sworn officers, 102 were female (24%), a number of whom were serving in senior roles, including two Deputy Commissioners. There were 11 female commissioned officers, 13 at Sergeant rank, 66 at Constable rank, and 12 in administrative roles (Tennant & Bernklau, 2016).

The Royal Solomon Islands Police Force (RSIPF) 2017 Annual Report noted that women accounted for 23% of the force (343 of 1491). Female officers had increasingly taken on roles 'in administration and operational areas including the Executive and supervisory roles in front line operational and General Duties including Acting Commissioner, Deputy Commissioner, Assistant Commissioner, Provincial Commander, Director and Deputy Director Roles' (RSIPF, 2017, p. 29). In 2019, numbers of female officers in the Solomon Islands had increased slighted to 24% (365 of 1520) of all police—non-commissioned officers and other ranks—and women made up 13% of commissioned officers across the following ranks: Deputy Commissioner, Chief Superintendent, Superintendent, Inspector, Senior Sergeant, and Sergeant (RSIPF, 2019). By contrast, in 2017, just seven of 100 police officers in the Tuvalu Police Service were women and, of those, six were constables and one was a senior constable (Melei as cited in Howes et al., 2021).

While this limited data gives some indication of the distribution of women across ranks and demonstrates that across policing agencies the numbers are increasing, little detail is provided in relation to their spread across each organisation. The information available indicates uneven distribution of female officers, shaped by perceptions of women as lacking the necessary strength and skill to perform certain policing roles (see Bull et al., 2021). For example, Tennant and Bernklau (2016) described how in Tonga, while there were female officers present within most police units—except for Search and Rescue—they were overrepresented in areas such as management, administration, and training. Tennant and Bernklau's (2016) evaluation was unable to determine whether women considered non-operational roles more appropriate for them, or whether such roles were the only ones available to them. Anecdotally, many of the female police officers were vocal and active in their roles, and had ambition to move up the ranks in the force (Tennant & Bernklau, 2016). At the same time, however, views that 'female police officers did not have "the skills or strength" to handle difficult situations' were also expressed (Tennant & Bernklau, 2016, p. 34).

INTERNATIONAL, REGIONAL, AND NATIONAL FRAMEWORKS FOR WOMEN IN POLICING

A range of linked factors have influenced and shaped the increasing numbers of women and the drive for gender equality and equity in policing. These include the growing number of international, regional, and national agreements, protocols, and plans that have stimulated the introduction of strategies that work to 'mainstream' consideration of gender equality and 'balance' gender participation across all levels of social life.

International Frameworks

The imperative to address gender inequality and discrimination in policing and more broadly in Pacific Island community contexts began in the early 1980s, when PICs started to sign up to relevant UN conventions. Key among these was the CEDAW, which was adopted in 1979, instituted on 3 September 1981, and ratified by 189 states (UN General Assembly, 1979). This convention defines discrimination against women, introduces principles of gender equality and non-discrimination, and obliges state parties to promote, protect, and implement women's rights. Its preamble refers to the importance of gender equality for enhancement of international security, stating that 'the full and complete development of a country, the welfare of the world and the cause of peace require the maximum participation of women on equal terms with men'. The international commitment to gender equality as a global standard expressed in the CEDAW was reinforced at the UN Fourth World Conference on Women in Beijing in 1995, when 189 governments adopted the Beijing Declaration and Platform for Action (UN, 1995) as a global agenda for women's empowerment and a 'policy framework and blue print for action' on gender equality (Mlambo-Ngcuka, 2014, p. 3).

The Beijing Declaration and Platform for Action 'imagines a world where each woman and girl can exercise her freedoms and choices, and realize all her rights, such as to live free from violence, to go to school, to participate in decisions and to earn equal pay for equal work' (UN Entity for Gender Equality and Empowerment of Women, 2015b). Signatories explicitly reaffirmed their commitment to:

> The equal rights and inherent human dignity of women and men and other purposes and principles enshrined in the Charter of the United Nations, to the Universal Declaration of Human Rights and other international human rights instruments, in particular the Convention on the Elimination of All Forms of Discrimination against Women and the Convention on the Rights of the Child, as well as the Declaration on the Elimination of Violence Against Women and the Declaration on the Right to Development. (UN, 1995, article 8)

The gender-sensitive guidelines created after the Beijing conference marked the UN's 'formal commitment to gender equality that includes a goal of achieving a 50/50 gender (male/female) balance' and 'of gender mainstreaming' (Hicks Stiehm, 2001, p. 42).

The strategy of achieving a 50/50 gender balance (referred to as 'gender balancing') is easy to understand and can be measured. It is often assessed with 'hard indicators', such as quotas that can demonstrate the efficacy of gender-focused initiatives. Simply increasing numbers, however, may not contribute to a sustainable change and can gloss over or disregard the perpetuation and regeneration of gendered power structures, even when the goal is achieving more gender equality. There is a real risk that reconfigured arrangements might provide the perception of new opportunities for women while giving rise to new power structures that obscure women's ongoing disempowerment (Curth & Evans, 2011).

It is well accepted that quantitative improvement in the representation of women alone will not necessarily increase sensitivity to gender issues. According to Hicks Stiehm (2001), gender balancing must be linked with effective 'gender mainstreaming'—an approach to policymaking that takes into account both women's and men's interests and concerns. She explains that gender mainstreaming is more complex, takes longer to implement, and can be difficult to comprehend. Even though mainstreaming addresses the concerns of both women and men, in practice such strategies tend to focus on women. This is because existing normative inclusion of men's needs and perspectives means that these are generally mostly well integrated into policies and programs. Women's needs are more likely to require explicit recognition. Critiques of such gender equality reform measures underline the requirement that gender balancing and mainstreaming should be treated as complementary, and adopted simultaneously to achieve meaningful change.

The CEDAW and the Beijing Declaration and Platform for Action have continued to be reinforced. In 2000, a five-year review of the Beijing Declaration and Platform for Action led to the publication of *Women 2000: Gender Equality, Development and Peace for the Twenty-first Century*—also known as 'Beijing + 5' (UN Entity for Gender Equality and Empowerment of Women, 2015a). This was the outcome document of the 23rd Special Session of the UN General Assembly. It recognised the need to overcome barriers to achieving women's equality in twelve critical areas: women and poverty; education and training of women; women and health; violence against women; women and armed conflict; women and the economy; women in power and decision-making; institutional mechanisms for the advancement of women; human rights of women; women and the media; women and the environment; and the girl-child. Consistent with the sentiment of each of these preceding frameworks, Goal 3 of the global UN Millennium Development Goals (MDGs) 2000–2015 (UN, 2000) promotes gender equality and the empowerment of women, and Goal 5 of the subsequent UN Sustainable Development Goals (SDGs) 2015–2030 (UN General Assembly, 2015) aims to achieve gender equality and empower all women and girls.

Regional Agreements and Accords

Since the adoption of the Beijing Declaration and Platform for Action in 1995, most PICs have ratified the CEDAW, and there has been increasing recognition that gender equality is an important part of economic, political, cultural, and social development. Commitment to this progress is reflected in an important body of agreements, reforms, policies, and initiatives. The goals of the CEDAW, Beijing Declaration and Platform for Action, and MDGs and SDGs, for example, are repeated at the regional level in a number of agreements, including the 2005 *Revised Pacific Platform for Action on Advancement of Women and Gender Equality 2005–2015* (Secretariat of the Pacific Community, 2005), which identified targets for and indicators on women's rights and gender equality, and was promoted as the reference point for 'developing national gender equality policies and supporting the integration of gender concerns in a broad range of sectors' (Secretariat of the Pacific Community, 2005, p. 1). This was followed by a stream of subsequent plans, declarations, and forums that sought to strengthen regional cooperation and integration through commitments to increasing the representation of women in legislatures and decision-making (42nd Pacific Island Forum) and bring about the eradication of sexual and gender-based violence (40th Pacific Island Forum).

Despite these repeated efforts (and some successes in relation to girls' education and positive initiatives to address violence against women) inequality has persisted, and in 2012 leaders of the Pacific Islands Forum expressed frustration with slow progress towards gender equality, restating their commitments in the Pacific Leaders' Gender Equality Declaration (Pacific Islands Forum, 2012). They explicitly renewed their pledge to implement the gender equality actions of the CEDAW, the MDGs, and the *Revised Pacific Platform for Action on Advancement of Women and Gender Equality 2005–2015* (Secretariat of the Pacific Community, 2005).

Pacific leaders also became party to broader regional accords, such as the SIDS Accelerated Modalities of Action (SAMOA) Pathway (UN General Assembly, 2014), which represents commitments made by 115 Small Island Developing States (SIDS) leaders at the Third International Conference on SIDS held in Apia, Samoa, in September 2014. The outcomes of this conference were especially critical to signal to the international community the fundamental issues for SIDS to be included in the Post-2015 Sustainable Development Goals that were agreed in September 2015. Gender equality and the empowerment of women were clear priorities among these issues. Paragraph 76 of the SAMOA Pathway recognised that 'gender equality and women's empowerment and the full realization of human rights for women and girls have a transformative and multiplier effect on sustainable development and is a driver of economic growth in small island developing States', and acknowledged that '[w]omen can be powerful agents of change'. Additionally, para 86 committed SIDS leaders to 'the development of action plans in [SIDS] to eliminate violence against women and girls, who are often targets of gender-based violence and are disproportionately affected by crime, violence and conflict, and to ensure they are centrally involved in all relevant processes' (UN General Assembly, 2014).

The Pacific Islands Chiefs of Police Women's Advisory Network (PICP WAN) is a unique feature of women's policing in PICs. This network originated after recommendations from the Australasian Council of Women and Policing conference held in Canberra in 2002. Acting Commissioner for the Fiji Police Force, Moses Driver, supported the constitution of a women's advisory body for the then South Pacific Chiefs of Police Conference (now the PICP). The first meeting of the advisory body was held in Suva in 2003, and a pilot women's advisory network comprising seven Pacific nations was approved. The South Pacific Chiefs of Police encouraged the network to report to them annually at their conferences (Eaton, 2005). The formation of the network, and its subsequent expansion, signalled recognition of the need to improve the representation and participation of women in Pacific police services. Strong networks of women have now developed within and across the 21 PICP member organisations, providing support to their membership at local and regional levels. The PICP WAN provides advice to the PICP in relation to issues impacting on women in policing in represented countries. It has a formal constitution (PICP WAN, 2020a), which provides a framework for its operation and interaction with the PICP, and regularly releases strategic documents that guide its activities.

For example, the *PICP WAN Strategic Direction 2020–2024* (PICP WAN, 2020b) commits to stronger and more meaningful partnership between the PICP WAN and the PICP. This is complemented by the *PICP Strategic Plan 2020–2024* (PICP, 2020), in which the PICP confirm their collective view that '[t]he recruitment, promotion and retention of women in policing is a high priority of the PICP' (p. 5), because—echoing Bastick's (2008) assertion on the importance of representation—'[p]olicing workforces that are diverse and reflect the communities they police are essential to gain and maintain the trust and confidence of Pacific communities' (pp. 4–5). The PICP WAN describes its mission as 'to strengthen policing across our Blue Pacific through the equal and full participation of women' (2020b, p. 4). This is to be achieved through an empowered network of women that works with police chiefs 'to share knowledge, solutions, resources and authority to make positive changes' for a safer Pacific (PICP WAN, 2020b, p. 6). According to *Strategic Direction 2020–2024*, this last goal can be achieved when '[m]anagement decisions are informed by WAN advice' and '[p]olicies and procedures support gender equity' (PICP WAN, 2020b, p. 7); for example, through the adoption of processes that serve to mainstream the perspectives of women and female police officers.

National Plans and Strategies

International and regional frameworks are reproduced at the national level. Across the Pacific region, various initiatives have been undertaken to build the capacity of public institutions and civil society in gender mainstreaming. *The Gender Mainstreaming Handbook of the Government of the Kingdom of Tonga* (Ministry of Internal Affairs, Women's Affairs Division, 2019), for example, begins with a statement describing how the government in that country 'recognises that sustainable development can only be achieved if gender considerations (i.e. the respective issues, concerns, and priorities of women and men) are factored into the work of the government, including service delivery, good governance and effective public service' (p. 1). The handbook explains that the approach is part of the Tonga Strategic Development Framework 2015–2025 (TSDF II), which envisions 'a more inclusive, sustainable and empowering human development with gender equality' (p. 1). It notes that operationalising these principles 'requires a system that supports a whole of government approach to gender mainstreaming' (p. 1). It commits to progressing gender equality through a range of government policies and strategies for action, including:

- *National Women's Empowerment and Gender Equality Tonga (WEGET) 2019–2025 Policy* and Strategic Plan of Action;
- *Revised Pacific Platform of Action 2018–2030*;
- UN Strategic [sic] Development Goals 2016;
- *Tonga Strategic Development Framework 2015–2025 (TSDF II)*;
- Small Island Developing States Accelerated Modalities of Action (SAMOA) Pathway 2014; and
- *Pacific Leaders Gender Equality Declaration (PLGED) 2012.* (Ministry of Internal Affairs, Women's Affairs Division, 2019, p. v)

Strategies of gender balancing and mainstreaming are a staple of security sector reform (Organisation for Economic Co-operation and Development—Development Assistance Committee, 2011). In the context of policing, eliminating gender imbalance within security institutions is intended to make them more representative and responsive to the needs of the community they serve. Bastick explains: 'A process cannot be people-centred if the needs of half the people are not represented'

(2008, p. 155). Gender balancing is promoted as improving the performance of security institutions and contributing to the level of public trust, both in specific institutions and in the sector more generally (Bastick, 2008; Huber & Karim, 2018). This—together with regional and national governmental commitments—means that gender balancing and mainstreaming are prominent in policing organisations across the Pacific region.

Improving the gender balance is evident in the increasing numbers of women in Pacific police training. In Tonga, for example, the 2014 recruit training program had a gender equity objective and accepted equal numbers of men and women (Tennant & Bernklau, 2016). In Solomon Islands, the 2017 recruitment course comprised 70 probationary constables, of whom 35 were women; all graduated from the Police Academy after 20 weeks of intensive training (RSIPF, 2017).

The RSIPF Annual Report 2017 demonstrates how national policies of gender balancing and mainstreaming flow through to shape institutional/organisational goals:

> Gender equity is one of the current Government's policy objectives to facilitate fair representation and equal participation of both genders in all areas of work. The RSIFP has therefore embraced the objective through its strategies including implementation in the areas of equal gender recruitment and engaging in roles and responsibilities in management, administrative operational duties. (2017, p. 29)

The RSIPF Commissioner's introduction to that organisation's Gender Strategy 2019–2021 described the aim underpinning the document as being to transform the RSIPF into a more inclusive workplace that offers fair and equitable opportunities for both women and men to make a difference, noting that '[a] fairer police force is a more capable police force' (RSIPF, 2019, p. 4). The mission of the strategy is: 'Improving gender equality to create a workplace that actively values and supports women in all aspects of policing to build a strong and professional police force for RSIPF officers' (p. 6). Here again, there is an appeal to the benefit that can be achieved by increasing the number of female officers. The strategy commits to having a higher representation of women across the organisation including in leadership roles. The desired outcome of this change is not just quantitative; rather, it is linked to a qualitative expectation that it will 'bring balance to the internal RSIPF decision making processes as well as in communications between the police and community members' (p. 9).

The RSIPF Gender Strategy thus signals mainstreaming as an important driver of change. It outlines a framework for an organisation-wide approach, which includes changes to systems focused on attracting and supporting female personnel; inclusive leadership and workplace culture; capability building and skills development; and advocacy supporting women to develop in roles across the organisation. Male advocacy is particularly important for changing gendered institutional and social norms. The strategy aims to strengthen and maximise support mechanisms for female officers. Key components are maximising the capacity of the RSIPF Women's Advisory Network to influence organisational change, fostering the contribution of women in the RSIPF, and forming a male advocate network to promote awareness of, and support for, the Gender Strategy and the initiatives and objectives of the RSIPF Women's Advisory Network.

Environmental Factors Influencing Increased Focus on Women in Pacific Policing

Environmental factors beyond institutional change at the international, regional, national, and organisational levels have also influenced the participation of women in policing in the Pacific. Conflict and instability in the region have opened the door for security sector reform, that includes gender-sensitive police reform. In the past, women's security needs were overlooked, but they have increasingly been recognised as an essential component of the reform process. Ignoring these security needs and thus violating human rights can compromise the inclusiveness and sustainability of peace and efforts to build democratic governance after conflict (UN Development Programme, 2007). Adding to this is the growing recognition of the important role played by women police in responding to gendered violence, which is experienced at alarming rates in many PICs.

Regional Instability

Instability in the Pacific region has been a factor contributing to increasing the numbers of women in policing. While the CEDAW does not refer directly to women's security needs during conflict and in post-conflict periods, according to the interpretation of the Committee on the Elimination of Discrimination Against Women, the Convention is applicable in such contexts and its regulations should be respected. Consistent with this assessment, in 2013 the Committee adopted General Recommendation No. 30 on Women in Conflict Prevention, Conflict and Post-Conflict Situations, which specifies that:

> Protecting women's human rights at all times, advancing substantive gender equality before, during and after conflict and ensuring that women's diverse experiences are fully integrated into all peacebuilding, peacemaking and construction processes are important objectives of the Convention. (Committee on the Elimination of Discrimination Against Women, 2013, p. 2)

Among other gender-related issues, this recommendation addressed such topics as women's 'participation' in the peace process (Committee on the Elimination of Discrimination Against Women, 2013, pp. 11–12), as well as their engagement in the security sector throughout processes of 'reform, disarmament, demobilisation and reintegration' (Committee on the Elimination of Discrimination Against Women, 2013, pp. 18–19).

In contrast to the CEDAW, in 1995 the Beijing Declaration and Platform for Action (and later the Beijing + 5) explicitly included the effect of armed and other types of conflict on women and girls as one of twelve critical areas of concern (UN Entity for Gender Equality and Empowerment of Women, 2015a). Subsequently, the UN Security Council Resolution 1325 (UNSCR 1325, 2000) on women, peace, and security in 2000 drew attention to 'the interdependence of post-conflict gender equality, peacebuilding and security' (Bastick, 2008, p. 149). It highlighted 'the important role of women in the prevention and resolution of conflicts and in peace-building' and stressed 'the importance of their equal participation and full involvement in all efforts for the maintenance and promotion of peace and security, and the need to increase their role in decision-making with regard to conflict prevention and resolution' (UNSCR 1325, 2000, p. 1). Since 2005, to ensure implementation at the national level, signatory states have begun to adopt National Action Plans that are intended to provide context for the expression of the resolution and translate its objectives into national and local realities (Women's International League for Peace & Freedom, 2016). The adoption of UNSCR 1325 initiated a wave of gender-focused security sector reforms (PeaceWomen, 2020), which make up the UN's broader women, peace, and security agenda (PeaceWomen, n.d.), and stimulated the production of a range of resources and toolkits.

Over recent decades, instability has been a feature of the Pacific region. Some key events have led to the deployment of peacekeepers to Bougainville from 1998 to 2003, with peace brokered between PNG and Bougainville in 2001; the mobilisation of RAMSI in 2003 to quell civil unrest linked to fighting between ethnic and regional groups in 2003; and the joint taskforce of troops and police (from Australia and New Zealand) sent to Tonga following serious rioting in the capital Nuku'alofa in 2006. These types of missions and deployments have left their mark on policing the region. While the nuanced nature of the legacy left by them is subject to debate, according to Huber and Karim (2018) the presence of multidimensional peacekeeping missions in a post-conflict country have had a positive and statistically significant effect, in that such states are 22% more likely to adopt a gender balancing reform. This type of legacy is evident in the case of RAMSI. Moreover, it is arguable the benefits of increasing the numbers of women in policing and building their capability (i.e., gender balancing and mainstreaming in police) were felt in PICs beyond Solomon Islands.

RAMSI was a police-led mission that was supported as required by armed peacekeepers (see Chapter 5). Its key priorities were restoring law and order, the integrity and the capacity of the RSIPF, and community confidence in national policing. The mission was in place for 14 years (2003–2017) and the Participating Police Force (PPF) included contingent members from 13 PICs: Cook Islands, Fiji, Kiribati, the Republic of the Marshall Islands, Nauru, Palau, PNG, Samoa, Tong, Vanuatu, Niue, Tuvalu, and the FSM. The size of the contingent from across these nations fluctuated over time, with the number of officers from each country varying depending on the overall size of the PPF, the size of the country's police force, and the numbers that particular forces could release from domestic duties. The size of the police organisations contributing to the Pacific Islands contingent ranged from PNG, with an estimated staff of more than 6800 in 2016, to Niue, which had only

15. During the second half of RAMSI, the largest numbers of contingent members were from Tonga, Samoa, PNG, and Vanuatu. While most members were male, between 2010 and 2016, 16% were female (Putt et al., 2018).

Initially RAMSI did not have a specific focus on women, but in 2009, the importance of including women was identified as a cross-cutting issue in the partnership framework between the Solomon Islands Government and RAMSI, and a gender advisor was appointed to provide advice across RAMSI programs and counterpart government agencies. RAMSI assisted the Solomon Islands Government to address gender inequality through measures including legislative reform and the collection of gender-based data. The Women in Government Program implemented through RAMSI focused on the removal of barriers to women's participation and representation in government by advocating change to policies, legislation, and employment terms and strengthening organisations that can foster women's leadership development (AusAid, 2012; Australian Civil-Military Centre, 2012).

In their report that investigated the legacy of RAMSI for policing in the Pacific region, Putt and colleagues (2018) described the experiences and views of Pacific Islands contingent members and assessed this multi-country police-led mission. Particular attention was paid to the lessons that could be learned about the role of women officers in the PPF, and the prevention of community violence and violence against women. Research participants—including former RAMSI leaders and current Pacific police commissioners—highlighted RAMSI's contribution to 'enabling and supporting regional policing cooperation, including in community engagement, women's empowerment and gender awareness, and complex investigations' and 'increasing engagement and involvement in regional networks, for example ongoing contact through the [PICP WAN], and the Pacific network of Transnational Crime Units' (Putt et al., 2018, p. 8).

Throughout the report there were many examples of the benefits of deployment through RAMSI for women in the Pacific Islands contingent. In relation to the mission objective of rebuilding community confidence in police, former Pacific Islands contingent members gave examples of where they had been able to take on leadership roles in community interactions and assist fellow RSIPF and PPF officers, usually as part of a small team based in police outposts. The report uses the example of a female police officer from Tonga (deployed in 2006–2007) to highlight the impact of female officers from PICs:

> She was working in general duties in Honiara on night shift when she and others were called out to a domestic violence incident. When they arrived, the women wouldn't open the door and told them to go away. The female police officer stepped forward and convinced her to open the door and work with them to solve the problem. The officer was of the view that the door would not have been opened if she had not intervened. Hearing from her voice that she was a woman and from another PIC, the female officer believed that the victim felt safe enough to let the rest of the police into her home. (Interview #50; 2006–2007 as cited in Putt et al., 2018, p. 43)

Putt and colleagues (2018) describe RAMSI's impact on gender equity, noting that most of the female members of the Pacific Islands contingent who were interviewed reported increases in their confidence, skills, and abilities as a result of their deployment to RAMSI. This confidence was linked to the presence of positive female police role models. For example:

> A PNG policewoman attributed her increased confidence in large part to the Australian women police officers with which she worked. She admired and was inspired by their attitudes, confidence and professionalism, and claims to have become more proactive and assertive since her return home. (Interview #47; 2008–2009 as cited in Putt et al., 2018, p. 51)

Prior to the intervention there were relatively few female police officers in the RSIPF. Putt and colleagues (2018) describe how this changed dramatically in the early recruiting rounds following RAMSI's arrival. Newly recruited Solomon Islands policewomen needed role models, confidence building, and supportive networks—some of which was provided by RAMSI. This was confirmed by women PPF members who reported that they helped female officers in the RSIPF during their deployment and in later years were able to provide ongoing support through the professional friendships that had developed. For example, one Fijian policewoman helped RSIPF women officers gain additional training on gender-based violence in Fiji at the Women's Crisis Centre (Interview #31; 2009 as cited in Putt et al., 2018, p. 51).

Not all participating female police officers made the same assessment of gender equity and opportunities within RAMSI. These varied depending on comparisons with their home police force. Putt and colleagues (2018) report that many Fijian and Tongan women police officers perceived that their home force already had opportunities for women. In contrast, according to a Kiribati woman, there were few female officers in her home country. For her:

> RAMSI was challenging and new. We were treated the same as men; we did all the same work – arrests and patrolling. We often were paired up with men, and that was good; it was safer … Really enjoyed RAMSI; it was like real policing, especially for the women. (Interview notes #93; 2004 as cited in Putt et al., 2018, p. 52)

This reflected the sentiment expressed by women participants in Putt and colleagues' (2018) study that both they and their male counterparts had benefited from seeing women members of the PPF involved in training and policing duties that were typically done by men in their home countries.

The other key contribution of RAMSI in relation to women was '[i]ncreasing the reach of regional networks: for example, ongoing contact through the PICP Women's Advisory Network' (Putt et al., 2018, p. 65). Female RAMSI deployees 'were able to utilise the [PICP WAN] to stay in touch and support each other in professional development' (Putt et al., 2018, p. 61).

With the end of the RAMSI deployment, the post-conflict context had an enduring impact on the development of policing policies in the Solomon Islands. The RSIPF Gender Strategy 2019–2021 (RSIPF, 2019) is explicitly framed in relation to UNSCR 1325 (2000), and provides a structure for the operationalisation of RSIPF responsibilities under the Solomon Islands National Action Plan. The strategy notes that it addresses the National Action Plan, which has four high-level outcomes linked to the agreed pillars of the UN Women, Peace, and Security agenda. These are:

- Women's participation, representation and decision making in peace and security are expanded at all levels
- Women's human rights are protected, and women are secure from sexual and gender-based violence

- Solomon Islands actively prevents conflict and violence against women and girls; and
- Women and girls' priorities and rights are reflected in development and peace building. (RSIPF, 2019, p. 8)

Repeating the sentiments expressed by Bastick (2008) and the *PICP Strategic Plan 2020–2024* (PICP, 2020), the RSIPF Gender Strategy explains that '[i]ncreasing and extending the role of women in the RSIPF can be expected to improve confidence, build trust and enhance the legitimacy of police within the Solomon Islands' (RSIPF, 2019, p. 9). The strategy states that '[w]omen often hold the position of neutrality within a conflict situation and there is evidence of women playing the important role of peace-keepers during and post-conflict in the Solomon Islands' (p. 9). This claim is further supported in the strategy as follows:

> Indeed, Melanesian women have a long history of intervention in conflict to prevent violence through invoking customary norms and taboos specific to women, as well as traditional perceptions of women as 'peacemakers'. Christian teachings – a pillar of shared Solomon Islands cultural identity – also provide a number of examples of women as peacemakers during times of conflict, arguably bestowing further legitimacy and acceptance of women's involvement in peacemaking. (Brigg et al. 2015 as cited in RSIPF, 2019, p. 9)

These factors contribute to the message that female officers have strengths in communication and peacemaking skills that result in less use of excessive force, fewer complaints, and more de-escalation of violent confrontations (Lonsway et al., 2002 as cited in RSIPF, 2019, p. 9). However, caution should be exercised in relation to the essentialising potential of these types of assessments. Mobekk (2010) rightly criticises the essentialist tendency of perceiving women in the context of security sector reform as peaceful and men as aggressive. Such oversimplification not only strengthens gender stereotypes, but also overlooks changes in traditional gender roles (such as those expressed by the female contingent member from Kiribati, above) that happen during conflict. Further, it has the potential to promote the false assumption that women are better equipped to tackle security issues that are traditionally identified with 'women's concerns', such as domestic and family violence and sexual violence, as discussed in the following section. And finally, it can contribute to the construction of police responses to such important and challenging problems as lesser than other policing activities. Adopting an approach of seeing women as 'different from men'—'[i]t is not about making everyone the same' (RSIPF, 2019, p. 9)—as a means of bringing women into the formal security sector as providers of additional 'soft' security services can reproduce socially constructed gendered differences, and consequently reinforce rather than dismantle or (at least) disrupt the traditional gendered protector–protected dualisms (Kunz, 2014).

An alternative interpretation of these types of strategies is that in strongly patriarchal societies they can provide a 'back door to equality' (Natarajan, 2008), and this can be valid in those traditional cultural settings that call for a rigid separation of women and men in daily life. Growing evidence from research focused on women and policing in the global South adds weight to this claim (see Bull et al., 2021; Carrington et al., 2019). Strategies that work through existing gender relationships in these types of settings can provide a 'foot in the door' to change social and institutional views and expectations in relation to women in policing (see Bull et al., 2021 on attitudes to women in policing in Tuvalu). This is pertinent in the Pacific region where, for example, the RSIPF Gender Strategy 2012–2021 acknowledges that 'cultural and social traditions may present some challenges for women's participation in decision-making and leadership roles in the RSIPF' (2019, p. 9). In this context, the differences between the policing styles of male and female officers and the types of authority they can exercise are seen as a 'great opportunity to use the traditional authority and respect afforded to women and elders to influence community tolerance of violence, especially which is perpetrated against women and children' (RSIPF, 2019, p. 9).

Researchers have identified primary challenges to women's engagement in security sector reform as patriarchal culture and entrenched gender norms, economic and social barriers, and women's potential participation being significantly curtailed by societal expectations and perceptions (Justino et al., 2018). Erzurum and Eren (2014), for example, point to the significance of pervasive gender norms of the given post-conflict society as hindering women's involvement in peacebuilding. A lack of status and the stereotypical perception of women as weak or vulnerable are sources of their systematic exclusion from decision-making processes, and this leads to women's needs being overlooked.

In addition, researchers highlight specific inequalities that present impediments to active participation in security sector reform by women.

These include unequal access to education; social norms that enhance restrictive gender roles; poverty and limited access to financial resources; high levels of gender-based violence; the double burden of women who are caregivers and work to generate income; and the rejection of women's skills by national governments, international community, and women themselves as relevant in peacebuilding. Even though gender equality norms are almost universally accepted at governmental levels (Kang et al., 2018), these assessments highlight the risk of relying on various international, regional, and national plans alone as vehicles for change, and alert us to the challenges and complexities that are associated with working with or through traditional gender roles and norms. The systems of particular institutions and organisations designed to operationalise these conventions, agreements, and plans often do not reflect the level of support needed, or they struggle to successfully translate them into practice; and the uneven implementation of the various standards and requirements results in their limited effectiveness (UNSCR 1325, 2000).

Experiences in Tonga, as part of the security sector reform process following the 2006 riots, for example, demonstrate the importance of committing to both organisational systems and monitoring to bring about change. The Tonga Police Development Programme (TPDP)—is a trilateral partnership between the Governments of Tonga, Australia, and New Zealand, implemented by Tonga Police, the AFP and the New Zealand Police in 2014. It aimed to reduce crime and increase public confidence in Tonga Police through professional, legitimate, and accountable policing. A cross-cutting theme of the evaluation of the TPDP was the extent to which it had 'appropriately addressed gender and human rights' (Tennant & Bernklau, 2016, p. 13). It found that the TPDP worked towards improved gender equality through increasing the participation by women in Tonga Police and through the implementation and enforcement of laws that seek to reduce criminal offending against women, specifically domestic violence, via the Tongan Family Protection Act 2013. However, the TPDP did not include specific gender equality outcomes or indicators, so improvements were difficult to measure. The evaluation identified some organisational shortfalls in relation to initiatives to improve gender mainstreaming and equality, identifying the need for:

- Targeted support to female officers in undertaking their duties through further training, including in areas that are non-administrative and are viewed as 'core policing' such as criminal investigations, responding to calls, general 'active duty' functions and forensics;
- Further training – from a range of providers, including civil society, on key gender issues not limited to domestic violence. Understanding of gender equality principles through further training and exposure would benefit the entire police force, and should be integrated into a range of training opportunities[;]
- Development and implementation of systems to monitor and report on the degree to which female officers are provided with the same opportunities and role responsibilities as male officers[;]
- … ensuring that gender equity is considered in all performance appraisals. (Tennant & Bernklau, 2016, pp. 8–9)

Gender-Based Violence

Initiatives to promote gender equality have been augmented by conditions associated with regional instability that have seen international deployments, capability building, and security sector reform, such as those associated with RAMSI. These interventions have had positive outcomes for the inclusion of women and their role in policing across the region. The imperative to increase the number of women in policing is also associated with preventing and addressing the high rates of gender violence across the region (see Chapter 3). In many of the international, regional, and national frameworks referred to above, the promotion of gender equality is linked to the prevention of violence against women.

Survey data indicates that lifetime prevalence rates for physical and sexual violence (by intimate partners and non-partners) among Pacific Island women are between 60% and 80%, which is twice the global average (UN Children's Fund [UNICEF], 2017). Because the police response to crimes of violence against women is so critical, it is worth noting that in the global North, female officers have long been viewed as more effective in this area than male officers (Chan et al., 2010; Schulz, 1995). This is a perception shared by the community (Breci, 1997), police training instructors, and female officers themselves (Beck, 2002; Martin et al., 1986). It is also supported by research on the value of female police officers in the context of international deployment. In peacekeeping environments, shame and related experiences around sexual violence mean that women are more comfortable reporting and seeking help from women (Bleckner, 2013; Mazurana, 2003; Pillay, 2006; Pruitt, 2013). Research reports that increasing the numbers of female police in peacekeeping and stabilisation missions has led to improved security outcomes for women and children, and increased reporting of and reductions in violence against women and children (Furnari, 2014; Greener, 2009; Harris & Goldsmith, 2010; Van der Spuy, 2011).

Interviews with female members of the PPF (Putt et al., 2018) on the legacy of the RAMSI deployment provided evidence that this also was the case in Solomon Islands. Many believed that their presence had helped with community policing in general, and responses to domestic violence incidents in particular. The women who were part of the RAMSI contingent reported that they were able to contribute to the prevention of violence against women through community-based policing work 'including police visits to schools, churches and villages' (Interview #39; 2012 as cited in Putt et al., 2018, p. 52). A PNG female officer described how in her view 'the women officers were better at communicating with local people than the men' (Interview #47; 2008–2009 as cited in Putt et al., 2018, p. 52). Several referred to the 'calming' effect their presence had. And a Tongan female officer noted how 'important it was to have female officers at provincial outposts as most incidents reported to the police involved domestic violence, and female officers were better placed to deal with women victims' (Interview #50; 2006 as cited in Putt et al., 2018, p. 52).

These views are consistent with community and police perceptions of the role of women in policing in other Pacific contexts. In Tuvalu, participants in a study that explored attitudes towards increasing the number of women in policing expressed views that align closely with those reported by Putt and colleagues (2018). Female police officers were perceived as more likely to adopt a community-oriented style of policing, and it was suggested that they were more effective at handling domestic violence incidents and crimes of violence against women (Bull et al., 2021). In Bull and colleagues' (2021) study, support for increasing the number of women in policing was explained in terms of their ability to deal with women-related issues, including customary matters. For example:

> [Women] understand the ladies' problems due to our traditions and cultures … Sometimes when there is a lady found drunk and they send

a police[man] but they are cousins or related and so [he] cannot do a thing because they are related … [I]t is better for male officer to counsel male and for female to counsel female it would be better that way. (Bull et al., 2021, p. 400)

Bull and colleagues (2021) concluded that according to their participants, female officers could navigate gendered social norms dictated by customary and religious authority, while still exercising the authority of the state to protect women, in ways male police officers could not. This suggests that both community members and police officers who supported increasing the numbers of women in policing valued the contribution that female police officers could make within the complex hybrid regulatory environment that is typical in PICs.

The benefits for policing gender-based violence that flow from including women in RAMSI have been felt beyond Solomon Islands. Female PPF members reported gaining experience in relation to gender violence issues during their deployment and then translating this into their local environment when they returned home (Putt et al., 2018). In recent years Family and Sexual Violence Units have been established in police stations in various PICs—in some cases, with direct input from officers who gained practical skills while deployed with RAMSI. In Kiribati, a Family and Sexual Violence Unit was headed by a former female RAMSI deployee, while Fiji strengthened its Family Protection Unit and developed training and reform initiatives led by a former PPF member (Putt et al., 2018). The transfer of skills and knowledge was not one-way (i.e., from Solomon Islands to the home state). Complementing these examples, a PNG female officer who was deployed in the final phase of RAMSI told how she was able to draw on her policing experience in PNG in training local police and raising community awareness about the newly introduced Family Protection Act 2014 in the Solomon Islands. Similar legislation had been introduced in PNG several years before. Having undertaken training in Fiji on the creation and maintenance of a family-based violence database as part of a New Zealand-run project, the police officer helped implement the system in Solomon Islands and later in PNG when she returned home (Interview notes #43; 2013–2015 as cited in Putt et al., 2018, p. 53).

In other security sector reform contexts in the Pacific region, instability has stimulated capability building targeting the prevention of violence against women. The 2014 TPDP supported the rollout of the Tongan

Family Protection Act 2013 training package, which was designed by a joint agency team involving Tonga Police, the Ministry of Health, and the Ministry of Information, as well as Tongan Crisis Centres and advocacy groups. The training package was delivered to 161 police officers—27 women and 134 men—across all police districts. However, security sector reform is not always smoothly integrated into everyday policing practice. Tennant and Bernklau (2016) explained that while most officers participating in the evaluation of the TPDP stated that they had received training and understood the new Family Protection Act, a small number expressed the view that the police should not interfere in domestic affairs and that the new law 'is bad' and against Tongan culture. The authors acknowledged that these beliefs may be more widely held among police; nevertheless, they were encouraged that only a few were prepared to openly express them. Research with police officers and community members in Tuvalu found explicit support for police involvement in domestic violence matters from both groups, even though such involvement was a relatively new development (Howes et al., 2021).

A final and important consideration in relation to the value of female police officers in responding to cases of domestic violence is the high rate of such violence committed by police officers themselves. Particularly high rates of domestic violence have been documented in police families in the global North (Neidig et al., 1992). In the global South, research conducted by ethnographers working within the PNG constabulary argued that members of this force were highly likely to be perpetrators of gender violence in their own conjugal relationships (McLeod & Macintyre, 2010). Further, they were frequently accused of perpetrating violence against women in the course of their professional duties, or when women approached them for protection from other sources of violence (Chandler, 2014; McLeod & Macintyre, 2010). It is short sighted to discuss the police response to violence against women without addressing the possibility that responding officers have committed these crimes themselves. Violence against women is much more likely to be committed by men than women, so increasing the number of female law enforcement professionals has the potential for lessening the chance that crimes of violence against women will be handled by an officer who has perpetrated such a crime (Tjaden & Thoennes, 1999).

Complexities arise not only due to competing forms of authority— state, *kastom* and religion—in PICs, but also because of gender norms in these contexts. Research has described how women officers may emulate the masculine gender norms that pervade police agencies generally, and thus they may police gender violence cases in ways no different to their male colleagues (Parsons & Jesilow, 2001). This suggests that in Pacific Island contexts, despite progress to date, existing gender norms—both within policing organisations and across society more broadly—can act as a barrier to increasing the numbers of women in policing. Moreover, such gender norms can limit the expected positive impact of increased numbers of women in policing on the reporting, prevention and reduction of violence against women and children.

Conclusion

This chapter has aimed to address the gap in knowledge about the role and experiences of women in policing in PICs. Little is known about their participation because they account for a small number of personnel in organisations across the region, with limited detail available in published data. The chapter has drawn together the information available from a range of sources, including published research, annual reports, evaluations of police development programs, research reports, and other grey literature. On the basis of these documents, it can be concluded that numbers of women police in the Pacific region are growing, and women are actively taking on operational roles across all areas of policing. This is apparent even when women's willingness to participate in policing may not always be matched by wider community support in strongly patriarchal societies. It is notable that in contrast to the gender breakdown of policing agencies in Australia and New Zealand, the information available indicated that the majority of women in policing in PICs are working in operational rather than administrative roles and have made some inroads at the executive levels of their organisations, working as commissioned officers.

The increase in numbers and the growing diversity of roles performed by women in policing have been aided by factors outside and beyond the initiatives of policing agencies within individual PICs. International frameworks such as the CEDAW, Beijing Declaration and Platform for Action, MDGs, and SDGs have supported the introduction of regional and national policies and practices that balance and mainstream gender inclusivity. Environmental factors, including civil unrest and alarmingly high rates of violence against women and girls, have also played a role. This is evident in the legacy of RAMSI, which delivered benefits to women in policing beyond Solomon Islands by providing an expanded range of opportunities that contributed to their inclusion across ranks and operational roles, positive mentoring, and the strengthening of the PICP WAN. Particularly important was the opportunity for both male and female officers to observe and work with women filling roles traditionally only occupied by men. Increasing the number of female officers achieved positive outcomes for survivors and victims of gender-based violence because of improved trust, which led to better engagement with police and higher rates of reporting.

This chapter has documented some of the specific strategies used by PICs to increase the numbers of women police and improve the conditions of policing for women. These have included recruitment practices that aimed to balance the number of female and male recruits, as well as mainstreaming goals, such as those embedded in the introduction of the PICP WAN, and support for Women's Advisory Networks in each jurisdiction that are well connected to their respective chiefs of police. It is important to recognise, however, that the geographical, colonial, political, and cultural contexts across the Pacific region are diverse, and the pathway into policing for women—and achieving equality and equity—is a work in progress. This continues to challenge, and be challenged by, the complex intersection of gender norms associated with professional policing and those that exist in cultures typically characterised by patriarchal power relationships, together with competing forms of regulatory authority that function alongside—and at times in competition with, or in the perceived or actual absence of—the rule of law. Working with and through traditional gender roles and norms to increase the numbers and roles of women in policing—as described in the Solomon Islands Gender Strategy 2019–2021—offers the potential of getting a foot in the 'back door' to changing organisational culture (Natarajan, 2008). With this strategy, however, there is a risk that must never be overlooked: it may at the same time generate new arrangements that can maintain and further entrench women's disempowerment (Curth & Evans, 2011). For this reason, striving to achieve gender equality throughout organisations and societies must be coupled with efforts to monitor and evaluate progress and actively address shortcomings.

REFERENCES

AusAID. (2012). *Regional Assistance Mission to Solomon Islands (RAMSI) annual program performance report 2011.* Australian Government.

Australian Civil-Military Centre. (2012). *Partnering for peace: Australia's peacekeeping and peacebuilding experiences in the Autonomous Region of Bougainville in Papua New Guinea, and in Solomon Islands and Timor-Leste.* Australian Government. https://reliefweb.int/sites/reliefweb.int/files/resources/ACMC-PFP-REPORT.pdf

Australian Federal Police (AFP). (2018). *International Command, gender strategy 2018–2024.* Australian Federal Police, International Command.

Bastick, M. (2008). Integrating gender in post-conflict security sector reform. In Stockholm International Peace Research Institute (SIRPI). *SIPRI yearbook 2008: Armaments, disarmament and international security* (pp. 149–171). Stockholm International Peace Research Institute.

Beck, R. D. (2002). *Integration or exclusion? Perceptions of gender equality in policing* [Doctoral dissertation, University of Wales].

Bleckner, J. (2013). From rhetoric to reality: A pragmatic analysis of the integration of women into UN peacekeeping operations. *Journal of International Peacekeeping, 17*(3–4), 337–360.

Breci, M. G. (1997). Female officers on patrol: Public perceptions in the 1990's. *Journal of Crime and Justice, 20*(2), 153–165.

Brigg, Morgan, Chadwick, Wren, Griggers, Cody, Murdock, Janet and Vienings, Tracy (2015). Women and Peace: The role of Solomon Islands women in conflict resolution and peacebuilding. *Sharing and exploring Pacific approaches to Dialogue: A compendium of case studies from Pacific Island Countries Suva.* UNDP Pacific Centre.

Brown, J., & Heidensohn, F. (2000). *Gender and policing: Comparative perspectives.* Macmillan.

Bull, M., George, N., & Curth-Bibb, J. (2019). The virtues of strangers: Policing gender violence in Pacific Island countries. *Policing and Society, 29*(2), 155–170.

Bull, M., Watson, D., Amin, S. N., & Carrington, K. (2021). Women and policing in the South Pacific: A pathway towards gender-inclusive organizational reform. *Police Practice and Research, 22*(1), 389–408.

Carrington, K., Sozzo, M., Puyol, M. V., Gamboa, M., Guala, N., Ghiberto, L., & Zysman, D. (2019). *The role of women's police stations in responding to and preventing gender violence: Buenos Aires, Argentina: Final report of field research.* (QUT Centre for Justice Research Report Series, Issue 1). QUT Centre for Justice.

Chan, J., Doran, S., & Marel, C. (2010). Doing and undoing gender in policing. *Theoretical Criminology, 14*(4), 425–446.

Chandler, J. (2014, August). *Violence against women in PNG: How men are getting away with murder*. Lowy Institute for International Policy.

Committee on the Elimination of Discrimination against Women. (2013, November 1). *General recommendation no. 30 on women in conflict prevention, conflict and post-conflict situations* (CEDAW/C/GC/30).

Connell, R. (2006). The experience of gender change in public sector organizations. *Gender, Work & Organization, 13*(5), 435–452.

Corsianos, M. (2011). Responding to officers' gendered experiences through community policing and improving accountability to citizens. *Contemporary Justice Review, 14*, 7–20.

Curth, J., & Evans, S. (2011). Monitoring and evaluation in police capacity building operations: 'Women as uniform'? *Police Practice and Research, 12*(6), 492–505.

Curth-Bibb, J. (2014). *Policing for development outcomes: Complexity in program management and monitoring and evaluation* [Unpublished thesis, University of Queensland].

Department of Foreign Affairs and Trade (DFAT). (2016). *Gender equality and women's empowerment strategy*. Australian Government.

Dodge, M., Valcore, L., & Gomez, F. (2011). Women on SWAT teams: Separate but equal? *Policing: An International Journal, 34*(4), 699–712.

Eaton, K. (2005). Pacific Island chiefs of police – Women's advisory network. *The Journal for Women and Policing, 17*, 42–44.

Elizabeth Broderick & Co. (2016). *Cultural change: Gender, diversity and inclusion in the Australian Federal Police*. Elizabeth Broderick & Co.

Erzurum, K., & Eren, B. (2014). Women in peacebuilding: A criticism of gendered solutions in post-conflict situations. *Journal of Applied Security Research, 9*, 236–256.

Faletau, L. (2005, August 21–24). 'Women in Policing in the Pacific Our Journey'. *Paper presented at the Improving Policing for Women in the Asia Pacific Region, Australasian Council of Women and Policing Conference*.

Furnari, E. (2014). *Understanding effectiveness in peacekeeping operations: Exploring the perspectives of frontline peacekeepers*. University of Otago.

Garap, S. (2000). Struggles of women and girls – Simbu province, Papua New Guinea. In S. Dinnen & A. Ley (Eds.), *Reflections on violence in Melanesia* (pp. 159–171). Hawkins Press/Asia Pacific Press.

Greener, B. (2009). UNPOL: UN police as peacekeepers. *Policing and Society, 19*(2), 106–118.

Guajardo, S. A. (2016). Women in policing: A longitudinal assessment of female officers in supervisory positions in the New York City Police Department. *Women & Criminal Justice, 26*(1), 20–36.

Harris, V., & Goldsmith, A. (2010). Gendering transnational policing: Experiences of Australian women in international policing operations. *International Peacekeeping, 17*(2), 292–306.

Heidensohn, F. (1992). *Women in control? The role of women in law enforcement*. Clarendon Press.

Hicks Stiehm, J. (2001). Women, peacekeeping and peacemaking: Gender balance and mainstreaming. *International Peacekeeping, 8*(2), 39–48.

Howes, L. M., Watson, D., & Newett, L. (2021). Police as knowledge brokers and keepers of the peace: Perceptions of community policing in Tuvalu. *Police Practice and Research, 22*(1), 745–762.

Huber, L., & Karim, S. (2018). The internalization of security sector gender reforms in post-conflict countries. *Conflict Management and Peace Science, 35*(3), 263–279.

Hunt, J. C. (1990). The logic of sexism among police. *Women and Criminal Justice, 1*(2), 3–30.

Irving, R. (2009). *Career trajectories of women in policing in Australia*. (Trends & issues in crime and criminal justice, No. 370). Australian Institute of Criminology.

Justino, P., Mitchell, R., & Müller, C. (2018). Women and peace building: Local perspectives on opportunities and barriers. *Development and Change, 49*(4), 911–929.

Kang, S. L., Barberet, R., Coronado, K., Kuisa Crivorot, A., Helwig, M., Jones, H., Merritt-Rogers, V., Ortiz, E., Osborne, E., Pukhovskaya, M., Rupchand, M., & Simmons, J. (2018). Engendering justice: The promotion of women in post-conflict and post-transitional criminal justice institutions. In J. I. Lahai & K. Moyo (Eds.), *Gender in human rights and transitional justice* (pp. 175–206). Palgrave Macmillan.

Kunz, R. (2014). Gender and security sector reform: Gendering differently? *International Peacekeeping, 21*(5), 604–622.

Loftus, B. (2008). Dominant culture interrupted: Recognition, resentment and the politics of change in an English police force. *British Journal of Criminology, 48*(6), 756–777.

Lonsway, K., Moore, M., Harrington, P., Smeal, E., & Spillar, K. (2003). *Hiring & retaining more women: The advantages to law enforcement agencies*. National Center for Women and Policing.

Lonsway, K., Wood, M., & Spillar, K. (2002). Officer gender and excessive force. *Law and Order, 50*(12), 60–66.

Martin, S. (1990). *On the move: The status of women in policing*. The Police Foundation.

Martin, S. E., & Jurik, N. C. (2006). *Doing justice, doing gender: Women in legal and criminal justice occupations*. Sage Publications.

Martin, C. A., McKean, H. E., & Veltkamp, L. J. (1986). Post-traumatic stress disorder in police and working with victims: A pilot study. *Journal of Police Science & Administration, 14*(2), 98–101.

Mazurina, D. (2003). *Do women matter in peacekeeping? Women in legal and criminal justice occupations*. Sage Publications.

McLeod, A. (2007). Police reform in Papua New Guinea. In M. A. Brown (Ed.), *Security in the Pacific Islands: Social resilience in emerging states* (pp. 73–88). Lynne Reinner.

McLeod, A., & Macintyre, M. (2010). The Royal Papua New Guinea constabulary. In V. Luker & S. Dinnen (Eds.), *Civic insecurity: Law, order and HIV in Papua New Guinea* (pp. 167–178). ANU Press.

Miller, S. L. (1998). Rocking the rank and file: Gender issues and community policing. *Journal of Contemporary Criminal Justice, 14*(2), 156–172.

Ministry of Internal Affairs, Women's Affairs Division. (2019). *The gender mainstreaming handbook of the Government of the Kingdom of Tonga*. Pacific Community.

Mlambo-Ngcuka, P. (2014). Introduction. In United Nations Entity for Gender Equality and the Empowerment of Women. *Beijing declaration and the platform for action: Beijing+5 political declaration and outcome* (pp. 3–4). https://www.unwomen.org/en/digital-library/publications/2015/01/beijing-declaration#view

Mobekk, E. (2010). Gender, women and security sector reform. *International Peacekeeping, 17*(2), 278–291.

Natarajan, M. (2008). *Women police in a changing society: Back door to equality*. Ashgate.

National Center for Women and Policing. (2002). *Equality denied: The status of women in policing, 2001*. US Department of Justice.

Neidig, P. H., Russell, H. E., & Seng, A. F. (1992). Interspousal aggression in law enforcement families: A preliminary investigation. *Police Studies: THe International Review of Police Development, 15*(1), 30–38.

Organisation for Economic Co-operation and Development – Development Assistance Committee. (2011). Section 9: Integrating gender awareness and equality. In *The OECD DAC handbook on security system reform: Supporting security and justice*. OECD Publishing.

Pacific Islands Chiefs of Police (PICP). (2020). *Strategic plan 2020–2024*. PICP. https://picp.co.nz/wp-content/uploads/2020/07/PICP-Strategic-Plan-2020-2024.pdf

Pacific Islands Chiefs of Police Women's Advisory Network (PICP WAN). (2020a, August). *Pacific Islands chiefs of police women's advisory network: Constitution*. PICP WAN.

Pacific Islands Chiefs of Police Women's Advisory Network (PICP WAN). (2020b). *Strategic direction 2020b–2024*. PICP WAN. https://picp.b-cdn.net/wp-content/uploads/2020b/08/WAN-Direction-2020-2024.pdf

Pacific Islands Forum. (2012). *Pacific Leaders gender equality declaration*. Pacific Islands Forum. https://www.forumsec.org/2012/08/30/pacific-leaders-gender-equality-declaration/

Parsons, D., & Jesilow, P. (2001). *In the same voice: Women and men in law enforcement*. Seven Locks Press.

PeaceWomen. (n.d.). *The resolutions*. PeaceWomen: Women's International League for Peace and Freedom. http://www.peacewomen.org/why-WPS/solutions/resolutions

PeaceWomen. (2020). *National-level implementation*. PeaceWomen: Women's International League for Peace and Freedom. https://1325naps.peacewomen.org/

Pillay, K. (2006). The proliferation of private security agencies in South Africa and its concomitant effect on crime prevention and crime reduction. *International Journal of Comparative and Applied Criminal Justice, 30*(1), 95–108.

Porter, L., & Prenzler, T. (2017). Police officer gender and excessive use of force complaints: An Australian study. *Policing and Society, 27*, 865–883.

Prenzler, T. (2002). Sex discrimination. In T. Prenzler & J. Ransley (Eds.), *Police reform: Building integrity* (pp. 67–82). Federation Press.

Prenzler, T., & Sinclair, G. (2013). The status of women police officers: An international review. *International Journal of Law, Crime and Justice, 41*(2), 115–131.

Prenzler, T., Fleming, J., & King, A. (2010). Gender equity in Australian and New Zealand policing: A five-year review. *International Journal of Police Science and Management, 12*, 584–595.

Prokos, A., & Padavic, I. (2002). 'There oughtta be a law against bitches': Masculinity lessons in police academy training. *Gender, Work & Organisation, 9*(4), 439–459.

Pruitt, L. J. (2013). All-female police contingents: Feminism and the discourse of armed protection. *International Peacekeeping, 20*(1), 67–79.

Putt, J., Dinnen, S., Keen, M., & Batley J. (2018). *The RAMSI legacy for policing in the Pacific region*. Department of Pacific Affairs, ANU.

Rabe-Hemp, C. (2008). Survival in an 'all boys club': Policewomen and their fight for acceptance. *Policing and International Journal of Police Strategies and Management, 31*(2), 251–270.

Royal Solomon Islands Police Force (RSIPF). (2017). *Annual report*. RSIPF.

Royal Solomon Islands Police Force (RSIPF). (2019). *Gender strategy 2019–2021*. RSIPF.

Schulz, D. M. (1995). From social worker to crimefighter: Women in United States municipal policing. *Journal of Criminal Justice, 23*(6), 571–572.

Secretariat of the Pacific Community. (2005). *Revised Pacific platform for action on advancement of women and gender equality (RPPA) 2005–2015*. Pacific Community (SPC) & Pacific Islands Forum Secretariat. https://pacificwomen.org/resources/revised-pacific-platform-for-action-on-advancement-of-women-and-gender-equality-2005-2015/

South Australian Equal Opportunity Commission. (2016). *Sex discrimination, sexual harassment and predatory behaviour in South Australia Police*. (Independent Review). Government of South Australia.

Standing Committee on Foreign Affairs and Defence. (2019). *Review report of the Fiji Police Force annual report August 2016 – July 2017* (Parliamentary Paper No. 1, 2019). Parliament of the Republic of Fiji.

Tennant, S., & Bernklau, S. (2016). *Tonga police development program evaluation*. New Zealand Foreign Affairs and Trade Aid Program.

Tjaden, P., & Thoennes, N. (1999). *Prevalence, incidence, and consequences of violence against women: Findings from the National Violence Against Women Survey*. US Department of Justice, National Institute of Justice, Centers for Disease Control and Prevention.

United Nations (UN). (1995, October 27). *Beijing declaration and platform of action*. Adopted at the fourth world conference on women. https://www.un.org/womenwatch/daw/beijing/pdf/BDPfA%20E.pdf

United Nations (UN). (2000). *United Nations millennium development goals*. http://www.un.org/millenniumgoals/gender.shtml

United Nations (UN). (2009). *2009 World survey of the role of women in economic development*. UN.

United Nations Children's Fund (UNICEF). (2017). *Situation analysis of children in the Pacific Island countries*. UNICEF. https://www.unicef.org/pacificislands/media/661/file/Situation-Analysis-Pacific-Island-Countries.pdf

United Nations Development Programme (UNDP). (2007). *Gender sensitive police reform in post conflict societies*. United Nations Development Fund for Women (UNIFEM); UNDP.

United Nations Entity for Gender Equality and Empowerment of Women. (2015a). *Beijing declaration and the platform for action. Beijing+5 political declaration and outcome*. https://www.unwomen.org/en/digital-library/publications/2015a/01/beijing-declaration#view

United Nations Entity for Gender Equality and Empowerment of Women. (2015b). *The Beijing platform for action turns 20*. https://beijing20.unwomen.org/en/about

United Nations General Assembly. (1979, December 18). *Convention on the elimination of all forms of discrimination against women* (United Nations,

Treaty Series, Vol. 1249, p. 13). https://www.refworld.org/docid/3ae6b3970.html

United Nations General Assembly. (2014). *SIDS accelerated modalities of action (SAMOA) pathway* (A/Res/69/15).

United Nations General Assembly. (2015, October 21). *Transforming our world: The 2030 agenda for sustainable development* (A/RES/70/1). https://www.refworld.org/docid/57b6e3e44.html

United Nations International Research and Training Institute for the Advancement of Women (UN-INSTRAW). (2007). *Integrating gender in security sector reform assessment, monitoring and evaluation*. UN-INSTRAW.

United Nations Security Council Resolution 1325 (UNSCR 1325). (2000, October 31). S/RES/1325.

Valenius, J. (2007). A few kind women: Gender essentialism and Nordic peace keeping operations. *International Peacekeeping, 14*, 510–523.

van der Spuy, E. (2011). Policing beyond the domestic sphere: The case of South African police in Darfur Sudan. *African Security Review, 20*(4), 34–44.

Victorian Equal Opportunity and Human Rights Commission (VEOHRC). (2015). *Independent review into sex discrimination and sexual harassment, including predatory behaviour in Victoria Police* (Phase 1 report, December 2019). VEOHRC.

Women's International League for Peace and Freedom. (2016, January 15). *National action plans: Localising the implementation of UNSCR 1325: Latest news*. https://www.wilpf.org/national-action-plans-localising-implementation-of-unscr-1325/

Open Access This chapter is licensed under the terms of the Creative Commons Attribution 4.0 International License (http://creativecommons.org/licenses/by/4.0/), which permits use, sharing, adaptation, distribution and reproduction in any medium or format, as long as you give appropriate credit to the original author(s) and the source, provide a link to the Creative Commons license and indicate if changes were made.

The images or other third party material in this chapter are included in the chapter's Creative Commons license, unless indicated otherwise in a credit line to the material. If material is not included in the chapter's Creative Commons license and your intended use is not permitted by statutory regulation or exceeds the permitted use, you will need to obtain permission directly from the copyright holder.

CHAPTER 7

Conclusion

Abstract Police organisations of the Pacific reflect the diversity and complexity of the countries and territories of the region, in terms of their size and the legitimacy and technical capabilities of these relatively young states. This short concluding chapter reflects upon the issues faced by Pacific Island policing organisations as discussed in previous chapters. It acknowledges the challenges police face in negotiating with diverse sources of authority and multiple actors in domestic settings and international settings, as well as the increasing vulnerability of Pacific Island countries and territories to transnational crime and insecurity produced through global mobility and communications technology, and the implications of changing gender dynamics on policing across the region. The chapter calls for further research on Pacific policing that adopts indigenous methodologies, community participation, and stakeholder partnerships to inform appropriately nuanced and contextualised policy and action on policing in the Pacific Islands.

Keywords Pacific diversity · Pacific criminology · Future directions

Policing in the Pacific Islands continues to be shaped and impacted by multiple factors within and beyond individual countries and the broader region. The region itself is a malleable construct and one whose successive framings by external actors have been increasingly challenged and reimagined by indigenous intellectuals and leaders (Hau'ofa, 1994). It is a region renowned for its traditions and resilience, as well as its sociolinguistic and cultural diversity, with significant variations in experiences of colonisation, independent statehood, and post-colonial development. This diversity is echoed in that between Pacific Island police organisations, including in terms of their size, domestic legitimacy, technical capabilities, and the security challenges they face. While a growing emphasis in recent years has been upon the external threat posed by transnational crime in an era of unprecedented globalisation, in parts of the region, as in the case of Papua New Guinea and Solomon Islands, the most pressing security challenges for domestic police forces remain internal in character, reflecting factors and processes particular to those countries.

Our discussions throughout the previous chapters provide insights as well as a selective overview of what we consider to be pertinent areas relevant to understanding the Pacific policing landscape. Given that police represent the most visible instrument of government authority, it is important to understand the challenges they face and issues they respond to, how they engage with local and international state and non-state social actors in the security space, and how they respond and adapt to shifting local, regional, and international priorities. Our overview aims not only to provide insights into policing in the Pacific region, but also to draw attention to the national and regional complexities of functioning within security spaces that have distinct and intricate histories, cultures, societies, and politics. The chapters also show the significance of the roles public police play and the extensive demands they face from a range of stakeholders.

In addition to the range of resource constraints common to all public service organisations, regional and domestic factors complicate policing in the Pacific, including significant differences between—as well as within—some countries, and enduring colonial and precolonial legacies in others. These factors include variations in the authority, legitimacy, and institutional capabilities of different states and the nature of their accommodation with alternate sources of authority within their territorial borders; for example, those premised on appeals to local *kastom* or tradition. Whereas a 'strong' state such as Fiji has little difficulty in asserting its writ through its monopoly of coercive power, state consolidation remains a work in progress in the larger Melanesian countries, with state authority regularly ignored or contested, or, in the case of Bougainville, violently repudiated. While by no means the only dynamic at work, the underlying friction between centralised authority embodied in the modern state and the continuing autonomy and legitimacy of alternative sources of authority at local levels remains a stubbornly persistent faultline in the domestic politics of countries such as Papua New Guinea, Solomon Islands, and, to a lesser extent, Vanuatu. Ideas about maintaining law and order across the region continue to shift not only as the jurisdictions are impacted by environmental, political, and international factors, but also as a result of the changing nature of crime and evolving categories of criminality, victims and perpetrators requiring police responses. While in some Pacific Island states there is acknowledgement of the role of other non-state stakeholders in responding to disputes and infractions, the police remain the official instrument of state authority with a law enforcement mandate. The modification of domestic legislation to accommodate international human rights and environmental obligations has resulted in the expansion of the policing domain to include areas previously neglected, or viewed as the purview of other local stakeholders operating primarily at the community level.

As police grapple to respond to existing challenges, they are also required to prepare for new roles borne of global mobilities. The region's relative isolation, its porous borders, and its geographic location at the centre of major transport (mainly shipping) routes linking different continents, as well as the frailties of its state institutions, make it an ideal transit point for international criminal activities. This is a growing challenge for relatively small and insular Pacific Island police organisations. Technologically enabled crime, crimes against the environment, organised and transitional crime, and crime against members of previously non-identified marginalised groups add to the pressures on these organisations to operate well beyond their functional capacities. This provides an imperative, as well as opportunities, for organisational adaptation and partnering with other agencies and stakeholders (domestic, regional, and international) to better respond to the changing demands of this evolving security-scape.

The plural character of policing provision in countries across the region, with the existence of multiple policing actors, makes partnering as possible as it is practical. Non-state actors, including the community-based and religious providers with a long history of policing and security provision in this region, can assist resource-constrained public police organisations as part of broader security assemblages with a shared goal of enhancing public security. The continued existence of older forms of self-policing, along with the emergence of more recent privatised, transnational, and other hybrid policing arrangements, suggests there is value in rethinking how policing capacity is both conceptualised and operationalised. This is also about moving away from conventional deficit approaches to developing policing capacity by recognising existing areas of local strength and resilience that can be drawn upon to facilitate partnering for improved policing outcomes in an intrinsically plural and rapidly changing policing environment.

Policing in the Pacific region requires not only an inward-looking approach to gain insights into domestic players in the security space of a particular country, but also an outward-looking approach to capitalise on regional and international partnerships and collaborative arrangements that can lead to better policing outcomes for all Pacific Island citizens. The evolving regional policing architecture is complex, with a multiplicity of partners and different organisations operating nationally and regionally with related mandates. Within these organisations, there are often subsections and specialised units with varied focal areas that may overlap with each other.

The uniqueness of different Pacific landscapes challenges police organisations to formulate policing strategies that align with national interests and also extend beyond state jurisdictions to prevent crime and fulfil their domestic law-and-order mandate. This type of policing necessitates the constant negotiation and navigation of relationships among varied security service stakeholders. Such manoeuvring is further complicated by the constrained coverage provided by the justice sector, the limits of national police organisations and the need to function within the broader international policing framework. What remains constant in the international policing space is the acknowledgement of the need to partner, and regional commitment both to maintaining existing partnerships and forging ahead with new partnerships as the policing landscape continues to evolve.

As police organisations continue to adapt to changing global and regional realities, it is also important to understand how the gender landscape is navigated in what continues to be globally viewed as a masculine space (though significantly more inclusive and aggressively contested as masculine spaces). Pacific policing literature remains considerably lacking in terms of presentations of gender—or, more specifically, women in policing—as a topical issue requiring further discussion. As the numbers of women in policing continue to grow, there is greater need to understand their experiences not only as a point from which to initiate dialogue about the unique challenges and opportunities faced by women in policing, but also as the catalyst for increased dialogue about the role of women in strongly patriarchal societies. The increasing numbers of women in policing and the expansion of their policing roles highlight shifts in gender inclusivity practices and dialogue, underscore discussions about increasing opportunities for women in Pacific societies, and slowly prompt further dialogue about the role women play in society, particularly in responding to crime and criminality.

The roles of history, culture, and geography cannot be underemphasised in discussions about women in policing. While we acknowledge the need to advance the gender agenda in Pacific policing scholarship, we stress the need for well-considered and carefully implemented approaches, as ill-conceived attempts may ultimately work in its disservice. What is important to note is how policing, gender, culture, and context intersect to action change.

Policing in the Pacific Islands draws attention to the gaps in research on Pacific policing and topical issues specific to security service provision across the region. The lack of systematic data on policing in the region not only highlights the complexities of researching and presenting scholarship based on a regional categorisation, but also raises questions about the suitability of regional one-size-fits-all policies and the impracticality of accurate regional generalisations. We subscribe to the idea of a Pacific criminology, as suggested by Forsyth et al. (2020), to more systematically cover common ground using appropriate methodologies and engaging all relevant stakeholders. Understandings of policing in the Pacific Islands require an approach cognisant of context and actors, and a flexibility to engage with and across different disciplinary ways of knowing and being. The concurrent thread throughout our discussions is the need to acknowledge the ever-changing and diverse landscape of policing in the Pacific, and to recognise that there is much ground to be covered in providing an all-inclusive portrait of policing in Pacific Island countries and territories. Our modest contribution provides a useful starting point.

REFERENCES

Forsyth, M., Dinnen, S., & Hukula, F. (2020). A case for a public Pacific criminology? In K. Henne & R. Shah (Eds.), *Routledge handbook of public criminologies* (pp. 163–178). Routledge.

Hau'ofa, E. (1994). Our sea of islands. *The Contemporary Pacific, 6*(1), 148–161.

Open Access This chapter is licensed under the terms of the Creative Commons Attribution 4.0 International License (http://creativecommons.org/licenses/by/4.0/), which permits use, sharing, adaptation, distribution and reproduction in any medium or format, as long as you give appropriate credit to the original author(s) and the source, provide a link to the Creative Commons license and indicate if changes were made.

The images or other third party material in this chapter are included in the chapter's Creative Commons license, unless indicated otherwise in a credit line to the material. If material is not included in the chapter's Creative Commons license and your intended use is not permitted by statutory regulation or exceeds the permitted use, you will need to obtain permission directly from the copyright holder.

Index

A
Alcohol, 44, 49, 50, 52
Australia, 19, 22, 24–27, 44, 61, 62, 64, 87, 88, 96, 98, 114–117, 122, 123, 127–131, 136–141, 167, 173, 178
Australian Federal Police (AFP), 22, 24, 25, 27, 97, 115, 117, 125, 127, 129, 131–135, 137–139, 152, 156, 173

B
Bilateral, 96, 115, 118, 125, 129
Boe Declaration, 136, 139, 141
Border security, 19, 63, 137
Britain, 91

C
Capacity development, 5, 25, 27, 28, 112, 119, 120, 124, 125, 127, 128, 130, 131, 133, 137
China, 24–26, 63, 97, 115, 118, 122, 123, 132

Christianity, 14
Civil society, 40, 42, 43, 54, 58, 63, 66, 70, 103, 163, 174
Collaboration, 17, 22, 39, 55, 71, 131
Colonialism, 10, 39, 86, 88, 89
Community policing, 18, 113, 131, 139, 175
Compensation, 10, 14, 122
Cook Islands, 24, 25, 41, 42, 56, 57, 60, 68, 114, 123, 132, 133, 135, 167
Corruption, 23, 38, 40, 43, 45, 66, 69, 122, 127, 136, 137
Courts, 15, 95, 102
Crime
    crimes against the person, 44, 47, 50
    cybercrimes, 44, 67–69, 134, 137
    environmental crime, 45, 136, 137
    property crime, 38, 41, 44, 46–48
    state crimes, 39, 43, 45
    violent crime, 38, 39, 43, 50–53, 60, 92

Criminology, 71, 191
Culture, 4, 11, 18, 21, 26, 28, 51, 70, 129, 152, 154, 165, 172, 175, 177, 179, 188, 191
Customs, 18
Cybercrime, 44, 67–69, 134, 137

D

Data, 2, 38–44, 48–50, 55, 57, 64–66, 68, 71, 92, 99, 128, 133, 136, 156, 157, 168, 174, 178, 191
Decolonisation, 86, 89–91
Department of Foreign Affairs and Trade (DFAT), 12, 19–21, 24, 27, 28, 94, 115, 130, 131, 152
Developing countries, 2, 23, 96, 119, 120
Dispute resolution, 10, 16, 20, 88, 98, 129
Diversity, 3, 11, 85, 86, 94, 101, 178, 188
Domestic violence, 25, 26, 42, 43, 52, 59, 133, 169, 173–175, 177
Donor aid, 26, 28
Drugs, 23, 44, 49, 50, 54, 61–63, 66, 70, 120, 136, 137, 153

E

Economic liberalism, 104
Enhanced Cooperation Program (ECP), 96, 124, 127–129
Ethnicity, 39, 52

F

Federated States of Micronesia (FSM), 24, 42, 43, 49, 53, 57, 60, 63, 123, 156, 167
Fiji, 12, 13, 15–19, 21, 23–25, 42–48, 50, 52–55, 57, 59–63, 65, 67, 69, 115, 116, 122, 123, 131, 137–140, 156, 167, 169, 176, 188
Firearms, 51, 61, 64–66

G

Gender, 2, 5, 18, 28, 39, 54, 55, 58–60, 70, 71, 103, 113, 131, 152–156, 158–174, 176–179, 190, 191
Geography, 18, 22, 88, 94, 138, 191
Geopolitics, 3, 39, 118
Globalisation, 39, 59, 60, 67, 86, 101, 104, 118, 136, 188
Global North, 18, 39, 68, 113, 116, 139, 140, 153, 174, 177
Global South, 39, 113, 117, 172, 177
Governance, 3, 5, 10, 15, 16, 29, 39, 65, 66, 85, 95, 102, 115, 116, 118, 122, 124, 152, 163, 165
Guam, 17, 18, 41, 43–47, 49, 52, 61

H

Homicide, 51–53, 95
Human rights, 17, 40, 43, 45, 51, 66, 85, 113, 116, 119, 159–161, 165, 166, 170, 173, 189
Hybridity, 10, 15, 16, 95, 102, 105, 113, 126, 176, 190

I

Independence, 16, 87, 89, 90, 92, 104, 114, 115, 127, 152
Indigenous, 3, 11, 15, 16, 38, 69, 71, 85, 87–89, 152, 188
International partners, 4, 190

K

Kastom, 3, 4, 64, 95, 101–105, 177, 188

INDEX   195

Kiribati, 14–17, 19, 20, 23–25, 42–44, 52, 57, 60, 62, 123, 133, 137, 167, 170, 171, 176

L

Law and justice, 24, 39, 93, 97, 127
Law and order, 3, 10, 14, 15, 20, 21, 123, 124, 154, 167, 189
Legal pluralism, 86
Legitimacy, 15, 17, 21, 29, 40, 102, 103, 126, 129, 171, 188, 189
Liberal peace, 96, 122, 124

M

Marshall Islands, 23, 24, 42, 43, 49, 53, 57, 60, 63, 64, 68, 123, 137, 167
Masculinity, 51
Melanesia, 4, 11–13, 17, 20, 21, 44, 52, 55, 60, 61, 65, 86, 88, 91, 97, 102–105
Micronesia, 4, 11–13, 17, 21, 43, 44, 61
Multi-island states, 20
Multilateral, 118, 126, 129

N

New Zealand, 24–27, 44, 61, 62, 64, 96, 97, 114–117, 122, 123, 130, 131, 133, 136–141, 167, 173, 176, 178
New Zealand police, 22, 25, 97, 117, 133, 137, 156, 173
Niue, 12, 23–25, 42, 65, 68, 114, 123, 133, 167
Non-government organisations, 67, 119, 139

O

Oceania, 52, 53, 115

Organised crime, 43, 45, 52, 60, 61, 64, 66, 97, 137

P

Pacific, 2–6, 10–14, 16–18, 21–25, 27, 29, 40, 42, 46, 50, 51, 55, 59, 61, 63, 68–71, 85–87, 96, 98, 104, 105, 112–116, 118, 126, 127, 131, 135–142, 152–157, 161–168, 172, 175, 176, 178, 179, 188, 190, 191
Papua New Guinea (PNG), 11, 12, 42, 65, 86, 93, 115, 154, 188, 189
Paramilitary model, 94
Partnerships, 5, 18, 21, 22, 25–27, 56, 113, 120, 125, 127, 129, 137–142, 162, 168, 173, 190
Peace building, 171
Peace keeping, 84, 116, 118, 119, 127, 152, 157, 167, 175
Plural policing, 5, 71, 84–86, 90, 94, 105
Police, 1–5, 11, 12, 15–22, 24, 25, 27–29, 38–45, 47–52, 54, 55, 58, 60, 61, 65, 67–71, 84–90, 92–97, 99, 100, 102–105, 112–114, 116–134, 136, 137, 139, 141, 152–158, 162, 164, 165, 167–172, 174–179, 188, 189
Police brutality, 45, 129
Police organisational culture, 4, 5, 11, 12, 17–19, 23–30, 84–87, 92, 96–98, 101, 104, 105, 117, 119, 126, 127, 132, 133, 136, 152, 167, 188–190
Police stations, 90, 176
Policy, 14, 17, 18, 24–26, 28, 38, 39, 41, 54, 60, 69, 71, 98, 105, 114, 117, 118, 122, 134, 153, 154,

158–160, 163, 164, 168, 170, 178, 191
Polynesia, 4, 11–13, 17, 21, 43, 44, 55, 61
Population, 1, 4, 11, 12, 16, 19–22, 27, 29, 40, 44, 47, 50, 52, 86–89, 91, 92, 94, 113, 124
Porous borders, 97, 189
Post colonialism, 12, 38, 39, 85–87, 91, 104, 114, 115, 188
Pre colonial, 12, 13, 188
Private security, 44, 48, 84, 91, 98–101, 103

R

Recruitment, 28, 152, 153, 162, 164, 179
Regional Assistance Mission to Solomon Islands (RAMSI), 96, 117, 122–127, 129, 130, 132, 156, 167–170, 174–176, 178
Regional bodies, 137, 140
Religion, 3, 4, 18, 59, 177
Resources, 2–4, 11, 20–23, 25–29, 39, 52, 63, 66, 67, 85, 88, 89, 92–95, 97, 99, 100, 113, 121, 126, 129, 136, 137, 139, 140, 162, 167, 173, 188, 190

S

Samoa, 17, 19, 25, 41–46, 49, 50, 53, 56, 57, 60, 63, 69, 70, 115, 116, 123, 130, 132, 133, 135, 137, 138, 156, 161, 167, 168
Security, 2–5, 11, 12, 16–19, 22, 25, 29, 48, 63, 65, 70, 84–86, 88, 89, 93–102, 104, 105, 114, 116, 123, 125, 132, 136, 139–142, 152, 158, 163–167, 170–177, 188–191

Service delivery, 3, 17, 122, 154, 156, 163
Small island developing states (SIDS), 3, 113, 161
Small islands, 3
Social media, 41, 54, 69
Solomon Islands, 11–13, 15–18, 20, 23, 26, 28, 29, 41–44, 49, 50, 52, 54, 57, 60, 62, 64–67, 69, 86–90, 94–96, 102–104, 117, 122–127, 137, 139, 155–157, 164, 167, 169–171, 175, 176, 179, 188, 189
State-building, 40, 86, 89, 97, 104, 112, 113, 119, 124, 126, 127
State fragility, 85, 90
Surveys, 40–43, 48, 50, 55–57, 92, 174

T

Taiwan, 26, 115, 118, 122, 123
Technology, 4
Tonga, 23, 41–44, 52–54, 56, 57, 60, 62, 63, 69, 70, 118, 123, 130, 133, 135, 137–139, 155–157, 163, 164, 167–169, 173, 177
Tradition, 4, 11, 12, 18, 103, 154, 172, 175, 188
Traditional leadership, 105
Trafficking
  drug trafficking, 61
  firearms trafficking, 51, 64
  human trafficking, 63, 64
  wildlife trafficking, 66
Transnational crime, 5, 23, 39, 43, 44, 51, 60, 61, 63, 65, 66, 70, 112, 113, 118, 120, 132, 136, 138, 142, 188
Transnational policing, 71, 86, 96, 97, 101, 112

Tuvalu, 14–17, 19, 23–25, 41–44, 47, 49, 51, 52, 56, 57, 60, 70, 123, 133, 157, 167, 172, 175, 177

U
United States of America, 27, 62, 97, 114, 152

V
Vanuatu, 16, 17, 23, 25, 42–45, 48, 57, 60–65, 67, 86, 87, 90, 94, 95, 101, 102, 104, 116, 123, 126, 130, 131, 133, 137–140, 156, 167, 168, 189

Violence
   domestic violence, 25, 26, 42, 43, 52, 59, 133, 169, 173–175, 177
   family violence, 42, 44, 171
   police violence, 44, 174, 178
   sexual violence, 42, 55, 56, 58, 59, 64, 91, 171, 174, 175

Y
Youth
   raskols, 47
   squads, 48, 90, 153
   youth gangs, 54

The manufacturer's authorised representative in the EU is Springer Nature Customer Service Centre GmbH, Europaplatz 3, 69115 Heidelberg, Germany. If you have any concerns regarding our products, please contact ProductSafety@springernature.com

Printed and bound by CPI Group (UK) Ltd, Croydon, CR0 4YY

25/03/2026

02078179-0002